Leadership in
Continuing Education
in
Higher Education

Leadership in
Continuing Education
in
Higher Education

CYNTHIA C. J. SHOEMAKER

To order additional copies of this book, contact:
Xlibris Corporation
1-888-795-4274
www.Xlibris.com
Orders@Xlibris.com
38319

CONTENTS

APPENDICES

Introduction: Challenges in Continuing Education in Higher Education

There are many new challenges in education in the 21st century and continuing adult education and life long learning are on the leading edge. People are living longer; they can expect to have a number of jobs and careers; and continual learning is a must for a long, productive and fulfilled life. Institutions of higher education are re-thinking who they are and what they are about as it becomes more and more evident that there are more adults than young people ages 18 to 22, and that ever larger numbers of them want to learn, and need to. Does the institution provide education services of many kinds or just the traditional in-class instruction education service for one age group? This is a question many institutions are addressing.

With the society, both global and national, moving into the Information or Knowledge Age, there is a major trend for adults ages 22 to 75, and older, to go back to school and learn. They are either enhancing their new or their old careers, or attempting to understand the rapid changes of this age better. To adjust to social, technological, political and economic changes, lifelong learning is seen as more and more of a need. By 1980 72% of the institutions of higher education had non-credit programs for adults. By 2007, over 75% of those enrolled in institutions of higher education were 25 and over and were 'non-traditional' students, which includes those married, with dependent children, over 22, or working full time. However, there is very little education for the management of this field which brings a peculiar need for the understanding of academic culture and mores, together with a need for excellent modern management which encourages creativity, and marketing knowledge and skills. The three together create a framework from which to pursue these challenges, and are needed in order to keep pace with a fast changing market, and the programs for it.

There are two major changes occurring in society today that impact continuing education, and, indeed, all formal education. These changes are also evident in the workplace. The first is the on-going transition into the information age as mentioned, which has resulted in technology not only being used to address problems but also being reviewed as an approach to enhancing the entire mission of an organization or enterprise. One example of this transition can be seen in federal agencies and corporations installing Chief Information Officers (CIOs) who sit at the highest levels and help to re-think the implementation of the organization's mission and goals as well as 'e-government' (Fose-Affirm Panel, 1996; AFFIRM Challenges Survey, 2003, 2006).

A subset of the information age or knowledge trend, as the 2,000 U.S. Census shows, is the fast growth of cities that attract creative, braindriven, energetic college graduates. This group likes the new-ideas-welcome environment of certain cities and are leaving other cities that have 'an inferiority complex' or are "stuck in the industrial age" (Harden, *Washington Post*, 2003). The emergence of these cities is usually linked to the presence of a large research university. Seattle is one of these cities, with Washington University, which has doubled its research budget in the last ten years. In Seattle 80.6% of the households have access to the Internet and 47% of the population have bachelor's degrees. Austin, Texas and San Francisco, California are also on this list of brains-attracting cities. In the question of talent luring technology to these cities, a well educated population and environment appears to draw the corporations, rather than the reverse. The success of U.S. cities, many demographers agree, is related to education levels and ambition, rather than to skin color or country of birth (Harden, 2003). These cities even have a significant population of college-educated people that have moved there and left other cities.

The second challenge is the rapidly expanding multicultural demographics on a national level (U.S. Dept. of Labor, 1989 to present). While cultural diversity in the classroom is not new and is robust in technology corporations, it may be newer among the ranks of senior faculty and administrations in institutions of higher education. Yet, even though it may not be new, this change in demographics is a challenge and a trend. Awareness and insight into cultural expectations, helps to ensure that each student's needs will be met in a way that is meaningful and understandable for the student, regardless of cultural background. This includes having appropriate same-culture models among the faculty and administration. Some senior higher education administrators will even say that a challenge is the many strong, vocal, multicultural constituencies that are telling them how to conduct their mission: by calling them, writing them, and even suing them (Trachtenberg, 1996).

A challenge in higher education is the management of a new division or enterprise for continuing education, and the framework for such management. Definitions, a mission statement, faculty expectations and attitudes towards non-standard scheduling, central university administration support and expectations, and budget objectives, will all need discussing along with the general goals, objectives and learning opportunities planned for programs.

Distance learning is a challenge and often a subset of continuing higher education. The planning for technology in support of the entire institution to enhance the general mission and its components, is usually a needed first step. Surprisingly, this planning is often not connected to actual distance education classes, although implications for administration and distance classes impact upon each other. Models for classes, library support, administrative use and other higher education support services using technological enhancement are more abundant. Legal issues and evaluative research lag behind but as more "best practices" become available, especially via the Internet, and through Associations for Distance Learning, some of the mystery about how to implement and manage distance education, has subsided. In Fall 2005 nearly 3.2 million students were enrolled in at least one online course an increase over the 2.3 million reported in Fall 2004. More than 800,000 enrollments were added, twice the number added in Fall 2004, a substantial number of which were at the community college level (Allen and Seaman, 2006). Blended learning and many mixed or hybrid models have now appeared which alternate live and online classes, or offer a choice of live or online sections, to serve classes or individuals at a distance.

The opportunities open to institutions of higher education as the global society moves into the Information Age are numerous. The educational problems and needs of adults in the workplace, for the leaders of the workplace, and for traditional college age students, bring the opportunity and challenge for institutions of higher education to rethink who they are and what they do. Providing education services for students with longer lifetimes and who are changing careers and jobs, in a high quality, accredited framework, will continue to be an endeavor worthy of the highest commitment. Intelligence is not static and the excitement of providing opportunities for the growth and intellectual development of all students will remain a leading goal of foresighted educators in higher education. Education does not only change the individual student's life, it changes all the lives this person touches and perhaps transforms (Hrabowski, 2003). It is indeed a privilege to make a difference in the lives of these students.

Chapter 1

Looking to the Future, Institutional Renewal and Implications for Future Study

Challenges and trends in continuing education in higher education are growing and expanding together at an amazing rate. More adults of more ages are going 'back to school' for more reasons, as human beings live longer, healthier lives and outside environments change. The kinds of continuing education needed, both credit and non-credit, plus the advent of distance learning and 'blended learning' approaches, require environmental scanning and a regular cycle of planning for the leader of a continuing education entity. The marketing sequence and cycle, and the finance and proposal writing and renewing cycle take time, but can be planned for on a time line. The opportunities for increased learning provided by a continuing education division of an institution of higher education are unbounded. The opportunity to share resources and expertise with students of all ages, including research and faculty expertise, plus multiple information resources, challenges educational administrators to present an appropriate and broad array of programs to serve their many constituencies. The chart in Figure 1.1 shows a brief overview of issues at many levels that should be considered. A good staff development exercise is to fill in such a chart at a brainstorming session for the home institution and even with regional applications. The futures discussion, reflected in Figure 1.1, draws from some of the main chapters in this book: Leadership, planning, decision-making, motivation, teambuilding and problem solving to help educational administrators to see applications for their own program futures.

Figure 1.1
Looking to the Future

	National	Regional	Institutional	Continuing Education Organization
1. Leading	U. S. will continue to be a world leader	IHEs help their regions to lead and to develop good economic growth & development	What should IHEs be teaching students? How? New technologies ? Mentorships?	What, where, who, when, and why – are or should be in the CE Mission statement?
2. Planning	Help plan where the US wants to be with its college graduates of all ages.	Be active in the IHEs regional planning	Do strategic planning Where should the IHE be teaching? Whom should IHE teach – graduate, undergrad, non-degree, non-credit?	Look at CE strengths & weaknesses, both external and internal
3. Decision-Making	Help decide what subjects are needed, and what expert resources are needed to develop intellectual and moral leaders for tomorrow.	Help decide where the IHE region wants to be in 15 years. What roads are needed? Intersections? Airport upgraded?	Encourage IHE staff to be knowledgeable & involved about decisions and motivations, e.g. do environmental scans, focus on external strengths & weaknesses.	Encourage CE staff to be knowledgeable & involved about decisions and motivations, e.g. do environmental scans, focus on external strengths & weaknesses.
4 Motivation	National economic development will be related to continuing education. Track this relationship for areas of growth, e.g. Boston, No. Va.; So. MD, CA etc.	Where does the region want to be in 15 years? -economic dev? – education/schools, IHE opportunities? -medical care? -social programs?	See economic development grow in IHE's region: track in future studies Why are fewer students studying math, science and engineering? Should an outstanding university contribute to the practical education of society?	Build Continuing Ed. and IHE strengths, minimize or balance areas of weakness to promote appropriate and sustainable growth.
5. Team Building	Regional and national team building to help plan and provide adequate education for life-long learning.	What special research teams might better enable the institutions in the region?	How should the institution of higher education collaborate with other institutions of higher education? Corporations? International partners?	What kind of team needs to be built in CE unit or division? What skills? talents? personality types? will be needed, and are they representative of your market? Encourage learning teams in the CE unit.
6. Problem Solving	Scan national trends and challenges, which might be quite different than regional & local.	Scan regional trends. (How should the IHE be organized to better enable faculty, students & staff to achieve their own and the region's goals?)	Numbers? Locations? use group problem solving models. What patterns of problem solving could be improved in the IHE? How? What models does the IHE want to build for the future?	Use group and individual problem solving models. Help the CE staff understand the institution culture and norms, mission and how CE fits in or could fit in with the IHE. What models does CE want for the future?

Leadership

The U.S. is predicted to continue to be a world leader and is known to be a leader in the number of institutions of higher education world wide. Furthermore institutions of higher education help their regions to grow, develop economically, and lead in their own areas. What should the institutions of higher education be teaching students? How? What new technologies, and styles of mentor-ships and internships should be used? These are some of the kinds of questions a new President of a large Ivy League university was asking all its stakeholders and alumni, to plan for the year 2015. Should there be new goals accomplished with old processes? Old goals enhanced with new processes? or new goals achieved with new processes (the most difficult to attain)? Continuing education organizations will need to be very clear in their leadership as to what, where, when and to whom programs should be offered – reflecting the "why" of their mission statement. This statement needs an annual review to keep it current.

Planning and Decision-Making

There are many causes for the need for planning and decision-making based on national trends. In all fields the previous state of the art is being replaced by new technologies at an ever-faster rate. Computers have fast become a part of the environment, rather than just tools. Wireless connectivity, faster, more powerful computers and newly emerging technologies give access to networked data wherever one goes.

Wireless links including satellite and Internet connections, simplify relocation of personnel and minimize delays in completing new installations and new projects. Within a few years, artificial intelligence, data mining, and virtual reality have helped most companies and most government agencies to assimilate data and solve problems faster than commercial applications could do in the past.

New technologies often require a higher level of education and training to use them effectively and efficiently. They also provide numerous opportunities for creating new businesses and jobs regionally, within the institution of higher education, and in their continuing education entities. Decision-making and planning will be needed to choose and prioritize which new degrees, programs and training programs will be provided first and then next.

Research and development spending is growing quickly in fields of information technology, electronics, biotechnology, aerospace, pharmaceuticals and chemistry. In the last decade research and development rose steadily representing 2.4% to 2.7% of U.S. gross domestic product (GDP) in different years, and the future increases will keep up the same percentage of an increasing GDP, it is predicted. The implications of this steady increase in research and development were predicted to be a national demand for scientists, engineers and technicians, especially in fields with an immediate business return on investment (AFFIRM 4/11/07).

The length of the design and marketing cycle: idea, invention, innovation and imitation, is shrinking steadily. This has implications for institutions of higher education and continuing education entities, as well as regional and national business and economic development. In the late 1940's this product cycle took 30 to 40 *years*, but by the year 2003 it often didn't even last 30 to 40 *weeks*, and today it is ever shrinking. Scientists, engineers and doctors today are exchanging ideas on the Internet. Furthermore these groups represent eighty percent of those practitioners who ever lived, which means more have studied in these fields, but now more will need to study in these fields. Some futurists predicted that all the technical knowledge being worked with in 2003 would represent 1% of the knowledge that will be available in forty-five years (Cetron and Davies).

Institutions of higher education including continuing education units or divisions, will need to continue to make provision for their faculty to keep attuned to the fast increasing body of knowledge. Those who adopt state-of-the-art technologies first will prosper – and those who do not will struggle, both in business and in higher education. Planning and decision-making will be required to move these adoptions forward at every level: business; institutions of higher education; and continuing education. Educators must ask questions such as: "Where does the U.S. want to be by 2015 with its college graduates of all ages?" "What subjects do they need?"

It is known that medical knowledge is doubling every eight years, and some say every five years. Today's young people will live much longer on the average, and in better health than anyone now expects. Eighty-five percent of the information in the National Institutes of Health computers is upgraded over five years (Cetron and Davies, 2003). This will have major implications for life-long learning, both for professional coursework and life enhancing courses for all higher education institutions, including continuing education and training divisions.

Internet based operations business to business (known as B2B), grew ten times between the years 2000 and 2003, to almost $4 trillion. These internet operations require more sophisticated, knowledgeable workers. People with the right technical background and training will find a ready market for their services for the next 15 years it is predicted. Rapid changes in work-related technologies require training upgrades for literally every worker. An impressive percent of the labor force will need to be in job retraining at any given time. Furthermore, in the next ten years close to 10 million jobs are predicted to open up for professionals, executives, and technicians in highly skilled service operations.

There already is a trend towards more adult education. There is not only a need to train for new careers, but also longer-living-adults grow bored with old careers and seek new careers, and healthy energetic retirees seek activities.

Education at all levels will be growing. It was recently predicted that 130,00 new kindergarten to grade 12 (K-12) teachers would be needed by 2010 according to the National Center for Education Statistics. National, regional and institutional planning and decision-making will be needed regarding more and better teacher education. In the U.S. all levels of education are using the Internet more, from rural elementary and high schools, to universities increasing their markets to distant and international students.

Small businesses all as well as large corporations, need to learn to see employee training as an investment rather than an expense. One company finds it reaps $30 in profits from each dollar it spends on training!

Corporations, management, employees and individuals are getting used to the idea of life-long learning as a significant part of home life and work life at all levels. An institution of higher education can help a region to lead and have good economic development but this requires being active in the region's planning and decision-making.

According to futurists, as minority and low-income households buy computers and join the Internet, they are increasingly able to educate and train themselves for technology and high-tech careers.

The information based organizations depend on teams of task-focused specialists and more independent specialists internationally. This creates many opportunities for small businesses, career choices, and continuing education units, as old careers and specialties become obsolete and new ones appear rapidly. People change careers on an average of every ten years. It has been found that generations in their 20's and 30's have more in common with their peers around the world than with their parents' generation. Computers, the Internet and wireless communication technologies are making national and international economies much more competitive. Workers are spending more time on the job in the U.S., which has become the trend in Europe as well (although this may be leveling out reported the U.S. Department of Labor in 2004 when the average work week shortened by two tenths of an hour). This high-pressure environment causes one and two worker families to seek out services and luxuries, which they now can afford, to ease this pressure.

The typical large business entity is working to re-shape itself and thus more and new management courses and programs are needed. Managing 'like the manager before you' as a model, just doesn't work well anymore. More planning and decision-making tools are needed as management changes and information-based organizations require more specialists and more research and development.

Corporations are predicted to have less than half the management levels they had in 1990 with one-third the managers – a trend that can readily be seen today. Well-trained executives are choosing to start their own companies rather than trusting in old fashioned corporate career paths.

With many new kinds of careers and training needed, institutions of higher education are also transforming themselves, although not as fast as other institutions, to be more transparent in their operations and to have fewer management levels. Whether this means enabling a continuing education unit to be more effective and efficient with institutional renewal, or outsourcing the continuing education and training function to one or more non-profit training organizations, institutions of higher education are being creative in seeking ways to serve the new and large constituency that includes life-long learning and career development. Like corporations and other institutions it is predicted that "the large will get larger and the small will get smaller". Paying attention to the over 75% of enrolled students in institutions of higher education that are 'non-traditional' (i.e. "traditional" being those ages 18-22, single and not working full-time), will help abate the trend of being 'squeezed out' predicted for small to mid-size colleges and universities.

All institutions of higher education may find themselves needing to help their region *decide* where it wants to be in 15 years. What roads are needed? What intersections or bridges need improvement? Is there an airport that could be upgraded? All of this planning and decision-making leads us to the next steps in looking to the future: motivation, team building and problem-solving.

Motivation, Team Building and Problem Solving

John W. Gardner (1963, 1995, 2003) argued that the ultimate goal of education is to shift the burden of pursuing one's education to the individual. Motivation for all ages to keep on learning can be seen at all levels: national and regional and most certainly at institutions of higher education and continuing education organizations. An interesting implication for future study would be to track economic development nationally related to the availability of continuing education in different regions. To mention a few regions: Boston, Northern Virginia, Seattle, Southern Maryland and many large metropolitan areas show a relationship between education availability and economic development. This relationship might even show up more clearly when tracked specifically for a region. For motivation and then necessary team building and team work, look further at a region that asks where it wants to be in 15 years in : economic development? education including school systems and higher education? medical care? social programs? transportation? For example, simply working to provide improved transportation security management across all the transportation modes requires teamwork: rail, highway, water and air.

Scanning national trends and challenges, especially those quite different from regional and local trends can give one clues as to where the future might be next taking an area. Problem solving skills will be needed and need to be taught in continuing education for both the national and regional changes that might be near-future possibilities.

Institutions will need to look carefully at where, when, and who are the students – taking which courses, and how this fits into their mission statement. Perhaps the mission statement will need to be broadened to fit actual or promising goals. Regular strategic planning looking at both institutional and continuing education goals, strengths and weaknesses, will help build the teams and the motivation needed to move in these promising new directions.

Encouraging staff and faculty will be needed in both in the larger institution and the continuing education organization, for them to be knowledgeable about and involved in decisions and motivations in their region. Focusing on external strengths and weaknesses and on internal strengths and weaknesses helps to develop and encourage learning teams and develop course work and degree programs needed for today and tomorrow's world (Galbraith 1997, Byerson 1999). For instance offering transportation security management combined from security management courses and transportation management courses, to use the earlier example of a need, is a possibility.

Institutions and continuing education organizations will need to look at group problem solving models and to consider: what patterns of problem solving could be improved in their institution of higher education? in the continuing education organization? and how? What problem-solving models do each of these want to build for the future? Furthermore this means helping the continuing education staff to understand the institution of higher education culture, norms, and mission and how continuing education fits into or spreads across all of these. What kind of team does the educational administrator/leader need to build in the continuing education enterprise? What skills, talents and personality types will be needed? Fewer students are studying science and engineering yet these fields will be needed in the future. What motivation can the institution of higher education or continuing education division offer them? Future salaries and rewards? Testimonials from those in the field? How might this be reflected in the wording of continuing education advertisements? As always, recognition, encouragement and praise help motivate continuing education teams to produce solutions to these and many other challenges.

Continuing Education Institutional Renewal

The identity of Continuing Education and its role in higher education is being questioned today. Isn't ALL education continuing? Continuing Education can be distributed across the entire institution of higher education and probably should be, due to local and global forces coming into play today. New scientific and technological changes which require complexity and flexibility are leading institutions of higher education to play a critical role in societal change.

All institutional change is dependent on context. One must consider the roots of the institution and institutional renewal, the communication needed, new ways of thinking and working, and know there will be challenges. For example the roots of many large universities include strengths in humanities, social sciences and natural science. How to re-invigorate these and align these strengths with the identity and mission of the larger institution and the Continuing Education entity? A new vision including knowledge, invention and creativity will be needed. Hopefully an opportune moment will appear such as a new President or new Dean or both, that wants to meet new goals and better integrate the enormous number of post-22-year-olds who are interested in higher education in this day and time. This will require clarifying and invigorating the core mission of the institution of higher education and enticing gifted individuals to learn and effect change – as there is a great desire to bring new ideas to market in a more timely way.

Challenges

Institutional renewal will not happen without challenges, of course, and one of these will be the home campus perceptions and past history with continuing education. Other challenges may include internal structures and the organization itself, and the continuing education staff's understanding of their roles, goals and relationships.

A main campus perception that doesn't encourage growth or risk taking and views the continuing education entity as separate but not equal, contributes to a poor self-image for the continuing education staff. Being "looked down upon" is not a strong path for growing larger. Some origins of this may be found in budget allocations that don't reimburse schools and departments for their efforts and inputs. One large university adjusted percentages going to schools and to their departments to address this concern. Another institution was able to fund new degrees and courses being offered through the colleges and utilizing the continuing education entity's sophisticated marketing and delivery systems.

The internal structures may be part of the problem and not a part of the solution. Is there an old data system that doesn't help staff to know much about the students?

Is there a marketing director? Are there goals focused on innovation rather than on limiting costs and *limiting* innovations? Is the core mission clear and understood by all? Is the staff knowledgeable about information technology? These are a few examples of questions to ask when considering institutional renewal.

Roots of Institutional Renewal

In order to break out of the 'traditional' vs. 'non-traditional' paradigm one university continuing education enterprise worked on building programs of distinction; aligning the strengths of the university with emerging professional audiences; building academic excellence and effective inter-departmental and cross-school partnerships, and actually helped the schools in the university to leverage their own resources with joint long term strategic planning. They further developed and maintained a strong continuing education alumni network, and lastly sought to retain the best outsourced services when they needed them. In short their goals were:

GOALS

FROM	TO
The periphery	The core
Maintenance	Change
Silos of staff	Integrated staff
Task oriented	Nationally and internationally oriented
Cost Center	Revenue Center

Communication of Transformation

A large transformation will have to start quietly with communication of plans beginning all on the same day with a formal meeting and than individual meetings, as some staff turnover will result. Not all employees will want to continue in a newly designed role but all can be given the choice. In planning the communication phase, attention must be paid to *the message*, the *target audiences* and *the messengers*.

The *message* should be carefully formulated with a long positioning document which includes what motivated the renewal, local and global forces envisioned, what the new vision is, and what the enterprise is doing, such as building on strengths, acknowledging challenges, recognizing opportunities, and taking action. Short sound bites of variations of the message need to be shared with all the staff, who will be the messengers, but first an email to all the stakeholders is the next step.

Target Audiences

Stakeholders include the faculty, the administration, and the students. Staged communication that is integrated and comprehensive will come together as the staff work on the flyers and announcements. Soundbites can come next, and focus on "how this impacts you" and generally **you-focused messages.** It is important that these steps happen within a short time when people are engaged and interested, and perhaps disturbed – as that is when they really want to know these answers and are paying attention.

Next take the show 'on the road' and meet with university standing departments, divisions, and school-wide committee meetings. One university group made a point to meet with new faculty orientation groups to capture their attention while they were still new faculty. The emphasis in all communication was the alignment of missing goals. The informal network of sound bites included all staff answers to phone queries and informal greetings on campus.

The Messengers

New ways of thinking and working will be needed for the staff in a large transformation. Re-defining a culture so that people work inter-dependently toward shared outputs requires goals such as: focusing on continuous improvement and being respectful and having fun. Staff were encouraged to be respectful of each other, of old staff, and of the students. They developed cross-team inter-dependencies that included formal and informal training, setting new purposes for old committees, forming cohesive teams for professional development, student services, and curriculum and instruction, elevating staff awareness of all of these and creating new structural IT solutions that would re-energize systems and track program development and enrollment information. New team meetings now focused on progress towards new goals and included: a new student manual, new website usages, and tracking information from an inquiry through to enrollment.

Playing a role in the core academic mission of the institution of higher education led to a focus on excellence including the quality and depth of the curriculum, training for new adjunct professors; collaborating in new relationships with university departments to give a voice to applied research and provide innovations. These included new design and delivery of program approaches, such as weekend courses and international travel programs. By adding value to the schools in the university, the continuing education enterprise provided process and infrastructure help, revitalized some old programs and helped field new program ideas. One institution even built cross-school collaborations for new degree programs with one or two early successes. Challenges include capturing the moment, translating the new vision into accomplishments and meeting operational deadlines while convincing skeptics that change *is* possible.

Summary

One can see there are many topics for future study encompassing the broad range of continuing education covered by institutions of higher educations. Tracking many kinds of results, and the cause and effect on economic growth and development, are but two of these. Analyzing the leadership, planning, decision-making, motivation, and team building, using many different models of problem solving, and looking at varying time periods (one year? five? ten?) could yield fertile results for future educational practitioners.

The future has a fast-moving impact on institutions of higher education as new technologies double and quadruple what can be done, and how. Reflective thinking and research will always be needed and now a new role as providers of life-long learning is emerging for institutions of higher education.

Chapter 2

Challenges, Issues and Trends in Continuing Education in Higher Education

The traditional mission of a university or college is teaching, research, and service. Part of the ability to achieve the mission of an institution of higher education can include extending its reputation and credibility for providing high-quality relevant courses, to reach out to and serve the surrounding populations. By empowering the adult community and alumni through life-long learning opportunities, an institution extends the learning community and the intellectual capital of the region as well as enhancing the quality of life. Preparing people to meet changes, empowering them, and helping them to improve their careers and their lives, gives the institution an additional link to the society and the community, and provides a balance to other academic initiatives as a service to their community.

The book *Built to Last* (2002) is about building something that is *worthy* of lasting, building something of such intrinsic excellence that the world would loose something if it ceased to exist. Most institutions of higher education *are* built to last this way, as they do more than make money, and they create something outstanding that makes a lasting contribution to the world in this global age. The research in that book shows that organizations like that make money over the long run despite hurdles. Most institutions of higher education choose to go this route – not settling for the mediocre but building an enduring and great institution that is worthy of lasting and is a noble cause.

The International Council of Distance (and Continuing) Education is in its infancy, but continuing education is coming into its own on many other continents. The market for continuing education in China alone is predicted to be $2.7 billion.

Now that translation through software and the Internet is easier, and the Chinese are willing to help, this market is open to continuing educators.

A university or college can be seen as not just a place with buildings, often with a distinction between the central campus and satellite or remote off-campus locations, but also as a resource that offers educational services at locations and times that best match the needs and interests of able students. Educational services are indeed expanding in the Information or Knowledge Age. What would happen if academia thought about programs that adults want and need, instead of merely extending convenient programs of what they are already doing, to adult and evening classes? According to futurists, the greatest unrealized job market is in unsolved problems, and solutions to unsolved problems often lie in insights gained through education.

There are many new challenges in education in the 21st century and continuing credit and non-credit adult education and life long learning are on the leading edge. People are living longer; they can and should expect to have a number of jobs and careers; and continual learning is a must for a long and productive life (Wee, 1996). Institutions of higher education are re-thinking who they are and what they are about (Trachtenberg, 1996) as it becomes more and more evident that there are more adults than young people ages 18 to 22, and that ever larger numbers of them want to, and need to, learn. Does the institution provide "education services" of many kinds or just the traditional in-class instruction education service for one age group? This is a question many institutions are addressing. By 1980, 72% of the institutions of higher education had noncredit programs for adults. By 2007, over 75% of those enrolled in institutions of higher education were over 25 and were 'non-traditional' students, which includes those married, with dependent children, over 22 or working full time. In 2003 the percentage of 'non-traditional' students had been around 55%.

With the society, both global and national, moving into the Information or Knowledge Age, there is a major trend for adults ages 22 to 75, and older, to go back to school and learn. They are either enhancing their new or their old careers, or attempting to understand the rapid changes of this age better. To adjust to social, technological, political and economic changes, lifelong learning is seen as not only a trend but as more of a need.

However, there is very little education for the management of this field which brings a peculiar need for the understanding of academic culture and mores, together with a need for excellent modern management which encourages creativity, and marketing knowledge and skills. The three together (knowledge of the academic culture, management and marketing) are needed in order to keep pace with a fast changing market, and the programs for it. However, as mentioned before in the Introduction there is little education for the field of management of continuing education that addresses the peculiar needs for academic institutions of higher educations that are developing continuing education programs as an additional way to stay in the black financially, as this has been found to be a revenue producing enterprise.

An editorial in *U.S. News and World Report* and Barak Obama (2006) call for the U.S. government to take the lead, with higher education and continual learning as a place to start, in correcting many of the ills in present day society including decay and anxiety. "Higher education is an investment in the greatest strength a country has – its people" it states and goes on to call for a GI bill type of funding for students who qualify for scholarships for higher education for the information age (Zuckerman, 1996). The GI bill itself was finally increased in 2006.

There are two major changes occurring in society today that impact continuing education, and, indeed, all formal education. These changes are also evident in the workplace. The first is the on-going transition into the information age as mentioned, which has resulted in technology not only being used to address problems but also being viewed as an approach to enhancing the entire mission of an organization or enterprise. One example of this transition can be seen in federal agencies and corporations installing Chief Information Officers who sit at the highest level and help to re-think the implementation of the organization's mission, goals and IT architecture (Affirm, 2006).

The second challenge is the rapidly expanding multicultural demographics on a national level. While cultural diversity in the classroom is not new, it may be new among the ranks of senior faculty and administrations in institutions of higher education. Yet, even though it may not be new, this change in demographics is a challenge and a trend. Awareness and insight into cultural expectations, helps to ensure that each student's needs will be met in a way that is meaningful and understandable for the student, regardless of cultural background. This includes having appropriate same-culture models among the faculty and administration. Some senior higher education administrators will even say that a challenge is the many strong, vocal, multicultural constituencies that are telling them how to conduct their mission: by calling them, and writing them. This can be seen as a part of varied chaotic daily happenings which Peter Vaill has called "managing in permanent white water."

In dealing with rapid change continually, circumstances can lead to a feeling of "being on a merry-go-round" or "the blind leading the blind" or any number of similar phrases. The pace of change itself is changing, and linkages and implications between changes can snowball. One effect is an absence of a sense of progress or of cumulative achievement, which actually might well be impressive, but the achievements are rapidly overtaken by other events. Some writers see "leading as learning" (Senge, 1990, Vaill, 1996) as the dynamic, rapidly changing situations require ad hoc thinking and the ability to face new issues. Individuals in leadership roles thus are put in a learning mode. Control may have been the goal in the 1980s but learning, continual learning, and new beginnings are likely to be the watchwords for the 21st century. Seeking perspective and leading "outside the box" or learning to adopt new paradigms, are some of the learnings and solutions that will be necessary in the decades to come (Kantor, 1983, Naisbitt, 1990, and Ackoff, 1970). Asking: "what can we do with our own enormous capacities to learn and think?" may be the necessary question for individuals as well as institutions. To gain perspective, the long yet short history of continuing education is illuminating.

Past Views of Continuing Education

The teaching of adults has been in evidence since the times of Plato and Socrates, and also goes back to the ancient Chinese and Hebrew cultures. But the concept that a different framework for teaching adults might be needed than the framework for teaching children, called pedagogy, (which means the art and science of teaching children), was discussed in the 1920s and 1930s and re-enunciated by Malcolm Knowles in 1973 in his book *The Adult Learner: A Neglected Species*. He sought a framework for the adult learner which included new methods of teaching as well as content that built on students' experiences. He called his approach **andragogy** and inspired adult education for years into the future.

As Katz (1993) says any educational goals that undermine the disposition to go on learning are miseducation. For many years conventional or traditional classroom methods were thought to do just that. Linderman in 1926, in *The Meaning of Adult Education* wrote that the resource of highest value in adult education is the learner's experience. Knowles thought that authoritative teaching and examinations which leave no room for original thinking have no place in adult education (1978). At that time concepts of intelligence were static; conventional education had standardized limitations; and higher educational facilities were frequently limited to a certain socio-economic/intellectual class (Knowles p.29). It was thought that the majority of adults were not interested in continuing education, or that they could go to public agencies for free short-course educational opportunities. Or else, adult education was viewed as supporting the cultural interests of the leisured classes. The search for new methods and incentives for adult education were partly aroused by the rigid, uncompromising, authoritative approach of conventional institutions of learning (Knowles p.30). Knowles' writings and search for new methods and incentives gave a foundation to the training industry which has grown explosively. New methods for adult learning with an emphasis on self-direction and life-centered student experience began to be used with great benefit in training classes in business and industry. While it is not the purpose of this book to describe that industry, much that is good and helpful to on-going continuing education in institutions of higher education can be found in these theories. Public school systems, county recreation departments, community colleges, labor unions, and state and local governments are all offering training/education courses to good effect. In fact, careful ground rules will need to be established where topics or areas might overlap from different educational or social institutions.

In 1872, George Washington University in Washington, D.C. started offering civil servants late afternoon classes at what was then the Colombian College, which was an early example of adapting to the needs of adult students. The college sensed a demand and made adjustments to scheduling to facilitate attendance. The president even extended the adaptation to include offering classes "where and when it would be convenient for the people who wanted it and were willing to pay for it" (Kayser, 1970 p.7) Other earlier higher education offerings came out of county extension efforts as the land grant colleges were formed, such as those at Cornell University.

Lawrence Jacks in 1929 envisioned a kind of education based on continuity of the learning, possibly called "continuation school" (Knowles p.32). The American Council of Education director in 1929 saw business and industry as *becoming* educational institutions (Ibid p.29). In 1930 a college president said that there was gradually emerging a concept of education as a life long process, "beginning at birth and ending at death," a process full of "reality and meaning to the learner." (*Journal of Adult Education*, 1930, p.123). Peter Drucker coined the phrase "life-long learning."

By 1940 most of the elements for a theory of adult learning had been discovered, but it was not until the 1950's that these elements were clarified and the knowledge explosion, which continues today, began to make continual learning a life requirement. In the 1950's Houle found three types of adult learners: goal oriented learners, activity oriented learners and the learning-oriented who seek knowledge and self enhancement (Knowles p.44).

Since the 1950's many institutions of higher education have developed some form of adult and continuing education whether for credit, non-credit or for both. Futurists see higher education as eventually having three main segments: undergraduate education, traditional graduate education, and continuing education. Whatever the source of the initiative, many institutions have some sort of adult or evening division and it is the purpose of this book to ease the growth and development of such a division or unit, especially for professionals new to this field. Some of the issues discussed in the next section also impact all age groups in higher education but the focus here will be on continuing education for adult students.

A Crossroads of Opportunities:
Leading Innovation

Continuing education can be said to stand at the crossroads of opportunities between academic innovation, traditional approaches, and new ventures and new initiatives. Sometimes it's easier to start new ventures, to act affirmatively and creatively, rather than to try to change a unit within a traditional institution of higher education (Whitaker, 2003). As new educational needs are felt in this information or knowledge age, academic innovation gives continuing educators a chance to share the intellectual opportunities that they are uncovering. However it's important not to loose one's hold on optimism, when ideas get stalled and one may be risking uncertain outcomes.

Thinking with insightful analysis, and acting in the presence of difficult circumstances, sometimes become part of the daily life of those educating all ages and stages of students, at new times and new places. New concepts and fresh thinking sometimes, or may often, run into obstacles in institutions of higher education. Continuing educators are in a most favorable position to challenge and help institutions of higher education lead, due to continuing educators' interest in serving. They sometimes find themselves compelling people to see education in different ways. This can be true in building, leading, and developing new organizations within institutions of higher education. How one responds to annoying or dissenting opinions within one's own organization is a key part of leadership. When continuing educators find the right opportunities, and the timing is right, they justly can be proud of change they helped to cause ((Whitaker, 2003).

Issues in Continuing Education

Up-to-date technology for curriculum, for administration, and for reaching students at greater distances, will definitely continue to be an issue in higher education. As more universities require adult graduate students and younger students to own, or have access to, a computer for a variety of degree programs, this requirement will seem less novel and more routine. Access to libraries and the Internet can be handled in many ways. Software packages for financial management, personnel administration and registration transactions are the norm rather than the exception, as is networking all the buildings of the institution, both local and distant. Groupware further enhances this capability as does client/server technology and data warehousing, data mining, and customer relationship management (CRM) software which are being used more and more (Kohl, 2003).

Distance Learning Issues

Internet users numbered 1,076,203,987 worldwide as of the end of November 2006. In 2003 this number was around 500 million, so that one can see this number has doubled to one billion plus in three short years with 200% growth. The international use of the Internet has been rapidly expanding. In 2000, Americans made up 42% of the total Internet-using population, but this percentage of the population dropped to 37% by 2003 or 185,000,000 U.S. users. In 2006 this U.S. Internet use was 17% of the total world use and numbered 205,161,706 users or 69% of the U.S. population. This is up from February 1996 when there were 24 million people on the Internet in the U. S. and Canada had a 26% increase from October to December 1994 according to the *Chicago Tribune*. This increase is still growing exponentially and is leading to a number of implications for universities and colleges, as well as issues. Firstly, institutions of higher education are getting used to the idea that they do not *own* information. The changing roles of higher education include moving to a culture of sharing, and sharing of "knowledge objects" between institutions of higher education.

The Hubble Telescope, for instance, produced a great deal of information that was not owned by an academic institution. Faculty may supplement, orient, refine and annotate information, but for some this will be a new role. The day may come when it is as unacceptable for a University faculty member to say "I don't use technology" as for a medical doctor to say "I don't use x-ray" (or other medical technology). E-learning and online library resources as well as continuing education and academic department collaboration are also increasing the capacity of institutions of higher education.

The concept of Distance Learning has many definitions but usually refers to technology enhanced offerings such as audio, video, computer-based or assisted instruction or instructional television via satellite, cable network, or online. T-1 lines can be added, to provide choices of audio and video components. Two-way video capability is a popular option so that the instructor can see the students as well as the students seeing the instructor. Online learning has moved to a new level with even composition courses given online. One institution has two instructors grade each composition (Kohl, 2003). These credit programs can also span several continents. Bringing more education to more people, without regard to their location, appears to be a meaningful service (and goal) in this information-age/knowledge age/global era. The argument that distance learning leads to less meaningful personal contact than that which occurs in the classroom may be a myth – it assumes that students have this 'meaningful contact' in the live classroom now. With e-mail contact, students have three or more contacts with the professor or teaching assistant *per week* in programs, at some institutions. However institutions of higher education may need faculty incentives to encourage willingness to teach courses with a distance technology component. These might include promotion, tenure, salary increase, course relief, or the assignment of a Teaching or Research Assistant for every 25 student section which is the most popular option at some institutions.

Institutions need to be alert to critical legal issues such as intellectual property rights. A number of workable models have been developed by universities in the western U.S. with great distances to cover. The University of Wisconsin-Extension's Instructional Communications System (ICS) is one of the largest. It may be that using client/server groupware, that ensures the security of courses so that they are only accessible to registered students, will be an alternative delivery vehicle to the less-than-private Internet. State supported pubic institutions will probably continue to lead in technological distance learning in order to provide equitable opportunity to all, as is their mandate.

A great need for careful, evaluative research still exists on the outcomes of distance learning. Highly technical or very distinctive degree programs, not easily available widely, seem to have been the best early candidates for success (Lynch, 1994). Considerations of student satisfaction and tolerance, when placed against lack of access to education, become less of an issue for many students. Furthermore no learning has well-demonstrated outcomes, according to some educators (Whitaker, 1995).

Distance learning can have a profound and positive impact on students with disabilities, allowing them access to learning that may have previously been inaccessible to them. Questions of access are still very much under discussion for the "information infrastructure" in general. There are sociological implications around different access for age, social class, gender and international expectations (NII, 1996). Some countries behind the "dollar curtain" without adequate telephone lines are using CD-ROM for medical and other professional libraries. Wireless technologies also are used widely in some of these countries. Many college courses are available on interactive CD-ROM.

Institutions of higher education must, however, guard against "vendor dictated solutions" in purchasing information technology. Seeing technology as enhancing the entire mission of the institution, and working back to solving particular problems with technology, will produce a more integrated (and inter-operable) set of solutions than the reverse. "Stovepiping" with different systems in a university not connecting (such as the registrar and student accounts), can lead to expensive problems in the future, as many government agencies have discovered.

An institution of higher education might address these problems with a task force such as an Information Management Advisory Group made up of heads of major departments and chaired by a Chief Information Officer. Next steps might include choice of a standard methodology with pilot projects and training; involving more interdisciplinary teams; and involving department chairs, managers and technical staff. Then technology acquisitions can support the framework. Information, orientation, and training can include communication institution-wide to reinforce the Information Management Framework (USDA, 1992). This might include an adjunct professor training program for using technology in the classroom, with an extra pay incentive for those who participate, as well as administrative training for all who come in touch with special systems.

Internal Issues in Continuing Education

Some (seemingly) large challenges to continuing education continue to exist within the internal environment of the institution of higher education in many institutions, and a large issue is in the area of faculty expectations, power struggles and intrigues. Faculty tenure and diversity issues further complicate these faculty challenges. Full-time faculty involvement and participation is often considered in addition to normal duties, and the amount of teaching may be limited. Further internal issues and challenges include budgets and resources, and space and facilities. Of course distance learning confronts space questions with new solutions, but it is expensive to launch. However appropriate faculty participation must be encouraged in order for institutions of higher education to maintain leadership in continuing education and to share it's resources with the public. All credit courses and instructors mostly must be approved by appropriate schools, colleges, or departments and faculty committees.

Historians note that internal challenges and other challenges are merely an extension of issues that have existed on the main campus or in residential programs over time. All of these challenges will be re-visited in various chapters of this book, as the need for the leadership to turn challenges into new opportunities for solutions emerges. Suffice it to say continuing education often has access to experts, academicians, researchers, master teachers and training professionals, and can offer educational experiences of the highest quality. Programs and courses can be designed to serve individuals and organizations alike, following a variety of formats and schedules throughout the year.

Challenges of Setting Up a New Continuing Education Unit in an Institution of Higher Education

Any innovation presents challenges and starting a new off-campus or continuing education unit in an institution of higher education is certainly a challenge. Accessible higher education for youth and adult students is a worthwhile goal and a continuing challenge (Birnbaum, 1988). As the unit often responsible for the design, coordination and teaching of a broad range of programs for the benefit of many groups and publics, these programs usually provide professional education to adults. Even if there is an "implementation dip" (the feeling of two steps forward and one step back), as things are getting underway, steady perseverance usually carries the day. At least six years are required to judge a program that impacts a wide audience. Rensis Likert (1961, 1972) calls this 'institutional lag' and describes the six years as divided into two year increments: two years of input, two years of attitude change and two years of output (see Chapter 3 for more applications of this concept). Five challenges enunciated by one Dean in the process of setting up a new, Off-Campus Learning Center in an institution that had only had traditional programs, may be useful to others:

Definition of Continuing Education.

Make sure two parties in conversation are using the same definition of continuing education early in the conversation. Does the phrase mean non-credit only? Credit only? Or both in a wider definition that includes all non-traditional education programs? Whole conversations have occurred with both parties talking about entirely different entities. This was seen as a crucial challenge in dealing with other deans and department chairs, especially if an institution is changing its approach to adult students and continuing education. A mission statement, such as the sample in figure 2.0 will help to attain the clarity needed. This can be printed in flyers, brochures, semester planning schedules and where ever else it fits and is appropriate.

Figure 2.0
Sample Mission Statement for Off-Campus Programs

Off-Campus Programs seeks to provide graduate and undergraduate programs of excellence, further developing the strengths of the University, at locations and times that are convenient for adults. Currently, more than (X) students are served per semester at more than (X) locations. Off-Campus Programs offer the most extensive off-campus Master's degree programs in this metropolitan area. Expanding professional opportunities and developing student potential are the foundation stones of the Off-Campus Programs Mission.

The University and the Off-Campus Programs Office continues to take pride in offering degree programs Off-Campus. These are identical in quality to those offered on campus in keeping with the Mission Statement of the University.

See Appendix A for an alternative sample of an Off-Campus Division Mission Statement.

Faculty Expectations.

Many faculty have had their earliest training with the 18 to 22 year old age group and many now find themselves at a more non-traditional institution with more adult students. Faculty will have different expectation as to how students will behave or should be treated if their previous experience is largely with the 18 to 22 age group. This can show in many ways, which can be surprising such as the words used in a syllabus, the attendance policy, or the make-up policy.

Formatting and scheduling of courses can be a source of expectations that are different: meeting one time per week for several hours versus three times a week for one hour can require different teaching styles and a variety of curriculum components to keep the rhythm of the class going and students learning and involved.

Attitudes toward Nontraditional Scheduling

In a survey of comparable institutions it was found that a period of transition to different semester starts and endings, different timing and pacing of classes, and to content that was appropriate to compressed formatting was needed for faculty. Several institutional representatives said that once these issues were discussed directly with the faculty the transition was eased. Such items as the need for break times in long blocks of class time and other logistical details, can be smoothed out with direct discussion. Adjunct faculty training to which full time faculty are also invited, can be very helpful.

Administration Support and Expectations.

An administration that has goals it wants to accomplish and is therefore very supportive is a help. Often expectations are too high for too short a period of time. But a few early successes and the informing of their opinions can help. Large systems may not accept the variability needed by continuing education: non-standard semester starts and endings; contract courses whose students are not billed in the usual way; or non-standard registration procedures that may be needed. If the registration program is linked to the billing program in a mainframe computer without a code that can be applied for contract courses, or off-campus differential tuitions, high level meetings with unit administrators may be needed to solve some of the resultant problems. A Chief Information Officer as discussed in Chapter 1 can help head off these problems when new technology is in the planning stages, by looking carefully at the business process of the institution before re-engineering it with technology.

Budget

Having a good sense of what the budget is at the start is important. As one new administrator said "know where the extra pots of money are." For example, if personnel pays for recruiting advertising, access this fund. If graphics and printing are fee-for-service departments, know this before large sums are suddenly deducted from the continuing education budget. It is important to know what the unit will be charged for and what it won't. Some institutions have cost-center budgeting and some have very separate income and expense budgets. Learning the historical reasons why this is the case, helps one to understand and deal with the limitations of different approaches.

Ethical Issues in Continuing Education: Possibilities for Leadership

With numerous non-accredited 'universities' and 'colleges' springing up on the Internet offering degrees for money and perhaps a short paper, maintaining a high ethical standard becomes even more important for institutions of higher education with regional accreditation and high academic standards. When one faces questions regarding equity, fairness, and students, stakeholders, co-workers, and community, ethical issues arise from questions with conflicting values and from the changing field of continuing education. Adult learners are:

- diverse
- seek to meet their own needs
- seek direct applications of their learning, and
- want parking, information technology, flexible book store hours, etc. with higher education services

Therefore educators need to re-articulate questions in ethical terms when conflicting values arise. One must look at the core values of the institution of higher education, of the community and of the profession.

When asked: What do ethical issues mean in one's role as continuing educators? Answers included that educators have to:

- take action
- consider one's role and responsibilities,
- help *students* be reflective practitioners.

A. Recognizing an Ethical Dilemma

Thinking of one's own professional life, recognizing an ethical dilemma is characterized by these statements from a focus group at a Continuing Education Conference:

> "it seems wrong";
> "clear inequity"
> "ask at gut level if it doesn't feel right";
> "would it be bad in the newspapers?"
> "does it affect larger issues? How?" and even "does it feel wrong in our culture and societal norms?"

They further listed some ethical issues they had encountered in continuing education:

- Unethical issues in the larger institutional organization, such as the provost vs. the treasurer;
- Income vs. program quality
- Professors double-dipping with travel re-imbursement
- Professors pushing social issues in class
- A student assistant enrolled in the same class in which he's assisting and copying other students' homework
- Using Ph.D. creditability in non-expertise fields
- Event planners being offered gifts from vendors
- Copying and copyright issues and "fair use" issues

In answering the questions as to where we seek answers to ethical dilemmas answers varied from "conversation with colleagues," "check with professional associations and professional literature" to "codes of ethics". The code of Ethics from the Association of Continuing Higher Education (ACHE) can be found in Appendix B.

B. An Ethical Perspective on Critical Challenges in the Profession in the Near, Mid-Term and Long Range Future

Great leaders who could *articulate* their core values helped their programs grow from "good to great" (Collins, 2001). Continuing education core values include improving lives and improving communities, as well as:

- Showing respect for and advocacy of adult students
- Fair treatment of all
- Concern for the integrity of the continuing education program content.

These core values are necessary if one is to lead, engage employees and define values for the organization. (See Appendix B Code of Ethics of the Association for Continuing Higher Education (ACHE).

Meanwhile there is pressure to increase enrollments without sufficient support and incentives for adjuncts to maintain quality; an overuse of adjuncts to save money; and a lack of 'normal customer concern' for adult students in many institutions of higher education.

There will always be production goals versus what is best for the student, financial vs. academic values, and the professional goals of truth, scholarship and standards vs. providing the public what it wants and the revenue that returns. There is a chance in the ethical arena to be leaders and educators within the continuing education organization.

Summary

As institutions of higher education are re-thinking who they are and what they do in the 21st century, there is a tremendous educational opportunity for them as the society continues to move into the information age. A number of Chief Information Officers both in the public and private sector believe that education is key to helping the Federal, state and local government agencies, and corporations move into the information age (Rand, 1995). Many lament that particular courses or degrees are not available nationwide by distance learning or other modes for their field offices. The need for more courses and degrees to be available to the adult workforce, is a still a continuing trend and a challenge to higher education. The use of information technology in support of the mission of the institution presents ongoing issues in many areas. Chapter Two presents more information on the many aspects of college life that can be enhanced by information technology. Dealing with multicultural demographics is another key challenge facing institutions of higher education, although many institutions have already integrated multicultural students successfully into their programs.

Clearness of definitions and a mission statement will help new programs get started, as will faculty and staff development about adult learners. The need to open up new opportunities, respond to individual needs, encourage community participation, improve the quality of life, create networks and linkages all are ongoing needs and providing these help people respond to changes in their world. Many kinds of adult and continuing education found in non-profit organizations other than colleges and universities, also can benefit from this clearness, a mission statement, and staff development.

Dealing with change easily and risk taking, have never been cultural norms of institutions of higher education and this has been true since the Battle of Hastings or even the Magna Carta, according to one university president. However, developing a better world and investing in people, have always been in the forefront of educators' ideals, and meeting the challenges of continuing education in higher education will help institutions to work towards these goals.

Chapter 3

Leadership In Continuing Education

Leadership principles drawn from management theorists can offer new insights to those responsible for providing well run, quality programs in Continuing Education in institutions of higher education. The divisions or departments that run Continuing Education programs are often non-traditional in structure and mission, but need to mesh with the traditional structure and organization of a college or university. There is, therefore, often a natural tension between the traditional organizational structure of most colleges and universities and the participative organizational structure of the continuing education-marketing-outreach division of the same institution. Leadership includes creating a vision and developing strategies to accomplish the vision, in addition to the management tasks of planning, implementing, operating and evaluating. Two-way communication is essential in continuing education, as the marketplace needs and economic trends change, which affect the programs' needs to be communicated to the institution, and the programs' availability to be communicated to the adult student market. Leadership principles can help with the meshing of the two structures, as the traditional institution of higher education is primarily affected by the ebb and flow of the 18 to 22 year old age group and the continuing education unit is serving the "non-traditional post 22 year old" students' marketplace needs, a huge group in the current demographic trend.

It's important to help the top levels of institutions of higher education to see their leadership roles in continuing education in the society at large. With new goals and new processes, the leader in charge of continuing education, often including distance education, has some new solutions to some historically difficult internal political problems, especially space and facilities power struggles. In the high context organizational culture of an institution of higher education, as described in the literature (Birnbaum, 1988), new numbers of learners in the over-22 age group will need to cause new solutions to be investigated, not old power struggles and intrigues to increase. The history of higher education shows some of the same issues of power and internal political influence and struggles as existing on the main campus or the residential campus, with continuing education issues as just an extension of some of these old issues.

Leadership

Leadership in continuing education administration is built upon planning for change. Leadership behaviors are designed to accomplish change for the improvement of the organization and/or the programs – not just for change's sake. Administrative behavior and responsibilities may be required of the same person as leadership responsibilities, but these just keep things going: systems, policies, regulations – these are the areas that fall under administration. Administration alone is not leadership, however, it is just using old processes to obtain old goals. Leadership would be using new processes to achieve on-going goals, or even new processes to reach new goals.

Diagram 3.1
Leadership vs. Administration

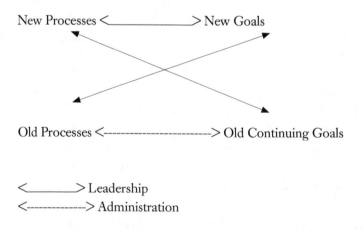

New Processes <————————> New Goals

Old Processes <-------------------------> Old Continuing Goals

<————> Leadership
<------------> Administration

In continuing education an example of an old goal might be the providing of numerous well-run courses. A new process to gain this might be to offer additional new formats, such as five Saturdays all day, or five weekdays, all day for one week, for courses with appropriate content. A new goal gained through old processes might be to add a lecture series for one credit or CEUs (Continuing Education Units) to a group of credit courses or a degree program. A new goal accomplished through old processes might also be to open another branch of a graduate education center in a new location, using the same administrative foundations and sequence of steps used to open the first center. An example of a new goal accomplished through a new process might be to set up new programs at a new off-site location, and then increase programs until there were several off-site and distance technology locations, identified by location codes or section codes.

Leadership in organizations and in society has been documented throughout history. Knowledge of the components of leadership is an invaluable asset to an individual charged with new kinds of tasks in higher education. Natural skill and ability in leading have always been an asset but knowledge of the various behaviors that increase the effectiveness of a group, in addition to planning new goals and/or new processes makes any effort needed more focused for leaders.

Perhaps a review of the basics would valuable. The original human relations management perspective sprang from experiments at Western Electric's Hawthorne Plant in the 1920's. The results of this experiment came to be known as the Hawthorne Effect in which a seemingly non-intrusive experiment produced striking results in human behavior. The basis of the study was to determine the relationship between working conditions and the level of employee productivity. It was found that no matter whether the lights were made brighter or dimmer the staff produced more (Gay, 1992). It was the attention the employees received and not the illumination of the workplace that made employees feel important and subsequently increased their productivity. The conclusion at the basis of this perspective is that leaders and managers CAN impact the behavior of their subordinates. In many cases improved morale and working conditions influenced peoples' productivity and attitudes more than financial incentives. It has always been assumed that faculty received stimulation and encouragement from each other and from their professional associations. This may or may not be true, but as staff and administrative employees fill many jobs in continuing education of all kinds, without necessarily having extensive backgrounds in higher education, peer attention and encouragement may not be sufficient to gain the results that a leader sees as goals. In considering leadership knowledge, skills and abilities, and leadership behaviors it is interesting to note the source of the material on leadership behaviors.

The behavioral approach to predicting leadership ability draws its data from descriptive observations of: (1) how managers/leaders spent their time at work; and (2) comparisons of the behavior of effective and ineffective leaders. The behaviors were documented through: job descriptions; direct observations; reviews of managers' diaries; anecdotes; and questionnaires. Researchers identified specific leadership behaviors which could serve as guides for effective leadership. A synthesis of these behaviors later became the basis of an instrument used to describe leadership entitled the *Leadership Behavior Descriptive Questionnaire.* This instrument was developed by Rensis Likert at Ohio State University and is still in use today.

Likert's early studies with managers identified other behaviors that made individuals successful. He identified five specific actions that managers and leaders took that made them more successful than their counterparts in the same company. These behaviors, with their specific associated tasks, created a climate of; (1) understanding; (2) mutual trust; (3) respect; (4) success among their subordinates; and (5) high task orientation. The five behaviors and their accompanying interpretations are discussed later in this chapter in the section on effective and ineffective leaders.

Likert determined that another important behavior involved informing. Informing is defined as a process by which a leader communicates the vision for the organization and task-relevant information needed by subordinates, peers, or superiors. A group eNewsletter or memo at regular intervals helps with this task, as well as the more traditional meetings approach. Likert believed that informing serves as a linch pin between the employees, the rest of the organization, and the outside environment. The situational approach to leadership which was developed by Blake and Mouton looks at: 1) work performed by the leader's organizational group; 2) the organization's external work environment; and 3) the characteristics of the followers. Their *Managerial Grid* has been used in organizations to assess the way that work is performed, and the relationship of these three variables to that work. Yukl emphasizes that the assumption underlying situational leadership is that different leader behavior patterns will be effective in different situations, and that the same behavior pattern is not optimal in all situations.

In his book *Leadership in Organizations,* Yukl (1994) identifies specific leadership behaviors that facilitate the management of the work and the management of relationships. Each of these functions was the result of studies of managers and leaders who had been successful ever since the early 1950's. Yukl compiled and analyzed the research and pinpointed the following behaviors as important. Leadership behaviors to manage human relationships include:

1. Supporting
2. Developing
3. Recognizing
4. Rewarding
5. Team building and conflict management
6. Networking

Specific behaviors to manage the work include:

1. Planning
2. Clarifying
3. Monitoring
4. Problem Solving
5. Informing

In summation, Yukl states that research on these specific categories of managerial behavior is limited. Nevertheless, the findings suggest that each of these categories of leadership and managerial behavior has the potential to improve leadership and managerial effectiveness if they are skillfully used in appropriate situations.

The Difference between Management and Leadership

Briefly stated, management provides consistency, control, and efficiency – with or without new ideas or processes. Leadership is needed to foster purpose, creativity, imagination, and drive. The specific roles of manager and leader have undergone a great deal of analysis in the field of business. This research points out that there are differences between these responsibilities and that the individuals who manage have specific roles that are determined by the organization. Organizational leadership, on the other hand, can come from a variety of people in a number of roles. In a time of continuing rapid change and innovation as is needed for the Information Age, managing well requires elements of leadership with creativity and imagination according to Peter Vaill.

Other definitions include Gardner's (1990), who proposes that leadership is "the process of persuasion by example by which an individual induces a group to pursue objectives held by the leader or shared by the leader and his or her followers" (p.1). He later describes managers as individuals who hold a directive post in an organization. They also preside over the resources by which an organization functions, allocate resources prudently, and make the best possible use of people. Gardner views leadership and management not as separate entities, but as a delicate balance between two roles. He calls individuals with the ability to play both these roles, leader/managers. Gardner does, however, differentiate between leadership and management with respect to the role the manager accepts in the workplace. He suggests that the word manager indicates that the individual so labeled presides over processes, resources and making the best use of people.

Yukl(1994), suggests that most definitions reflect the assumption that leadership involves a process of social influence as does Jacobs (1971). Yukl and others view effective leadership as a "group or organizational process that contributes to the overall effectiveness of a group or organization" (1994, p.8). Administration and management are similar in the description and in Figure 3.1 given earlier. However leadership differs as leaders must deal with the issue of implementing long-term change, and must use new processes to achieve on-going goals (such as helping young people and adults reach their full potential plus technology and alignment as two new processes); old processes to achieve new goals, or new processes to reach new goals. A new goal might be outreach to the many adults who never completed a four-year degree.

How does a Dean or Director enhance alignment? Leadership includes knowing that student requirements will change and sometimes are hard to interpret. While adult students may speak in the present tense, institutions of higher education must anticipate the future. Unfortunately few employees actually have direct contact with students, especially adult students, and understanding them is not seen as a collective responsibility. However many institutions are finding that they must be more student-focused or do poorly, according to the 1997 book *The Power of Alignment*, and also according to their own enrollment statistics. This need for alignment and a student focus is creeping into traditional, home-campus institutions but the slowness is often a frustration for continuing education schools and divisions. Sometimes, the student/customer voice is heard and ignored or perceived differently by professors and student assistants (e.g. 'change my own course' or 'it's not my job') resulting in no shared understanding with institution administrators. This lack of shared understanding impacts the institution, its strategy, its processes and its employees.

Institutions might well ask: 'What are the best-of-the-best doing?' How does the way we operate right now make us 'difficult to do business with?' Think of the 77% of those enrolled in higher education today that are "non-traditional" students and while thinking about them ask: 'How well are we satisfying our student/customers right now in what they care about? What are one or two things we could do differently?'

How does a Dean or Director make significant changes to achieve better quality results? Usually this requires long term changes that may take one or two years to plan, and two to three years to implement. This requires leadership. Under the terms of social exchange (Jacobs), leadership is:

An interaction between persons in which:

1) One presents information, of a sort, and in such a way that
2) the other is convinced that the benefits to him/herself will be greater than to you (cost-benefits improved), and,
3) the interaction avoids direct confrontation
4) and moves the persons or groups towards goals without making status or power differentials obvious.

A good example of this can be found in the story of a Midwestern state college Dean of a large continuing education center. Her center was in a small town in the middle of flat, hot, dusty farmland. She always managed to hire crackerjack Assistant Deans – competent productive people. How did she do this? She told them that if they would do their best work for her for four years, she would then write a top letter of recommendation to the

Dean of any of the biggest Continuing Education Programs in the country that they chose. (They could see their cost-benefits as being improved). The Dean made it clear that she didn't expect them to stay with her forever, just for the four years. Without this leadership gesture which provided the young professionals with a chance to see their own direct benefits in giving their boss their best efforts, this Dean might have had assistants quitting in one year. Or she might have had a hard time enticing able people to her locality at all.

Obviously this type of leadership requires interpersonal interaction skills to persuade persons (Kotter, 1999,1996, 1990). Some prefer an *authoritarian* type leader and some prefer a *humanitarian* type of leader. The choice will depend on: the situation; the leader; or the followers.

Sources of Power

There are five different *sources* of power described in management theory, and leadership can be helped by combining two or three of these to 'widen it's power base'. Remember, power is the *ability* to influence others and is always granted from below in this definition. Authority is granted from above, but power has to be earned. These sources of power, therefore, are ways one can seek to influence others' behavior:

1) *Reward Power.* This derives from the capacity of one person to reward another person in some way in exchange for their compliance with desired behavior. This compliance is expected to happen without supervision and works best when the results of the person accepting direction and providing effort *can be seen.* If it has been reinforced at the time, then it can easily be referred to later when the Director is giving the person a raise, or selecting a 'staff member of the month' to be a featured in some way.

2) *Coercive power.* Coercive power is not just withholding rewards, but it is the capacity to actually inflict something negative on a person. The outcome of the use of this kind of power is not good and it tends to cause people to 'cover up', to lie, to turn in false reports and in general to sabotage the goals of the organization.

3) *Legitimate Power.* Legitimate Power is just that: the Director is the Director (holds that job) so people *expect* him or her to lead and ask them to do things. However, the efforts to change made by the leader must appear to be 'reasonable and correct' to the group or else the leader will need

to 'inform them of his or her point of view' or have them understand more about his or her responsibility. Elected officials also have 'legitimate power'.

4) *Referent Power.* The source of this power is that people find the leader so attractive, competent, and understanding, that they want to *identify* with him or her. They wish to please the Dean or Director by seeking to do as he or she asks. This is the kind of leader who 'inspires' people and often they have no idea of the power that person ever has over them. This is one of the most powerful sources of power and a valuable one for all continuing education leaders, as it is important for staff and administrators to also model ways to inspire the faculty and students.

When a person models his or her behavior after a leader, it allows the leader great influence over the person. People do things then because: they like the leader; they want to do something the leader might like; and they want to *be* like the leader. People will have different areas in their lives, or groups of reference, which might each have a different referent person, such as: work life, social life, family life, and/or religious life.

5) *Expert Power.* This lies in the peoples' view that the leader has more knowledge and ability in a given area. This is an easy power source to add to, by updating knowledge with workshops and conferences, and keeping up with professional reading – *and talking about it* – whether in staff training or informally. People will provide support and follow directions without supervision in relationship to how expert they think the leader is.

When dealing with other peoples' ideas, work, or property expert leaders try to should always maximize the person's self-esteem and give credit at the end of a project when it is successful. On the other hand an expert leader knows that a person will be grateful to be saved from the embarrassment of constructive criticism in a public setting, if that is needed.

Social Exchange – How to Make Interactions Work for You

This concept is particularly useful to new leaders in continuing education in higher education confronted with a myriad of issues and charged with the task of creating new growth (in many ways). Social exchange can be a very helpful concept and can aid in deciding how fast to move on new initiatives.

The basic concept behind social exchange, which can be applied to leadership, is very much like a checking account. A leader can have a plus or minus balance of 'credit' and he or she can add to this or subtract from it. In exchange theory the central question is *why* a group member subordinates himself or herself to someone of higher status. When a leader starts out, he or she usually has a neutral balance. Then:

1) Everything the leader says builds plus or minus credit.
2) The follow-up on what he or she says builds plus or minus credit – getting resources as promised, etc.; and,
3) The reward or sanctions for those doing well or poorly towards organizational goals, builds plus or minus credit.

Many times the leader starts off with a slight plus credit, because he or she is 'the leader' unless the leader or director before him or her has done an unusually poor job. In the latter case, a leader would start off with a slightly minus credit and must allow a longer time to 'build trust' remembering the three categories above. Two major new initiatives every six months builds this trust – as people notice 1,2 and 3 above. However more than two changes in six months may strain this newly-formed trust and become a minus. Therefore saving smaller, surface new changes until later can help prevent using up this "plus credit" in advance, thus depleting the 'trust balance' into the following year or two.

When a leader begins his or her job, the organization can put a publicity item in a newsletter or college paper to help give him or her a plus credit start. However, there is only limited carry-over effect from past leaders, as credit is mostly based on the new individual, and what he or she does. A new leader also has a small plus credit as people just assume he or she has access to resources.

Good change is often slow and deliberate. A new Dean or Director needs to have the group at least not in opposition to him or her. If the group doubts the leader, they may try to split the cohesiveness of the group. Some individuals will work slowly and cautiously to split the staff. This of course, ruins the organization. In order to prevent this, the leader:

1) Has to make the proposed reward great enough to keep people positive and engaged.
2) Shouldn't promise anything he or she can't deliver.

The leader always gets more credit:

1) He or she has a plus to begin with and it grows, but he or she also gets more criticism. Deans and Directors should decide if they want this and have the competency for it.
2) Maybe a given individual has other competencies.

Social exchange is popularity-based. Mostly it is based on people *liking* to be with the leader. This leader makes people feel good about themselves. The followers feel that they are helpful to this kind of leader and like being helpful to him or her (referent power). Popular leaders can tolerate, accept, and appreciate a wide range of values – they are not dogmatic.

A leader of course can never know how employees will interpret his or her behavior, or what they'll do. Leaders can hope, though. Most groups develop fairly strong informal organizations. The goal is to have the goals of this informal network be the same as the formal goals of the division (for example: being the best continuing education unit in the area or region).

Getting the Minimum Effort or the Maximum Effort

Usually when an employee goes to work there is an 'employment contract' either written or unwritten in which the employee will accept direction and provide effort without question. This is called a 'minimum effort' – basically what must be provided without serious risk of getting fired. In continuing education this concept might be applied also to departments and professors, as their cooperation is essential to most new program initiatives. It's important to look to the incentives that exist for cooperation with the continuing education unit, and address them directly if necessary. Is there a revenue incentive? Does the department get a percent of the net income from new programs? Do they get research opportunities? More teaching assistants? More marketing exposure and infrastructure support?

One goal of leadership is to obtain, at least part of the time, group or individual effort that far surpasses the minimum. To obtain this greater effort, there must be some sort of process that leads the group or individual to be concerned about the achievement of organizational objectives for reasons other than just his or her pay and fringe benefits or immediate short term return to the department such as research, consulting, and publication opportunities. One could explain the benefits of long range marketing and showcasing of their content area as one possible incentive. The employee or department must be genuinely concerned about the goals of the Continuing Education Division itself (must have identified with it – usually related to finances) or must feel that the goals themselves are right and proper (e.g. the worth of the work – helping people/students develop to their full potential). Either will lead to a superior effort. This person or department takes pride in saying, "I work for a top university (or college) with a continuing education program that reaches far and wide".

Perhaps the most important aspect of the interaction between adults and the higher education institution is that the interaction must reflect to the adult that the institution considers him or her important, and of personal worth in himself or herself whether student, staff or faculty. Each person has a strong need to feel accepted and esteemed by others. To the extent that the institution communicates a feeling of personal worth and support to the individual or department, staff or faculty, they will feel rewarded and *in exchange* will feel motivated to repay the institution through greater cooperation and encouragement of other adults, whether students or employees. (However, this happens best when he or she knows that he or she or the department will get even more esteem or income – or both – if this behavior is continued and improved upon).

An interesting system of improving rewards to professors who perform extra services, in this case, offering engineering courses on compressed video, on-line and on satellite for down-link, can be seen at a large state university. The professors are given a teaching load of just one course on-campus that is also on distance technology, and are also given a half time research assistant. In addition, 10-month professors are paid also for the month of August. They come for some hours of training and practice in front of the TV camera in August. Interestingly enough, the school finds that good instructors can practice very little and still do well, and poor instructors are not helped much by the training. The goal is acclimatization to on-line presentation, however. Commitment in the marketplace and with faculty and students is very slow to build but commitment *is very easy to destroy.*

Rensis Likert in his two books, *New Patterns of Management* (1961) and *The Human Organization* (1967), found that organizations have three sets of variables. If you want to effect long term change you must have input into the first set, which then affects the second set, and that affects the third set. These variables are:

1) *Causal Variables* – The organization has some control over these: policies; interpersonal relations; salary; fringe benefits; rules and regulations; and hours.

2) *Intervening Variables* – These include perceptions, attitudes and loyalty which build, based on the causal variables.

3) *End variables* – These result from the attitudes and loyalty in a continuing education department or division, and include as an end goal competent students and profitable programs (one definition of productivity); cooperative staff or faculty; or on the negative side, waste, pilfering, turnover of employees, non-cooperation of departments, and absenteeism.

Chart 3.1
Likert Model

VARIABLES

Causal —————————————— *Intervening* —————————— *End Variables*

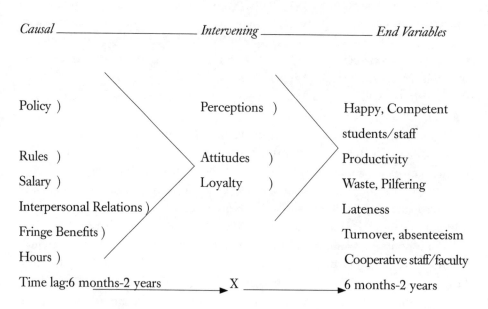

Policy)   Perceptions)   Happy, Competent students/staff

Rules)   Attitudes)   Productivity

Salary)   Loyalty)   Waste, Pilfering

Interpersonal Relations)   Lateness

Fringe Benefits)   Turnover, absenteeism

Hours)   Cooperative staff/faculty

Time lag:6 months-2 years ———→ X ——————→ 6 months-2 years

Remember the need to consider the *time* factor in the above process. The time lag or 'institutional lag' needed is six months to two years between sets of variables for each column to effect a change in the next column. A full total of six years may be needed for a change affecting a large market or a large university.

If undesirable behaviors in the end variables are found when this chart is applied to a specific division or center, or even to an entire institution, plans can be made to start a change in causal variables. Perhaps it is time to have the leadership as a group review and update staff and faculty policy. Salary is a problem in the higher and continuing education world, but almost all of the other causal variables can be changed to better benefit or accommodate the faculty and staff, and to create better feeling and more loyalty.

An example of a simple change illustrating the effects of causal variables can be seen in the story of Mary, a staff assistant. Mary needed to take a summer waitressing job to help pay the taxes on her graduate tuition benefits at a private university. Her boss adjusted her schedule two afternoons a week so she could leave at 3:30 p.m.

Mary was very grateful (intervening variable) for this understanding attitude on the Director's part and was loyal to the division and polite and enthusiastic with the students and faculty for the rest of the time she was employed there (several years).

The time lag in this change in Mary's perception from feeling that this was just a job with inconvenient hours and low pay, to a feeling of gratitude occurred considerably faster than the six months on the chart, but then this was a small change.

Unfortunately, this chart works in reverse, too, and where there is waste, absenteeism, staff turnover, unhappy students, and uncooperative departments, a director or an observer might find disloyal staff or faculty, who perceive the policies and regulations as harsh and unfair or have other complaints (whether justified or not). This would be a larger problem and might take the full two years for attitudes to change, after some of the causal variables had been changed.

Because of this time lag, it is important never to judge a program or initiative, and perhaps drop it, after only one year. When a new dean or director comes in, he or she sees many things he or she might want to change. He or she should write these in a file or notebook and start changing the two most important choices the first six months. This is a 'building trust' time so the changes should come gradually. However, after a year if he or she looks at the four areas he or she has chosen to work on, (two every six months), noticeable improvement may be hard to find. The Likert Model and the idiosyncracy credit concept, discussed in this chapter, suggest the benefits of waiting another year before dropping these efforts, as attitudes and perceptions change slowly, but are well worth waiting for.

Characteristics of Successful Leaders

In studying large companies with many branches, Likert compared the thirty most successful leader/managers with the thirty least successful leader/managers in the same company as mentioned earlier. He found that the major factors of difference between the two groups fell into five categories as mentioned earlier. The successful leaders and managers were able to:

1) *Provide social support for people and groups.* This was found to be the most important characteristic and is a causal variable that a leader can control to build good attitudes.

2) *Provide high task orientation.* These leaders were always clarifying the overall goals of the organization, translating the vision, and reminding people of their importance.

3) *Provide a high degree of technical expertise.* These leaders knew their fields. They took courses and workshops, and read books to keep up professionally, and thus they were able to be problem solvers and help train their people.

4) *Maintain a high degree of role differentiation.* While these leaders were friendly with their staffs, they didn't go out and get drunk with the staff or share details of their recent divorce. By being sure to do the things that only a leader can do and not always being tempted to 'pitch in with everyone' they served their organizations better. This is not to say that they did not pitch in sometimes but they reserved time for planning and keeping up with professional reading.

5) *Provide general supervision.* This means not close and specific supervision, but meeting with groups of people in a *general* way. The concept here is that people are hired because they are competent, and are trusted to do a good job. General training and direction is offered at staff meetings. It was found that specific, close supervision makes people feel mistrusted. Even nosy praise can 'hem people in'. People who feel mistrusted immediately develop attitudes of disloyalty and non-support for the organizational goals.

Providing these five conditions created a 'climate' that led to happy, competent employees and other positive results.

People want a leader who can be a focal point. A leader who:

1) Gets supplies (increases resources)
2) Provides goal orientation and facilitates group attainments
3) Resolves conflicts between people

Likert divides organizations into four types:

System 1: 'exploitative authoritative';
System 2: 'benevolent authoritative';
System 3: 'consultative'; and
System 4: 'participative group'. (See Figure 3.2)

Figure 3.2
Rensis Likert's Four Systems of Management

Which are You?

(1)	(2)	(3)	(4)
People afraid to talk to management or are told not to. 'Head in the sand'	People less afraid to talk Closed – door policy	People fairly free to talk	*Extensive friendly interaction* People really working with you *Productive* problem solving not Win-lose *Management* knows what peoples' problems are

In extensive (300-400) studies, Likert found that when organizations changed from system one to system four management, their income/revenue changed from 15% to 20% *less* than the projected budget amount, to 15% to 20% *more* than the projected budget amount. This benefit of a system four management style, characterized by extensive, friendly interaction and problem solving with people, reflects the fact that the most valuable asset of any organization is its people. When a Dean or Director gets 'over task oriented' he or she is selling short his or her most valuable asset – people. In fact, when the 'let's run a tight ship', 'clean up the budget', 'follow the organizational chart (stovepipes)' or hierarchical attitudes come in, the most productive employees leave first, as they get offers elsewhere.

Comptrollers and budget officers often do not have the vision to build towards a system four management, and suggest short-term budget oriented solutions to problems. The specifics of how a leader applies system four management goals, varies with the individual organization. People have to be treated well in order to want to put any extra effort into changes and organizational improvement. The essential fact is that leaders need to respect each individual's human dignity, within his or her *own* framework.

If a Director or Dean would like to find out what system his or her program is, he or she can ask any employee "How much confidence and trust do you feel your superior has in you?" The formula for a successful organization is supportive relationships (including opportunities to advance), plus high performance goals and technical competence.

Supportive Relationships + High Performance Goals + Technical Competence =
Successful Organization

Most of Likert's research is based on *perceptions* which *may not reflect what's really going on*, but the *perceptions are what counts* (they affect the end variables).

When one first starts to build attitudes, loyalty, and perceptions, 'productivity' may decline in the first six months.

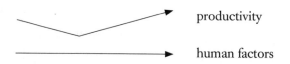

productivity

human factors

This has also been called the "implementation dip" in the change management literature. Because resources previously *all* were put into productivity. Some people may have been 'just waiting' to let you know their problems.

But in this phase of 'building attitudes' to survive you can:

1) Use up inventory
2) Borrow
3) Cut back in other ways

In the long run, a person that feels respected will be much more willing to give the organization and institution his or her maximum effort. This leads to it really becoming the best continuing education program in the area, and to everyone associated with it taking pride in providing really excellent programs for adult students.

The Use of Power

Sometimes power is erroneously defined as negative and coercive because the positive aspects of power have been listed under leadership. However, the following definitions of power as distinct from authority, will be used here.

Definitions of Power:

Power is – *The Ability to Influence Other's Behaviors*

(Always granted from below, that is, by the people over whom it is exercised.)
People will die – rather than change for some people, as in the American Revolution.

Authority is – *The Vested Right to Try to Influence Others*

(Always granted from above.)

Power has to be earned.

Power actually increases when you give it away. There are more ideas and more people involved. Some people think the more power they give away the less they have. (A few powerful academic deans are good examples of this). For example, suppose Dean Joseph Jones approaches his staff and says "We need more active showcasing and marketing of this program. I want you each to call ten companies." What happens? Two people find suddenly that they are much too busy with administrative duties, two others have car trouble and another thinks it's a bad idea and will never work and says so (politely). However, if Dean Jones turns the power of deciding how to solve their marketing problems over to the professional outreach or marketing and counseling staff, he may find that he winds up with four or five components to an elaborate marketing campaign: an education fair; a direct mail piece; advertising; corporate calls; and highlighting the course description and schedule on their Web site. Since each person is confident about the success of their component (and knows how to get help to make it work), and likes their own ideas so well, he or she is ready to work on it and the unit benefits. The total amount of "power" is multiplied. To have new growth in changing times, this participative approach is almost an imperative. The collaborative learning that can result from the participative approach also produces increased learning, creative insight, higher productivity, higher achievement, and a higher quality of decision making (Johnson and Johnson, 1989).

Figure 3.3
Amount of Power and Number of People

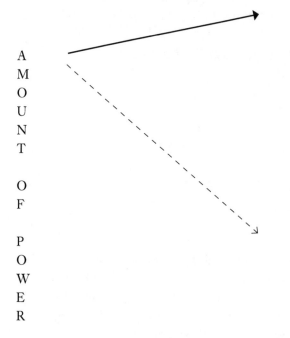

A
M
O
U
N
T

O
F

P
O
W
E
R

Power actually increases when you give it away. (More ideas and people are involved).
 – Some people think the more they give away the less they have.

NUMBER OF PEOPLE

There are times when a Director needs to take the lead and be 'in charge'. Two things determine whether or not power attempts will work:

1) The potential costs and the potential consequences of the change the leader is initiating, and
2) The staff's view of the Director's responsibility.

The Director needs to consider the staff's view and change it by giving them information about his or her responsibilities if necessary. This is a good time to develop joint goals to solve the problems creating the need for changes. Working as a group to develop joint goals also implies that positive potential consequences of the change being initiated, include the leader's valuing the staff's input and ideas. Naturally, this would help to offset a potential cost of the change being initiated – large or small – such as the rearranging of schedules or classrooms, or even coffee breaks.

If you get the staff into coalition in your favor they will accept many more of your ideas. To do this talk one-to-one with staff members. Hopefully, this coalition would include the entire staff, but if the majority or even a few people understand the change and have had time to make suggestions in informal chats, the coalition will help the leader reduce his or her costs. A coalition risks costs to the leader, but it more often will help the leader to avoid costs. (That is, the costs involved with presenting an idea and having it turned down).

Idiosyncrasy Credit

Idiosyncrasy credit, sometimes called personality credit, develops slowly, over time. It's important for new leaders to remember this, as mentioned earlier. The term idiosyncrasy directly refers to the number of idiosyncrasies (or peculiarities) the Director, or new leader, is allowed to have.

A new Dean or Director may come in and see room for innovation in the program. In workshops for Deans and directors, experts advise new leaders to write down all these good ideas for later use when their fresh perspective may have worn off and they cannot identify the needs as clearly. Then choose only two new ideas to begin implementing the first six months. The second six months he or she can choose two more. One director handles this in a 'letter to the staff' which is the first page in her staff notebook. (In this staff letter following the paragraph on philosophical topics she includes a paragraph on her two idiosyncrasies, plus thanks for each person's special efforts.) These idiosyncrasies can be anything from how the telephone should be answered to the start of a re-organization.

The idea here is that she gets to have two idiosyncrasies – even if they are a little unusual – just because she *is* the director. This builds with time and with her abilities in social exchange and interactions. Generally, leaders have a greater positive balance of idiosyncrasy credit. Studies show over and over again that people at least want a fair exchange or even that they prefer getting more back in return, for their efforts. If they feel they gain self-esteem and status from working in a good work climate where their extra efforts are especially valued, they will begin to feel that they are getting a fair exchange. The amount of credit a leader gets is based on the *perceptions* of the group members relative to the accomplishment of group goals. A leader, therefore, should let the group know when the division or unit is praised or group goals are being met in a way in which the staff may not be aware.

To Gather Credit A Leader Must:

1) facilitate group attainments and the group has to know it. (Remember though, they get their perceptions through interactions.)
2) resolve conflicts
3) increase resources

Exchange behaviors for *leadership* are partly learned in early childhood. Children build high self-esteem and a strong self-concept at an early age. They learn that they are desired, loved and popular. This in turn helps them to take risks and to make decisions. Because they are popular they are asked to make decisions or to take risks first. This may be the source of charisma and what seems like leadership "natural ability".

But adults as well as children can learn to value the pay-offs which result from risk taking (such as asking the staff to implement one change). Adults can learn to accept failures that can also result from risk taking. By learning from their mistakes, adults and children can say, "I won't make the same mistake twice" or "I can usually do *something* to help correct a wrong decision."

Adults can learn leadership behaviors, to take risks, and to value the payoffs. It is difficult to change one's behavior and to maintain it over a long period of time. In stress situations one's behavior won't change too much, so that if it's fairly consistent with one's most comfortable style, whether it is "people oriented" or "task oriented," there is less disruption.

Some leaders understand how others perceive them and some don't. The ones who don't, keep going out on a limb and getting no support. To read perceptions, leaders have to read peoples' behavior, their slouches, for instance. They need to be sensitive and "read" people. If a leader doesn't feel he or she has support it is better *not* to take a stand but discuss the issue more and more ahead of time, informally, in one-to-one conversations. Stress can block some of this discussion, or perceptions, so a relaxed situation, over coffee or food of some kind, might be in order. (At one spring staff meeting the Director provided fresh strawberries and powdered sugar to dip them into. He had just gone out at noon to pick up the two items at the store. The originality of the idea gave everyone a lift.)

The more valuable the leader is perceived as being, the greater the credits, rewards, and money or salary can be that he or she receives. Just as directing one graduate education center can help students develop to their full potential, directing three continuing education centers will help more students and thus provide more return to the institution of higher education.

Organizing Structures

There is no typical organization of a Continuing Education Division, Department, or Unit in higher education, but it is usually different from the traditional college or department organization. A college or department organization might look like A or C in Figure 3.4 "Organizing Structures". Other useful structures look like D, or E, arranged by geographic area, by school or program, or less useful B, a minimal or "burn-out" structure, in a humorous representation.

Figure 3.4
Organizing Structures

A. Total Institution

- = Prof. staff & coordinators

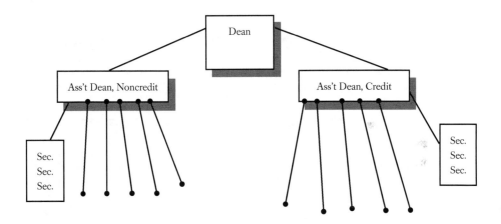

B. Minimal Structure (Leads to Burnout)

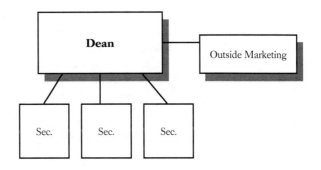

C. By College and Department

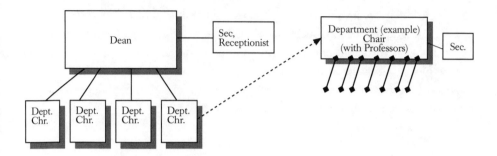

D. By School or Program;

- = Professional staff/marketing and counseling (associate managers)

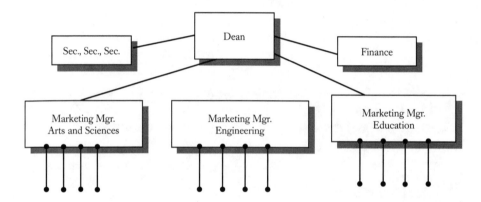

E. By Geographic Area

- = Professional staff/associate directors

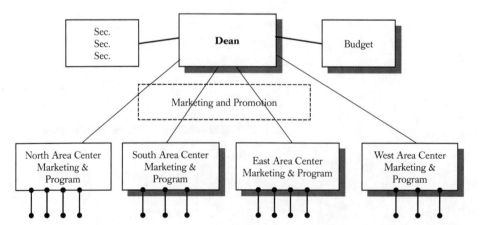

These last two models, whether organized by area or school and program (or in a matrix combination of both to meet special requirements), allow for the programs to grow. Directors or Managers can be added by program or area, and Associate or Assistant Directors can be added for professional level marketing outreach, counseling, handling information sessions, and off-site course administration.

Management "by walking around" (Peters and Waterman, 1982) is more necessary for the leader using this structure, as professional staff may be dispersed into several locations. Attending prospective student information sessions when possible and in general being in touch with the staff, the faculty, and the market in each area, will yield benefits.

As a program grows and changes, re-assessment of areas, programs and duties will be needed. A large contract program with 150 students in six or eight courses may be added. Another program may saturate and need to be closed down. This ebb and flow can be accommodated but is quite normal in continuing education. The role of the Associate Director is most frequently overlooked in the staffing up of continuing education programs and Deans and Directors wind up attending education fairs and giving information sessions themselves, as more and more companies outsource their training and education needs, which has now become a fast growing new market for higher education.

Summary

As risk-taking is an inherent part of leadership, but is not a traditional cultural norm in higher education (Birnbaum, 1988), many Deans or Directors of Continuing Education accept the position only if they are tenured professors in their own disciplines. Therefore knowledge and understanding of higher education are inherent in the individual, but the person has to rely on personal discretion and local tradition for leadership knowledge and skills, for management, and for marketing strategies and techniques. Often the individual is a likeable, entrepreneurial type of person, who may see the need for delving into the literature on marketing and on leadership or management. One successful Dean, a Ph.D. in Management, overcame the gaps between the three fields of higher education, marketing, and management. Understanding that the framework for continuing, adult education needs a leader with higher education, leadership, and marketing knowledge and expertise, helps to support a successful (and growing) continuing education unit within the institutional context. The unit usually works better with its leader chosen for these multiple backgrounds and experiences. Balanced risk taking with risk assessment can be done; understanding the institutional lag in a large institution and a large market is possible; and utilizing persuasion and idiosyncrasy credit, all help the leader to be successful.

Faculty tenure, for instance, is a nationwide issue, and the resulting problems of tenure can be addressed when one looks at the main incentive of tenured faculty. Is it educating students? Doing research? Not seeking more than the allotted number of full-time-enrollments(FTEs)? Or is the main incentive retaining enough time to do outside consulting? If the latter is true, institutions of higher education have lost control of internal incentives for faculty, except that of spending less time at the institution. When institutions maintained a monopoly view of higher education, faculty wishes were largely ignored, and perhaps this is a contributing factor to faculty attitudes today. This certainly works in opposition to the goals of new (read energy-consuming) programs, courses, locations, and technology. As one large department chairman said "universities are the last bastion of individual entrepreneurs" (referring to individual consulting work). This person had been re-elected as a Department Chairman for 18 of the last 20 years. The huge new market for college level continuing education in India, China and the rest of Asia is just coming into its own.

Budget and resource allocation issues are also not new to higher education with the advent of continuing education, but again, a new revenue stream from adult students can help bring new solutions to old problems. Diversity of students and faculty are newer but on-going issues, as the demographics of the nation change, and the changes are reflected in public and private institutions.

It is interesting to note international approaches to continuing education. Australia encourages the involvement of all family members in the continuing education program. Australia and Bangladesh let the community plan and design programs that respond to their needs. Other countries such as Malaysia and Indonesia set up committees for this planning. Flexibility, as in all continuing education, is often linked to innovation when new practices are quite different from traditional educational approaches. In Australia they find that the capacity – building these programs provide, with the knowledge, skills and abilities necessary, results in helping people become more self-reliant and confident. Many international continuing education programs, while being non-credit, value sustainability so that learners participating in programs can develop skills and knowledge and thus become more self-sufficient (UNESCO, 2003).

Careful planning and decision-making, with the group of staff members or the group in an academic department cooperating whenever possible, also help, and are addressed in the next two chapters. Leadership behaviors that follow as leadership skills and knowledge are acquired, help the internal group and even the institution, become more effective as they, and it, define the mission and develop a vision for continuing education.

Chapter 4

Planning for Continuing Education in Higher Education

Good planning is the key to smoothly running programs for continuing education in higher education or in any setting. Planning can help anticipate decisions; it can help handle interdependent decisions; and it can provide a process by which staff and faculty can have input and buy into goals and strategies.

One point of view stresses that the main value of planning does not lie in the actual plans produced, but in the process of producing them. The interaction of people and ideas as they think about mid-range and long-range goals for a program or educational center is the main benefit. Therefore planning cannot be done *to* or *for* a group but must be done *by* the group. Many "best ideas" of staff and faculty in a planning session, may surface and can be suitably adapted onto a time line joined with other "best ideas." The implementation of every step of the plan is less important than the habit developed of sharing good ideas and planning for the future within a framework structured enough to allow good ideas to be captured and thought through. As with students, the process of learning can be more important than the product.

Since both the program being planned for, and its environment, change during the planning process, it is nearly impossible to consider all the variables. Therefore it is necessary to continuously update and maintain a plan, both individually and in a group. To prevent being "sandbagged" by change it is important to try to understand the environment systematically on at least five levels: global, national, community, workplace, and individual. When changes in each of these levels are considered in relation to the impact(s) they might have on the programs for adult students, new insights emerge and actions and contingency plans can be developed. One can also:

1) try to alter the course of the change.
2) decide how to capitalize on the advantages of the change
3) plan to resist the change.

Anticipating change and predicting it helps an organization and its people feel more "on top of things" and therefore maintains morale. Long range planning that is hard to reverse, and that effects many functions of the organization should also be considered in the light of techniques for decision making given in the chapter on Decision-making. This strategic planning must be done with both external and internal considerations. Planning next week's classroom use schedule is an example of short range planning and hopefully can be delegated to another person or group, along with most short range planning. Opening another education center across town is an example of long range planning and it could require a lot of the Continuing Education Administration's resources, and also those of the total institution of higher education involved: money, person-hours, and equipment and materials.

Three Philosophies of Planning

Three major philosophies of planning include: satisficing, optimizing, and adaptivizing (Ackoff, 1970).

Satisficing is when one solution is arrived at that meets objectives and goals that are feasible and desirable. It implies "being satisfied." The satisficing planner sets a few simple goals and is happy to satisfy them. This has dangers in not being long range enough, or not considering the outside environment enough, but for some problems it is appropriate. An additional danger of satisficing is that sometimes at the end of a long meeting, when there is pressure of time, the single solution can look more and more attractive when it is not the best or the most appropriate solution.

Optimizing is similar to the rational approach taught in business schools. The goal in optimizing is to do as well as possible and many, many alternatives can be generated. Unfortunately this takes more time than one always has. In the rational technique, criteria are developed after the problem is defined and only three to five alternatives are considered against these criteria. The consideration of several alternatives can surface some variables that may be combined in yet a new way. For example a 'hybrid course' that alternates weeks of live and distance instruction might solve instructor travel problems, by reducing the frequency of trips. There are always variables that are uncontrolled, such as weather, economic conditions, the competition, technological developments, and preferences of students or employees. Unfortunately the optimizer sometimes ignores these variables, and often ignores goals that cannot be quantified. (For example: the financial bottom line can be more important than the academic excellence, integrity or applicability of the programs.

Adaptivizing is the name given planning that "gets outside the box" or considers solutions from a very different perspective than satisficing or optimizing. Often this happens when the problem is redefined and looked at in new ways. The chapter on problem solving suggests a number of ways to do this.

Adaptivizing provides for five different sets of plans based on our knowledge of the future which can be: certain, uncertain, or complete ignorance. The planning for the future that is fairly certain, is called commitment planning (plan set number one) and the administrative budget might be an example of this. The other four sets of plans will be described as follows.

Planning for uncertainty of the future that is a little better or a little worse than the present situation is called "contingency" planning and requires two plans: one for the somewhat better (plan set number two) and one for less good or somewhat worse conditions (plan set number three). The aspect of the future that cannot be anticipated, or that represents ignorance also requires two sets of plans: one for much better conditions (plan set number four) and one for much worse conditions (plan set number five). This is called "responsiveness" planning, and is frequently overlooked. It's labeled "responsiveness" because this planning builds responsiveness and flexibility into the organization. The chart in Chapter Eight leading to Saturday, and weekend programs, shows how responsiveness planning might be done for scheduling in a situation that was much more favorable than previously thought. A responsiveness plan for conditions being much worse (such as a major plant or military base closing near your town) might first require additional classes, and then might need financial emergency measures such as plans to rent out one or two classrooms for other uses and/or for small business incubators. Another emergency measure would be to eliminate the most expensive, least effective, part of your program, such as a programs that had saturated the market in their present location. New formats, new locations, updated course descriptions and titles, all help programs be responsive to new circumstances, whether much better or much worse.

The adaptive planner tries to change the system or the structure so that efficiency follows as a result. Organizations that plan this way tend to use their employees' best potential and therefore are very effective.

Scenarios and Objectives for Managing Change

Commitment planning sometimes is called "reference projection" and is essentially what can be predicted if nothing new is done. What one would like to have done can be referred to as a "wishful projection" and the difference between the two defines the gap that needs to be filled by planning and setting objectives onto a time line.

Sometimes it is difficult to get at the aspirations of those involved, in order to learn "what kind of Continuing Education Program do we want this to be?" An effective way to uncover these aspirations is through the use of scenarios.

A scenario in the motion picture industry describes what people will do when acting out a story. Scenarios in continuing education management planning describe different models of what people will do or what must or might happen to reach different goals. They also allow for wishful thinking in various areas to be quantified so that decisions regarding possible goals can be made. Deans and Directors usually have many aspirations for their organizations and these can be called "wishful projections." The steps that will take a Program or Division from their reference projection to a wishful projection are called "planned projection." A schedule can be attached to the attainment of each step or objective in the planned projection.

A good way to get at the wishful projections of a group and to determine if there are possible goal conflicts is to develop scenarios around different topics. Identifying and resolving possible goal conflicts *early* further enhances any project, by reducing conflicts and encouraging useful discussions.

It is possible to develop scenarios around policies, programs, procedures, practices and courses of action. In each case draw a picture (model) of the existing policy, course of action, or other item that needs to be examined. Put a box around each existing step. Then brainstorm alternatives for the step described in each box of the model. A group or an individual can do this. As the four or five (or more) boxes are reviewed and brainstorming occurs, a scenario begins to emerge. Some ideas may clearly be inappropriate but lead to other possible suggestions.

Deciding How to Increase an Education Center's Enrollment Income, Quality and Morale, and Other Scenarios

In identifying problems and solutions for an education center it is helpful to be clear on the style or values of the education center. Discussion of the philosophy with both the staff and the Faculty or academic departments will help to define the programs to be presented, more clearly. This can be done by brainstorming statements for the philosophy and then the market needs and requests, first in a staff meeting, followed by a vote on the five or ten most important elements in the philosophy. This list can then be taken to a meeting that includes faculty and faculty can brainstorm *their* ideas about the philosophy and the program that are recorded on a flip chart. When a final consensus is gathered on the faculty list, by the faculty, and then the two lists are taken together, usually an impressive goal statement results. This can be placed in the publicity brochures, on bulletin boards and wherever else information on good higher education continuing education is needed. A sample program goal statement can be seen in Figure 4.1.

Once the philosophy and programming goals are developed, the "style" of the educational center will be clear and possible scenarios for improvement and advertising of one aspect or another can be generated. We have developed a few here as examples. A scenario is a description of what an organization might look like at some specified time in the future. It is a description rather than a financial plan. Use of scenarios is based on the idea that what an educational center becomes depends more on what it does than on what is done to it. It builds on the idea of making the future happen rather than letting events slide and then saying "what happened?" The steps in developing a scenario are given here but first it's important that the philosophy and programming goals of the educational center be clear so we've listed the following as an example.

Figure 4.1
Philosophy of a Continuing Education Division or Center

The philosophy of the Higher Education Continuing Education Division is based on the belief that students are individuals, learning and growing. Within the framework of the current world situation, the focus of the Continuing Education Division (or Continuing Education Center) will be:

1. to provide programs which, in balance, enhance a student's development intellectually, and build career abilities as appropriate
2. to provide programs that are requested in the community and marketplace
3. to provide an environment conducive to learning
4. to provide and environment in which students can learn actively through research and hands-on experience, (this could mean facilitating library resources, Internet use, project teams, internships, computer labs, text books, etc.)
5. to provide individualized attention within the context of a group setting

6. to provide specialized student services including informal counseling, expediting administrative matters, and making higher education 'user friendly'.
7. to work with faculty as active partners in their students' learning

---

The opportunity to vote on elements of the philosophy gives faculty a true feeling of involvement and can be repeated every spring during the planning-for-fall period. This philosophy can also be communicated in a one-to-one situation by the Dean or Director of the Continuing Education Division or Unit, calling on the heads of the academic departments, or by presenting it at academic department or school meetings. Faculty also hear the many expectations other faculty have for the education centers or unit, and in voting for the elements favored by the majority, they see that not all wishes can be met. If a faculty member feels strongly that his or her students should be allowed photocopier or even camcorder privileges, for example, he or she if an adjunct, may wish to look for another institution of higher education in which to teach. This will save the center director and adjunct faculty member a year of complaints and unhappiness and thus can be a benefit. Or the faculty member may see that photocopying by students cannot be worked into the budget, and suggest students use outside photocopy or camcorder rental shops.

Once the philosophy and programming goals are decided upon, the Dean or Director can begin translating them into goals for the Division and staff, and then into a schedule for attainment of these goals. A Director's list of goals may look quite different from the philosophy, while still remaining relevant. These goals might include:

– Remaining financially afloat and producing a surplus by increasing the Division or a particular Center's income
– Building quality into the program by focusing on specifics in the philosophy
– Improving safety and security throughout the center
– Building staff morale and student service

An effective way of working on these goals is to develop a "scenario" for one or more of them. A Continuing Education Division and its centers can design almost any kind of future it wants for itself, given careful planning and involvement of staff and faculty. A scenario allows room for wishful thinking in the future.

The first step in developing a scenario is to draw a model of the activities done throughout the planning cycle in a continuing education division or center. See Figure 4.2.

Figure 4.2
A Model of the Continuing Education Planning Cycle

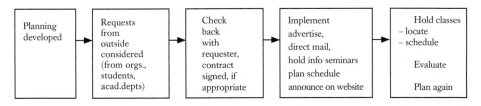

| Planning developed | Requests from outside considered (from orgs., students, acad.depts) | Check back with requester, contract signed, if appropriate | Implement advertise, direct mail, hold info seminars plan schedule announce on website | Hold classes – locate – schedule

Evaluate

Plan again |

The second step in developing a scenario for a particular goal is to brainstorm alone or perhaps with a group how that goal could be implemented in two or three ways around each box in the model. For instance for the goal "Increasing a Center's Enrollment and Income," the scenario might look like this:

Figure 4.3
Increasing a Continuing Education Center's Enrollment and Income

| Direct mail goes out | Ads run | Information sessions held | Students register and attend | Students graduate |

Direct Mail

1. Plan on 3% return
2. Use best lists possible, plus in-house lists
3. List program content and information session dates.

Ads run

1. Run ads in targeted/general newspapers and radio, 2-4 wks after direct mail goes out.
2. Put briefing dates in ads, plus in direct mail. List phone and fax numbers for Reserveation' option.

Info Sessions /Briefings held

1. Schedule 2-3 per program mid-fall, mid-spring, & mid-summer. Vary the weeknights held.
2. Faculty and Deans describe content of courses, how to be accepted etc.
3. Have refreshments if possible
4. Hold at 5-6, 6-7 pm for working adults

Register and attend

1. Have reservations at convenient places & times.
2. Develop Internet & telephone & registration systems.
3. Ease finding classroom and parking first night in many ways – list all of them

Students graduate

1. Have an Alumni Assoc. after graduate
2. Alumni Assoc. tasks:

   – help in job & social networking
   – serve on Advisory Board to faculty
   – mentor current students

This scenario then gives a Director lots of ideas from which to choose three to five logical projects for development, that might increase the center's income. Other ideas stay in the back of people's minds, and the director may hear more ideas or more possibilities about a given idea next year.

A scenario which might maintain and build quality into the program according to the Philosophy in Figure 4.1 and would also work towards building staff morale, might look like Figure 4.4. Space doesn't permit all the ideas that can be generated from the philosophy when it is applied to the model of the planning cycle. More equipment, more imaginative use of what is there, or a visiting speaker at a Staff meeting, are a few that come to mind. The possibilities are limitless and generating them makes a good exercise for beginning-of-the school year staff meetings. If the staff can help choose two or three goals for staff training for the year, and then even the improvement of quality and morale have a good start.

Figure 4.4
Scenario for Maintaining Quality and Staff Morale

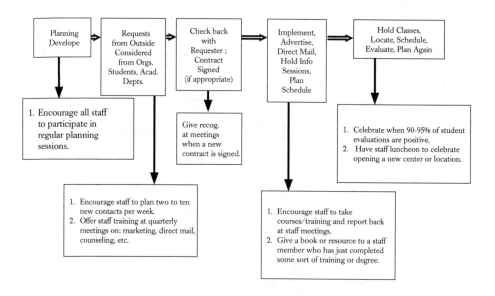

Scenarios are a tool for helping people to take a long view in a world of uncertainty. They are NOT predictions but are vehicles for helping people learn. The end result is not an accurate picture of tomorrow but of better decisions about the future. Scenarios can also be used to change others' view of reality. This use of scenarios visually demonstrates future possibilities or possible realities, with a 'better', 'the same', or 'worse' scenarios such as the following three in Figures 4.5, 4.6, and 4.7.

Figure 4.5
Scenario for More Growth

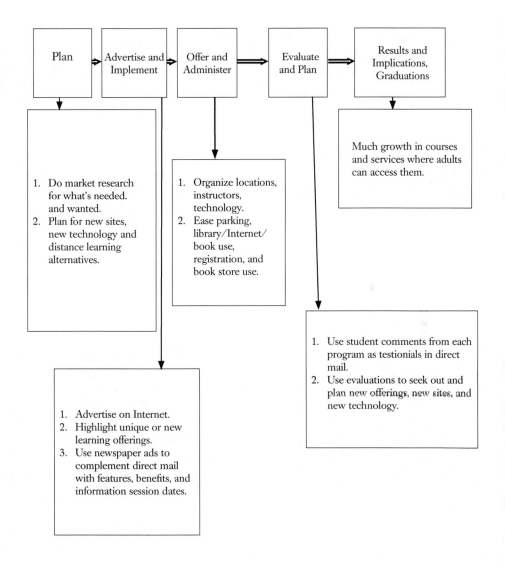

Figure 4.6
Scenario for Less Growth (Worse)

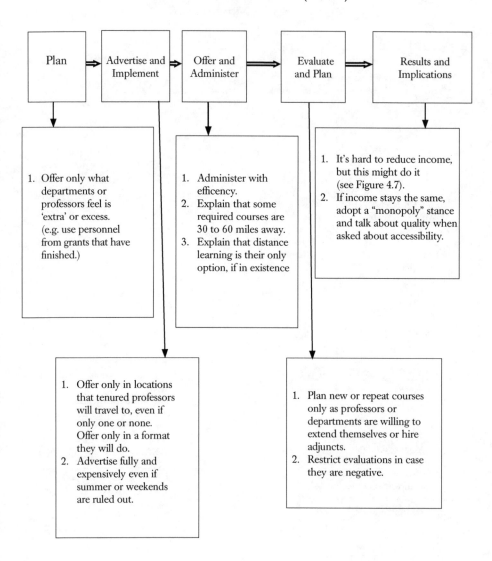

Figure 4.7
Scenario for No Growth (The same)

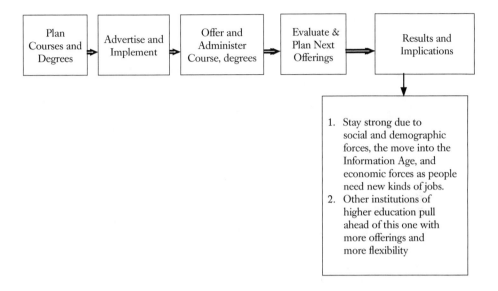

Use the "Decision Making Tree" in Chapter 5 to help decide with which projects one might invite the group to become involved. Some ideas generated would benefit from outside funding, or would need cooperation from another group, of course.

Strategic Planning

Strategic planning is the name that has been given the process of looking first in an organized way at outside environmental opportunities and risks and then at the continuing education unit's strengths and weaknesses (i.e. available resources). Strategic planning can become a very useful tool for educational administrators who need to respond to the ever-increasing challenges accosting or competing with their programs. In a rapidly changing and less predictable environment it is better for a unit to develop plans and opportunities and not to just respond as outside events have an impact. This helps the administrator to avoid being a perpetual 'crisis manager'. At the very least, this process has the effect of adding some predictability to outside impacts. A first step might be for a planning group to think of two or three significant events in society that will impact continuing education in higher education. It is not necessary to agree on these, but as the leader/facilitator goes around the group for each person's list, some consensus does emerge. This is called the 'External Analysis' and is shown as I on Figure 4.8.

Figure 4.8
Strategic Planning Steps (counter-clockwise)

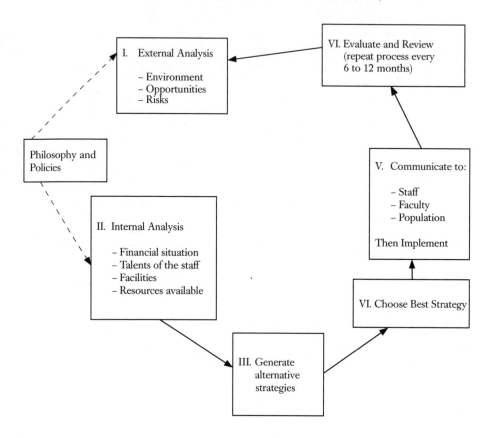

Responses might include such things as changing demographics, the society moving into the information age, and an economic downturn requiring new job or career skills.

At this point a "visioning" exercise of some type might be useful. Simply asking people what they envision being able to tell people about the continuing education unit or center in five years is a good start, or use the scenarios approach just described. With this information recorded, a review of the mission or philosophy statement for the unit or center, possibly re-writing it, and adding some policies might be in order. This done, the group can review the external analysis done earlier, and then review internal strengths and weaknesses to develop the Internal Analysis, II on Figure 4.8. These include a weak or strong financial picture which would allow or would not allow for expansion. The depth of professional and managerial talent also must be considered.

It isn't necessary to reach a consensus on the internal analysis either. Setting priorities and then writing objectives for the next three to five years comes next. Then the group is ready to write strategies for new programs and processes.

Generating alternative strategies can be done alone or in a group brainstorming session. The choice of strategy and its implementation requires group involvement and communication outward, to be most effective. Figure 4.8 shows a model of these steps. This planning time can be the most valuable that a Dean or Director spends and prevents management by default. Failure to plan can result in ineffective, undirected action (also called planning to fail from failing to plan).

Once the alternative strategies are generated for accomplishing priorities, the best choice of strategy can be agreed upon. At this point it is important to keep a record of the other strategies generated, as they may become useful as outside events change. The best choice strategy is then communicated widely, to staff, to faculty and the public, as appropriate (V on Figure 4.8). Hopefully, all but the general public will have been involved in one way or another before this juncture. A last step after these plans have become operational, and which may begin next year's planning session (or next quarter's) is to evaluate and review this strategy and these choices (VI on Figure 4.8), to build for the future. Therefore there is a continuous circle as shown in Figure 4.9:

Figure 4.9
Planning and Evaluation Cycle

Evaluate & Review

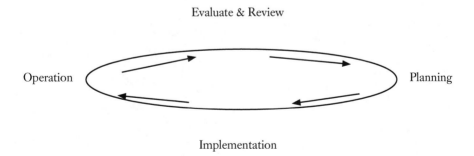

Operation   Planning

Implementation

For better alignment in the Continuing Education organization during institutional renewal consider Figure 4.10.

Figure 4.10
Plan for a Self-Aligning Continuing Education Organization

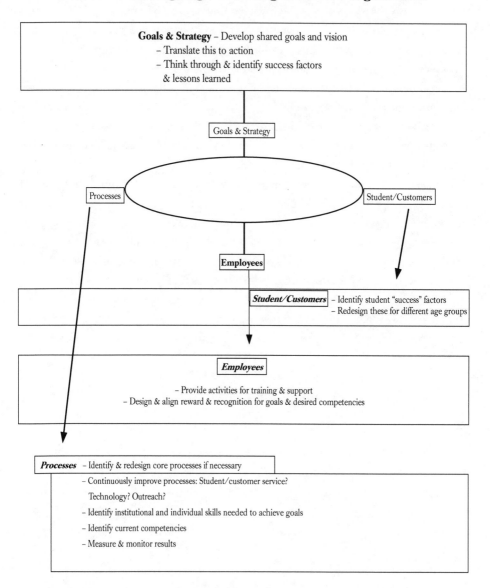

Since programs for adult students are affected by outside trends including demographics and economics, planning becomes essential. Figure 4.11 on "Sources and Impacts of Change" showing the results of a brainstorming session on the "Sources and Impacts of Change in Programs in Continuing Education" shows how even global and national concerns can be interpreted in the workplace, and for individuals, in order to manage the impact of such change. This makes an interesting exercise for staff meetings, as the information or ideas in the boxes may change every few months. This also could be a first step in a strategic planning exercise in considering all levels of the environment as demonstrated here in Figure 4.11. A second meeting, or a meeting using Figure 4.11 as a handout could go through more of the strategic planning steps: considering the opportunities and risks, perhaps beginning with impacts of change at the national and community level. The staff might choose one category to develop more fully for the workplace or for the individual level, such as social, physical or technological. After considering possible alternatives such as the ones listed for the workplace and the individual shown on Figure 4.11, and to which the group has added alternatives, the group can vote on one or two best alternatives to pursue. If you are working with the staff you skip to that level of communication in the Strategic Plan Figure 4.8. For example, the Division could communicate to the public that it is having an initiative in technology (or another theme for the semester or the year) that will include credit and non-credit courses, with the lead feature being a non-credit series in multimedia and web and gaming technology. Then list the degrees and courses and their various locations that fit into this theme. Different teams might work on each alternative. More ambitious plans, using more resources, such as opening a graduate education center across town could be tested on the scenario process, which helps a group (or an individual) to simulate possibilities and probabilities for the new idea.

Summary

Planning is an essential and integral function of continuing education leadership if those in charge do not want their days filled with crisis management. The use of planning and management techniques by leaders in continuing education helps to ensure the viability of their programs, and to enhance their visibility and effectiveness. Strategic planning with its core activities of redefining (or clarifying) the mission; forming overall objectives looking at strengths and weaknesses, opportunities and threats both external and internal – helps to develop an action plan, implement this plan, and monitor and evaluate the plan. If done carefully the analysis of the external environment will reveal opportunities open to the program as well as threats to success that continuing education leaders must consider. The major task then becomes to optimize the benefits presented by the opportunities, and reduce the threats or even convert them into future opportunities. Steps for improving the strengths while working on the weaknesses can be put onto a timeline, once they are identified.

Strategic planning, while an extensive process, can ensure program survival in a changing environment while providing a rational basis for allocation or re-allocation of resources to categories of issues. It also offers insights into both rational and political approaches to issues.

The excitement and friendly interaction in generating these ideas in a brainstorming session helps staff (and faculty members) learn and also helps them to feel stronger, more helpful, and more "empowered". Designing situations in which people can succeed, such as these, for considering hypothetical scenarios and strategies, unlocks creativity and puts some of the joy and energy back into the sometimes taxing work of being in continuing education in the higher education setting. As people come up with ideas, they will be more likely to offer help. Innovation is attractive and new ideas, even generated by an individual, will be interesting and draw support. As was stated in the chapter on Leadership, Chapter 3, if things have been discouraging for a while, two or three idea sessions may be needed to get useful planning under way. Educational institutions have not historically been strong in defining priorities and moving into the future, confident of their course. The application of strategic planning techniques helps educational leader-administrators find success.

If a continuing education unit allows its innovations to be high quality they will be "ahead of the game" when competition becomes stiffer. The programs will also have great "word of mouth" publicity and possibly more students in the center(s). It might be necessary to have special programs to help pay for some innovations, but feeling more in control of the continuing education unit's future will be worth it.

Figure 4.11
Sources and Impacts of Change in Continuing Education

Sources:	Political	Economic	Social	Physical	Technological
Global Impacts	New configurations of countries on the globe are causing changes.	Global economic cooperation is more of a reality creating many learning needs.	Families and individuals will be moving to follow jobs & education needed for jobs. Offer Continuing Educ. courses internationally?	Transportation is faster and better. Easier to transcend physical distances with email & distance learning.	Faster and better communications. Use of computers and technology is world wide. Include Cont. Ed. schedule on *Web Home Page.*
National Impacts	Federal & State cutbacks are causing institutions IHEs* to look to Continuing Education units and alumni for additional income	Businesses partnering with IHE*s initiatives are becoming the norm.	U.S. demographics becoming more international. Have a partner IHE in another country?	More IHEs are opening satellite locations in other cities and states.	More information network linkages. IT learning is a national need on all levels.
Community Impacts	Political support for state-funded IHEs will be needed. Fewer funds-dependent projects will be needed.	More and better Cont.Ed./life-long learning will be needed for all economic levels.	Some communities have a higher need for ESL courses (English as a Second Language).	Place education centers near the students, e.g. in suburbs or on transportation routes.	Communities are networking services and will help advertise continuing ed. programs available.
Impacts for Continuing Education Programs	Invite local legislators as guest speakers. Remind them that education is the 'bridge' into the knowledge age and to economic development.	Offer different tuition or fees for different locations, populations or contract groups. Consider offering deluxe services to offset costs: such as resume writing & counseling.	Provide social interaction times at Info Sessions and other events. Offer multicultural management courses as needed.	Regularly share news about different segments of your geographic marketing areas.	Network all locations in one geographic area. Offer Information Technology courses at all (or most) ocations.
Individual Impacts	Do regular scan on Federal, state and local political issues.	Always tie economic benefits of programs into new student information sessions.	Have regular staff eNews – letter. Include a section on coming events and public relations opportunities.	Encourage staff to come up with new ideas for a 5-year plan for serving new locations.	Encourage staff to stay current with new computers, soft-ware and other technologies.
*IHE: Institutions of Higher Education					

CHAPTER 5

Making Decisions in Continuing Education

Leadership involves decision-making. To lead effectively one needs to plan for change that improves the organization. As discussed in Chapter 3, this change may involve achieving new goals using old processes, continuing to work towards old on-going goals using new processes, or aiming for new goals using new processes. Research has shown that at any time the leader involves staff, faculty, or students in the planning and decision-making, the leader builds commitment. But how is one to do this? And when? Furthermore, planning should be a continuous process as new resources, goals, policies, needs, or changes in the environment arise. This is especially true in continuing education in higher education with changes in the economy, changes in the demography of the student body, and new calls on public institutions for scrutiny and accountability from legislative and governmental bodies. A plan can be considered an interim report, so it is essential that the planners get together at regular meetings to adapt and improve plans that have been made, and to generate new plans to address these many issues.

The Greek word for administration is "kuberneseis" which refers to the work of ships' pilots who steer the ships through rocks and shoals to the harbor. All administrators have days when they say, "Where is the harbor?" "The fog is too thick!" "Why are there so many rocks?" Administrators and leaders of all kinds need to have wisdom, for if the administration of an organization is not well done, the organization cannot meet its goals. The fog rarely lifts. Peter Vaill (1989) called this "paddling in permanent white water". Administrators and leaders also need to generate encouragement, confidence and commitment on the part of staff, faculty, and students in order to have an excellent and growing continuing education enterprise. It is rewarding to be a part of an organization about which staff and faculty can be proud and enthusiastic.

Having an outstanding Continuing Education Division and/or Education Center(s) requires leadership and decision making. Other in-depth continuing education leadership and management materials are available in the chapters on leadership and motivation and throughout this book. However, a basic premise behind leadership is that the more power a leader gives away by involving others in decision making, coordination, or supervision, the more total power a leader has. Command and control management does not mix well with the Information Age. Not all decisions are appropriate for group involvement, however, so further analysis of the decisions to be made, and the decision making processes, are needed.

Simple Decisions

In a decision with only two possible outcomes, and in which the leader has no preference, the leader can flip a coin. Listing the pros and cons of a decision in separate columns on a paper, is a useful strategy for slightly more complicated decisions. The benefit of decision making strategies is that they help the decision maker look at a problem in a more systematic way, and consider relevant questions which may not at first have been apparent. The context in which higher education decisions are made is also a factor. As a leader of an organization, it is hoped that most "simple" decisions can be delegated to an appropriate staff member, after parameters have been set by the leader. For example, "The holiday party can be held in any of these three ways. Let's have a vote." (Or have a committee investigate, or have Mrs. Smith choose this year, etc.) Much has been written about the benefits of delegating decisions to the lowest feasible level, to build commitment all through a staff's organizational system. For example, "This year the staff will vote on where to have the holiday party."

More Complex Decisions

A decision tree is useful for decisions that are a little more complex. A decision tree can be generated with staff and faculty participating in a meeting setting, and can be a helpful tool to encourage discussion and inform persons, before a vote is taken. Or a simple tree can be used at home, alone, to solve personal problems such as whether to buy a new car, repair the old one, or buy a used car.

A simple decision tree for the annual holiday party might center on whether the meal was lunch or dinner. The tree might start out like this:

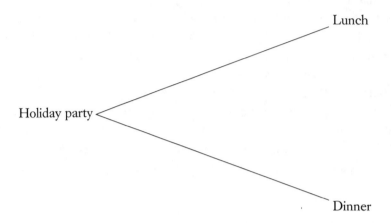

Then discussion (or information getting) focuses on whether Restaurants B and C take groups, at what hours, and with how much advance notice. The tree begins to look like this:

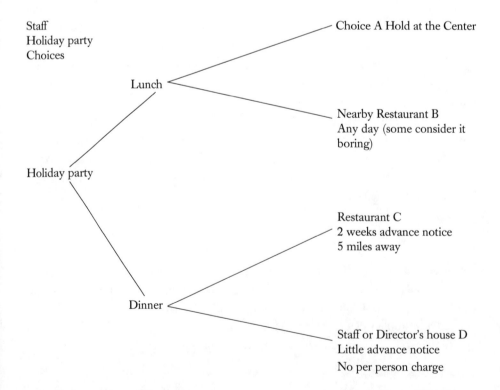

This tree could have additional branches placed to the right as one considers more details, possible gift exchange, entertainment, or car pool arrangements. In dealing with this chart the group or the decision maker first decides on the boxes the farthest to the right. To start deciding one might first rank all the considerations on a preference scale of + 1 to + 10 or - 1 to - 10. The tree then looks like this:

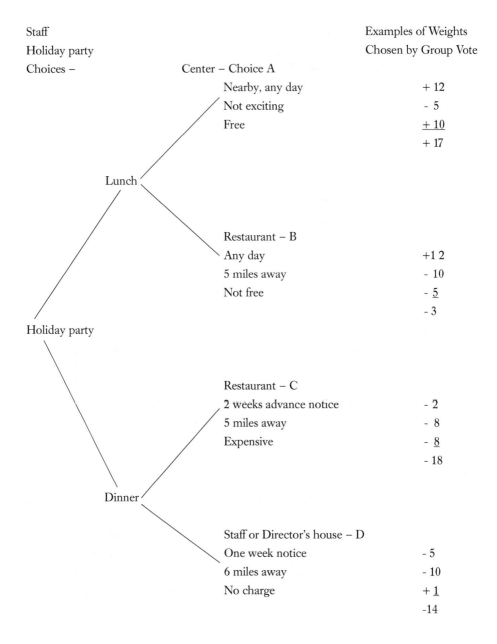

Staff
Holiday party
Choices –

Examples of Weights
Chosen by Group Vote

Center – Choice A
Nearby, any day — + 12
Not exciting — - 5
Free — + 10
+ 17

Lunch

Restaurant – B
Any day — +1 2
5 miles away — - 10
Not free — - 5
- 3

Holiday party

Restaurant – C
2 weeks advance notice — - 2
5 miles away — - 8
Expensive — - 8
- 18

Dinner

Staff or Director's house – D
One week notice — - 5
6 miles away — - 10
No charge — + 1
-14

Restaurant B becomes the favorite if people want the event to occur during work day hours. If they still want dinner, Restaurant C seems better. This question could now be presented to the large staff meeting with a choice between Restaurant B and lunch or Restaurant C and dinner. Having it in a home was not an issue as it became obvious that lunch during the workday was preferred over dinner. Some employees commuted long distances and a later night drive was undesirable. The factor of whether the same people consider Restaurant B exciting or not, or whether that is even important to the attendees, did surface. After deciding on lunch or dinner, decide who should be invited from the institution at large outside the Continuing Education group, if anybody. This example may seem very simplified, but in today's workplace with the diverse group of people in various ages and stages in life, with different backgrounds and cultures, who make up an excellent continuing education unit staff, it is a "safe" practice exercise in group decision-making.

Using a simple tree of this sort is helpful in making other group decisions either with staff or faculty. For instance, in the above example, it also gets people interested and they will go out and research other restaurants and bring in new information for next year. This is building commitment and interest. This formula worked quite well, in one true story, for several years.

Then an autocratic decision maker became Dean and just selected the place and set the hours. Results included leaders, not involved in the choice coming, but coming quite late and not eating. Others came late or left early, and there was no generalized 'buy-in' into the activity. However good effects in employee relations and interaction did result, as is further described in Chapter 7 on Motivation under 'hygiene factors' needed to keep employees from being dissatisfied, (but, please note, this is not a 'motivator factor' only a 'hygiene factor'). The remaining question for a leader, however, is how many people should be involved in a given decision? And HOW does the leader involve them?

The Fish-Bone Decision Making Tree

The Fish-bone Decision Making Tree can be used to suggest a series of questions to be asked about a decision in order to decide how many people to involve in the decision-making process. These questions appear on Figure 5.1 in each section of the 'fishbone' on the following page, but they will be discussed here first for clarification. The issues around topics that can usually impact a decision are: People, Resources, the surrounding Environment, and Technology. These are headings for each section in Figure 5.1. More sections can be added to the 'fishbone' for more factors in a particular decision.

Figure 5.1
Fishbone Decision-Making Tree

Surrounding Environment
1. Does it use a large amount of resources? Is it easily reversible?
2. Is conflict likely among staff members and colleagues in chosen solutions?
3. Do they have enough information to help decide?

People
1. Do I have enough information to make this decision? Who needs to be involved?
2. How many people are needed to decide? Is it easily reversible?
3. Do staff members or colleagues have to accept my decision for this to happen? Is this likely?
4. Do they share the goals of the organization?   **GOAL**

Resources (time, materials, money)
1. Will scarce resources be used?
2. Is it easily reversible?
3. Do I know where to get the information I need? Who does or where is it?
4. Do I know where to get the money or materials or people-time I need? Who does?

Technology
1. Does it use a large amount resources? Is it easily reversible?
2. Can technology be used to help staff or colleagues gain more information? To stay in touch with each other?

The first question is: Is one solution better than another in that a large amount of resources would be used, and/or is it not an easily reversible decision, so other options cannot be 'tried out'? Examples of answers to this question might include opening a new education center across town (this would use a lot of money and time), changing a major part of the programming, or changing in a major way the information processes the university or the center uses to track its students. Since "people time" is a very scarce resource in continuing education programs, the amount of time a dean or director would have to put in is always a consideration. More hallmarks of a high quality decision, in addition to the percent of money, man/woman power or materials, are: does the decision use scarce resources? And is it easily reversible? This question should be asked *first* in all four sections to uncover additional elements that might be present.

The next question in three of the sections, People, Resources, and Technology, involves information about the challenge or problem and the decision one needs to make. Do I have enough information to make this decision? Do I know where to get more information? Who does? Where can they or I get it? Who needs to be involved? Can technology be used to gain this information or share it? Again since 'people time' is a very scarce resource in the workplace, the amount of time a leader would have to put into a decision is important. Marks of a major decision, in addition to the percent of money, man/woman power or materials needed, are: does this decision use *scarce* resources? Is it easily reversible? Often the leader does not have sufficient information to decide alone, but knowing that much, at least, is a start. For example, if a leader knows he or she wants to start another education center across town, but also knows that he or she does not know all of the necessary steps, (or can't decide between one closer in or one 3 to 4 hours drive away – with good reasons for both –) he or she can then start reading professional materials about others' experiences, looking on the Internet, and asking people for more information. If he or she has gone through the Fishbone decision-making tree and decided to involve his or her staff at this point, the dean or director may invite guest speakers to staff meetings that have successfully started second centers. He or she might also ask the staff to start researching this problem as "the Division is looking into it," without necessarily stating that the Division plans to open a satellite branch. Alternatively, the administrator might talk informally at a professional conference with an administrator or two from other institutions of higher education who have started new education centers in satellite locations.

The question(s) under 'Resources' asking "Do I know where to get the information, and the money, materials and people?" means – does the leader know exactly what information is needed, who possesses it, and how to collect it? In terms of starting a new center the answer would probably be no. If the question were, "What is the LCD projector with the lowest price?" the answer would probably be yes, the leader does know *how to get* that information. This is a very important question as one may need the resources of the group or information the group may have about resources, in order to move forward. If the answer to these two questions is "no" than it is likely that the group will need to be involved. However, "knowing what you *don't* know" is a great strength because at least you can start to find out the answers (or the right questions that need to be asked). By opening the problem to the group, more resources and more ideas will be brought into the whole initiative. Looking together for information and then for solutions, builds commitment and interest of employees in any project.

Is acceptance of the decision by employees critical to effective implementation? This question is very important to ask about many decisions as are the questions about 'Is conflict likely if *I* decide?' and, 'Do they (staff and faculty) support the goals of the organization?' If staff members and colleagues will be the ones carrying out a decision (such as implementing a new academic program or a new student relations program) then giving the staff members and colleagues enough information and a range of choices to gain their acceptance, will be the key to success or failure. In the question of opening a education center across town, this question of needing staff support may have a yes or no answer, depending on whether a totally new staff would be sought, or whether two top staff members would be asked to transfer for one or two years or longer.

If I were to make the decision myself, is it certain that it would be accepted by my staff and colleagues? This question relates to the previous question, obviously, but serves as a reminder to a leader who might be tempted to go out on a limb. It is always better to allow more time for understanding and discussion if it is apparent that the limb could be sawed off. It also helps the leader to assess the climate of feeling around a given issue.

Does the institution or the staff share the Continuing Education Division's goals to be attained in solving this problem? Hopefully, in a continuing education organization the answer would be yes: the staff members and colleagues are working toward a goal of satisfied students gaining knowledge and competencies in their programs. However in reality, some persons may take a job just to earn money, and if that is the majority of the staff's attitude, staff training, motivation helps, and perhaps some selective hiring and firing are needed. If the majority of the staff does identify with the goal of an education center being the best education center in that location (or any goal that benefits students, faculty, and the institution of higher education, and agreed to by all or most), then involving staff in decision making will enhance staff commitment and the organization. When staff members and colleagues share the goals, the group can look together for solutions that are in the best interests of the organization. In any organization, people tend to share the goals that they helped to select.

Is conflict likely among colleagues or staff in preferred solutions? This question will be skipped on the Fishbone decision tree if colleagues and staff share the Continuing Education Division's goals. But if colleagues and staff do not share organizational goals it is important to pre-plan how to handle possible conflict. Or to decide if one even wants conflict to arise. Think through how you would deal with various objections.

Do colleagues and staff have sufficient information to make a high quality decision? Often they do not, and this leads to a natural opportunity for new learning and staff training on a given topic. Faculty members can be invited to attend, or even to speak about the programs, at the staff training too, if that is appropriate. In discussion, or ahead of time, the leader can identify the problem more clearly and, by using the Fishbone tree, decide which solution and degree of staff involvement is appropriate.

The first question is: Is one solution better than another in that a large amount of resources would be used, and/or it is not an easily reversible decision, so other options cannot be 'tried out'? This occurs for instance, when an organization moves to a new location. This question should be asked first in all four sections to uncover additional elements that might be present.

After looking over the Fishbone tree (on it's side), the leader turns to the questions for possible decision methods for group or individual problems. Sometimes involving the group is the *fastest* method for solving the particular problem just "broken out" on the Fishbone Tree. For instance, in a move to a new location, if it is just announced as a flat statement (the autonomous, autocratic method), members may complain for two to five years after the move. If three to six months of discussion occurs, complemented by subscribing to the newspaper in the new location and researching the resources in that area (gaining more information), the fastest solution of three to six months may be the best and the smoothest.

How Much to Involve the Group

The group becomes involved in more and more ways as the solutions progress from autonomous to group decisions. In *autonomous* decisions the leader makes the decision herself or himself using the information available, at the time. Or, if the leader needs more information, the decision maker can obtain the necessary information from employees and then decide alone. One could ask staff "Where would be a good location in this town?" and so forth. The leader can tell them his or her plans or not, as the leader thinks best, but they are not part of the decision, only information providers. In a cooperative solution, the leader talks one-to-one with the staff without meeting with them as a group. This can be done informally, at a dinner or at a social gathering, over time, or in a number of ways. Finally the leader makes the decision which may or may not take their views into account.

Or in a *cooperative* solution variation, the leader may finally decide alone, perhaps not even using the employee's advice, but this time they come together in a group to give their suggestions. This allows everyone to be familiar with the question and also provides a situation in which they can build on each other's ideas. If one should decide later that one does need their help, at least they would know what one was talking about. Of course, if one does follow their advice, one lets them know and praises them for their help. If one doesn't use their advice, one can explain that circumstances were such that another solution seemed better at this time, if an explanation is appropriate or needed.

A *group* decision maker shares the problem with the group and then acts as a discussion leader while everyone generates as many solutions as possible. The majority vote on the best solution is one the leader is willing to adopt and implement, and, of course, it has the support of the entire group. This might be very helpful if the leader knows he or she wants to move the center or open a branch of the education center across town, but is not sure where to locate. The leader would want to have it fairly convenient for students. This group solution is especially useful when one knows that one wants to do something big, but one doesn't know how to go about doing it or even where to learn how. By opening the problem to the group, more resources and more ideas can flow in from the whole group. They may decide they want to know more and guests or guest speakers can be invited and literature provided, as everyone learns more and has time to solicit information from friends and acquaintances. Interesting problems attract able people, and the leader will find all sorts of resources becoming available. Also allowing some time gives 'the grapevine' time to work, and a staff person might ask a neighbor or some other informal network person, key 'how-to-do-it' questions, which would be inappropriate for the leader to ask.

Solutions for individual problems follow the same pattern but are appropriate for one-to-one problems. As usual, politeness in seeking information or asking advice is essential.

Risk Management and Decision-Making

A good decision-making process includes understanding that good decisions can have bad outcomes. One needs to remember this in considering risk and decision-making. Consistent decision-makers can choose a level of risk tolerance and put that in their decision model or tree and use the level every time. Consider a list of four steps in a good decision: 1) What is the sequence of decisions and uncertainties? 2) What are the payouts? 3) What are the probabilities of payouts? and then 4) Put them all together. For example in making a movie, you have to decide 1) to make the movie; 2) then decide about making a sequel; 3) look ahead to where you may end up, and 4) do the analysis backward. In other words, you have to think about the kind of future decisions you'll have to make and work backward to where you first decide whether to make the movie. One can make a decision diagram or tree that reflects choices and uncertainties and then following choices and uncertainties, as shown earlier in this chapter with the tree. Then look at the payouts, or positive results for all possible paths.

An easy example is standing in a cafeteria line and choosing between soup and salad. One doesn't draw a diagram, but one gets into the mind-set of thinking through consequences of choices, without drawing a tree or diagram. Some times, there is Choice A, and you look at the range of outcomes and look at choice B and it's range of outcomes, and B doesn't overlap A. One can then make the decision. The decisions one spends more time on are the decisions that overlap. You must ask WHY they overlap. What are the various components? Even with a spreadsheet of everything that relates to the decision, one must sort out what items are important and ones that are not. (Bodily, 2007). The tree shown earlier helps with this, but any model that splits out the components will be an aid.

Frame Blindness

It is well to keep in mind that decision research over the last 20 years has shown that people in a wide variety of fields tend to make the same kinds of mistakes in decision-making (Russo and Schoemaker, 1990, p. xvi). Ten of the most common errors include:

1. **Plunging in**. Gathering information and reaching conclusions before taking time to think through the crux of the issue – and to think through how you believe this type of decision should be made.
2. **Frame Blindness**. Trying to solve the wrong problem because the mental framework that you hold has allowed you to overlook some of the best options or some important objectives.
3. **Lack of Frame Control.** Failing to consciously define the problem in several ways (always more than one), or being influenced by the mental framework created and held by others. *Your* framing of decisions is important.
4. **Overconfidence in One's Own Judgment**. Not collecting key facts and looking at the evidence, because one is too sure of one's own opinions and assumptions. (Experienced Directors need to be wary of this one.)
5. **Taking Short Cuts for the Short Run**. Relying on 'yardsticks' or 'rules of thumb' and/or trusting too much in information that's easily and readily available and convenient. Coming to conclusions requires looking at mid-term and long term goals, too.
6. **Winging It and Shooting from the Hip**. Thinking one can keep all the information in one's head and rushing ahead rather than using a systematic procedure for making a final choice. Information gathering is important.
7. **Failing to Manage the Group Decision-Making Process.** Assuming that good people will make good choices without using a method to arrive at this desired result can be costly.
8. **Inaccurate Interpretation of Feedback**. Not interpreting feedback for what it really says – whether one is protecting one's own ego or the egos of others, or because of being 'tricked' by hindsight (e.g. 'It seemed to work last time'). Learning from feedback is important.
9. **Not Keeping Track**. Failing to keep track of results of past decisions and to analyze these results in ways that reveal their key lessons.

10. **Failing to 'Audit' the Decision Process.** Failing to develop an organized approach to understanding one's own decision-making, leaves one exposed to mistakes numbers 1 to 9 above. To begin to do this, list the frames and 'yardsticks' or 'rules of thumb' you usually use and your preferred strategies for arriving at conclusions. Ask which phase of the decision process is the hardest for you? Which of these areas can you improve on by becoming more aware of them, and which require formal steps? These might include changing how you make estimates; formalizing processes; analyzing learning after making major decisions (perhaps in a group); or keeping better records. List the steps you should take. Rank yourself from A to F on these 10 areas or 'decision traps'.

Think what your present frames emphasize and minimize. How do you measure success? Frequency of problems? Sense of partnership? Usefulness of other people's input? This chapter broke down some of the parameters to consider when approaching a decision, and the following chapters on teamwork, motivation and problem-solving provide additional tools that may be useful.

Power, Roles, and Goals of Administrators and Faculty

Decision making is complicated in higher education due to differences in the perceptions of administrators and faculty members about the power, goals, roles, objectives, status and work load of the opposite group. Many administrators, of course, have been faculty members and so understand the differences on both sides of the equation. However, when administrators come directly from another institution or organization and have not served as faculty in their present institution, wrong assumptions can creep in as to how business is done in *this* institution (or in *this* organizational culture). Many of these differences in perception could be called 'structural conflicts' (Kotter, 1979) as the 'structure' of the higher education organization has conflicting components built right into it.

There have been few institutions of higher education with faculty representation on the Board of Trustees since the early days at Harvard when faculty lived in the dormitory. When the two faculty members got married and moved out of the dorms they were taken off the Board of Trustees. Today living in the dorms is not the general practice nor has it been ever since that early time. Since that time a gap has grown between 'administration' and 'faculty' as the faculty usually has no *formal* representative on the Board of Trustees which traditionally hires the President and sets policy. In the labor relations field this situation is akin to the classic category of labor not being represented to management which generates a number of predictable problems, and sometimes even unions.

It is helpful to look at the understandable differences in focus between the two groups as an aid to decision making dynamics. See Figure 5.2 for a summary of these differences, much simplified.

Figure 5.2 Perceptions of Power, Roles, and Goals of Administrators and Faculty

In a generalized way each group thinks the other has more '*power*'. The *goals* of the faculty are usually life-long, career goals, whereas the administration often has one year (or five year) goals and budgets to worry about. The *role* of the faculty is a professional role and while the role of administrators is also professional, there is more need for personal discretion and local tradition to be used as guidelines. This can be seen in the refusal of a senior professor to travel to a satellite center to teach a required course in the degree program offered there. He did not see this as part of his role, and certainly not as one of his goals. Yet he had been in agreement when his department approved offering this degree at that location, as this would reflect well on the department and bring administrative credits for income earned. The Dean of Continuing Education used a great deal of tact and pointed out that the tradition of this institution was to offer a whole degree at satellite centers when it had been advertised. Later, this degree may have been closed down at that site since all the required courses were not offered.

The *objectives* of faculty are again related to 20 and 30 year, or life-long goals: publish more, research certain specifics, etc. The administrators' objectives tend to be tied to yearly goals for marketing, enrollment, and income versus expense concerns. The *pay* is perceived to be different by the two groups, but there is variability in who thinks the other gets more. The *status* differentials also vary, with faculty having a professional status (and using a 'status veto' when individual members feel their power is low, Birnbaum, 1988 pp.170-171), and administrators, except for the highest levels, having a lower status. This can be of particular importance in continuing education as administrators may be dealing with several 'layers of prima donnas' as one observer put it. Lastly, the *workload* of each group is frequently misperceived, as the faculty work long hours and feel high pressure at paper grading and exam time, and administrators feel a more generalized, year-round pressure. These areas are necessarily simplified here for reasons of space, but the discussion is summarized in the chart in Figure 5.2

These dynamics bear reflection as often the key to understanding an interaction lies somewhere on the chart, and can be developed with more detail for a specific situation. Furthermore, the answers to the differences lie in getting to know each other as people, with real human needs and aspirations. Using this knowledge, framing a decision that is likely to be successful, becomes more likely. Hypothesizing faculty responses in a scenario will become more realistic before discussing possibilities with faculty, from blocks in a scenario as described in Chapter 4 on Planning.

Figure 5.2
Perceptions of Power, Roles, and Goals
of Administrators and Faculty

	Perception of Faculty	*Perception of Administrators*
POWER	'I have less, they have more'	Same/ ditto
GOALS	lifelong or career	One year
ROLES	related to lifelong goals	Often related to
		one year or one semester
PAY	professional pay	Some lower, some higher
STATUS	high (when this is lower,	Lower
	faculty may become less	
	creative, seek fewer grants	
	and research opportunities)	
HOURS OR	24 hour pressure, but time for	8-10 hour a day
WORKLOAD	Summer travel, writing and	Yearlong pressure
	Consulting	

Summary

Decision-making is indeed key in leadership processes in an organization. However, the ability to structure decisions and then break them down into manageable parts is necessary in decision-making, and these skills can be learned. Sometimes making a decision one's self can be the *slowest* way to a resolution when group support is needed and group involvement would be better (and faster). Taking three to six months to involve the staff, is often the fastest decision approach possible when a large decision is involved and when an individual decision might result in years of back-sliding or controversy. The key decision team needs to be well-versed enough in the particulars, especially the core issues, to agree with any of the decisions that are very important and thus to deal with the later consequences. If each is convinced it is a good decision, it will be one which he or she can support wholeheartedly. This means they must possess knowledge and comprehension of the significance, the nature, and the implications of a situation or a proposition. This chapter breaks down some of the parameters to consider when approaching a decision, and the following chapters on team building and problem solving provide additional tools that may be useful. Focusing and thinking through new initiatives in an organization helps the group move into the information or knowledge age more smoothly and with prosperity. Making a conscious effort to relate to others and involve others, whether at home or at work, in this age when time is spent so often one-to-one with a machine (a computer) pays great dividends in this new age that builds on the strength of information-providing machines combined with the spiritual energy, initiative and motivation of people linked and working together.

Chapter 6

Team Work, Team Building, and Small Groups

Small groups, whether in the workplace or in voluntary organizations, provide a source of satisfaction to the group or team members that is of great importance. What goes on in small groups is a vital factor to any leader. It is necessary to understand some of the processes that go on in small groups (or teams) in order to help develop group stability, group health, and group effectiveness. Internal dynamics and factors within a group can make it more or less productive. A small group is usually considered to be less than twenty, and is often less than twelve. Many small continuing education units' staffs comprise just one "small group" so it is important that it be productive.

Dynamics of Small Work Groups

The basic reason for group membership is that groups provide their members with social support and a feeling of personal worth. The foundations for mature social exchange are established early in life through child-child, and child-adult interactions that are favorable, thus indicating acceptance and approval. Acceptance and approval continue to be important in adult life and in the workplace.

It has long been found that small groups or teams in the workplace will be more effective if they contain "friendship groups", that is if they take into account the small groups that exist in the "informal organization". Individuals like to be surrounded by people who like them, even if it is a small number. Sometimes the attitudes and opinions of others are the only basis on which a person can evaluate his or her own opinions and attitudes. People like to have a feeling of certainty about their beliefs, opinions and attitudes and gain affirmation through shared values in a small group.

A negative aspect affecting small groups is that people with low self-esteem tend to find frustrating conditions MORE frustrating than those with higher self-esteem. Those with very low self-esteem may give up in a situation in which a person with higher self-esteem might stay.

Stages of Small Work Groups

In any new small group there are three observable stages: "forming", "storming" and "norming" (Tuckman, 1955, Jacobs 1971). Norming is defined as creating a social norm for the group. In the workplace a "norm" can be a performance standard or a standard of behavior expected of informal group members. These stages can be observed during the planning of an evening information session or briefing for inquiring students, or on a three month work-group assignment, such as a marketing campaign.

The forming stage occurs as the group gets going and a status hierarchy develops in the group. Status can be based on a person's performance skills, interpersonal skills, or the job he or she holds. Emergence of different roles can be seen in the group during this stage: the tough leader, the friendly helper, and the clear thinker. Clear expectations help speed this process, for example, by having an appointed discussion leader (or Chair), a discussion group will get into a discussion more quickly. Sometimes the leader is just the person who has the pen and paper or some other needed resource.

The storming stage can cause tensions, and occurs when one or more group members think the leader of the group is going in a direction with which they disagree. An example of this occurred during a staff training small group activity for which the assigned task was to write out a philosophy for an education center. (Several groups were working on the same task as a first step towards developing a unified written statement). One person started the group off with a strong statement about her views favoring a fairly harsh philosophy of: no eating, no drinking, no moving of chairs or rearranging furniture, etc. Another person said, "Now, *wait* a minute." A "clear thinker" type in the group suggested checking other written philosophies, and thus broke the possible deadlock and also, incidentally, became the leader. It should be noted that this is an "unclear task" according to the definitions given later in the chapter, which contributed to the rough start of the group.

The third stage or "norming" stage follows quickly for an information session planning meeting or can last several weeks or years for a work group assigned to a large task such as settling into a new education center. Norming is based on shared beliefs and opinions in at least some areas of reference (social, work, church, political). Group members need to feel that their objectives are worthy of attainment. They develop expectations about how people should feel about certain issues. There is usually some agreement about what is relevant and what is not. Interestingly enough, if group members perceive a difference in one of these areas they will talk *more* about it rather than less, perhaps trying to persuade the others to their point of view.

Group norming leads to pressures for conformity which include defining "a fair day's work" in the office. Group norming can increase group effectiveness when the goals of the group are lined-up with the goals of the organization. On the other hand a negative group norm can be detrimental to the organization. If the informal group, for example, defines a fair day's work as very limited, it can pressure other workers to not go beyond that "norm."

Rules or norms can help group or team effectiveness and make the group fairer for all. They reduce the need for decisions on routine matters and also reduce the need for the use of personal power. A more elaborate model of the stages of small groups comes from Drexler and Sibbet (1995) with a seven step model. This model addresses additional elements of the early establishment of trust and acceptance; agreement about goals, procedures and timing; and the exchange of information. The interdependent elements, which are not necessarily chronological, are: orientation, trust-building, goal/role clarification, commitment, implementation, high performance, and renewal and return to orientation.

An interesting exercise for a class, a staff meeting or just a review of an interaction with persons, is to check off behaviors on the following Figure (6.1) that occur. These show behaviors that can be seen in the progressive steps of these two group-forming models. This is also good practice in observation that helps sharpen one's observation in any small group. The behaviors that move towards numbers nine and ten are the most beneficial: clarifying group goals and facilitating group attainment. Comments such as "What date shall we set for our next meeting?" demonstrate facilitation of group attainment. Noticing that number six, "awareness of the high cost of coercion" sets back the whole interaction, this awareness helps persons avoid this approach. These behaviors might be seen as a sequence in a new Directors' first six to twelve months on the job, also.

Figure 6.1

Behaviors Demonstrating Social Change

Tally
Behaviors
Used

1. To obtain approval of others agreement, compliments, conformity – generally spontaneous.

2. To reward others asking advice, compliments, positive responses – generally calculated.

3. To reciprocate interacting or responding on the same level.

4. To obtain marginal return supplying rewards that benefit, yet obligate the other person.

5. To maximize benefit/cost ratio consulting indirectly, i.e., talking about a problem to get advice rather than asking directly for it. Seeking advice from a group member perceived to be more like self.

6. Awareness of the high cost of coercive attempts. Shrewd manipulation of the group toward the leader's point of view, perhaps using debts from past exchanges.

7. To indicate superior bargaining position such as having the only copy of a book or CD in the library checked out to you or a skill in a technique or knowledge needed by the group.

8. To make unique and valuable contribution in return for status. Presentation of knowledge which is superior to that given by other members of the group. Taking more responsibility than other members.

9. To develop or clarify group goals. Action to ascertain that a group member is certain of group goals.

10. To facilitate attainment of group goals. Structuring the group. Keeping the group to goal-directed behavior.

Questions a leader might ask after using Figure 6.1 are:

- What happened? What did they do? Observe? Think? Feel?
- What insights did observers gain? What did we learn? Relearn? How does this relate to the 'real world'?
- Now what? How can we use these insights in our Continuing Education unit?
- How can we extend the learning we had?
- What challenges do we think we're going to have using these insights? – How can we plan for these? Can we do a simulation of presenting this?

Specialized Roles in Work Groups

As a group emerges two, or even three, types of leaders can be seen. While one person focuses on the task and competes for, or takes over, the position of power and influence in the group, another person can be seen reducing tensions in the group and having a high interaction rate within the group. The first person could be said to fill the role of "tough leader" and the second to take the role of "friendly helper." A third role can often be seen in the "clear thinker" which occasionally is combined with the "tough leader." Some writers call these behaviors, goal behaviors and (group) maintenance behaviors, or task specialists and social specialists.

These roles are so important for group or team success that a certain individual might find herself or himself filling different roles with different groups, just because it's so obvious that the group won't be effective without someone stepping into the role. Also a particular person might fill different roles at different stages in his or her life. A person in a beginning career might be the "friendly helper" more of the time, for example. A person, new in the education community, might offer to be on a telephone committee. These different role structures in a group permit the rapid attainment of assigned tasks.

Prediction of Work Group or Team Performance

Frederick E. Fiedler (1967, 1995) integrated other work he had done and developed a model that would predict group or team effectiveness based on leadership style, group variables and task variables. He found that three main factors within a situation affected group performance:

* Leader-member relations, or how well they got along
* Task structure, or clearness of task (e.g. can it be written down?)
* Leader position power, or the actual power to hire and fire.

The task variable was further defined showing four ways a task might be clear or unclear: (1) If a decision could be shown to be correct in an impartial manner (such as with enrollment statistics or other quantitative measures or measurable behaviors). This is called decision verifiability. (2) If the group members understood the requirements of the task. (3) If more than one procedure can be used to accomplish the task (such as different marketing strategies). (4) If the problem has more than one correct solution. The goal or task of higher education continuing education is not a clear task – there are several right ways to do it and several correct solutions to most problems. Anything that adds clearness will be a help.

Fiedler (1971) found that any group that had two out of three of the major factors (leader-member relations, task structure, leader position power) would probably be effective. If one looks at education and sees the task as unclear, one can see that leader-member relations (also called collegial relations), and leader position power become essential. Conversely, anything that can be done to make the task clear (written goal statements, course descriptions, checklists, Faculty, Student and Staff Handbooks, or anything that is written), will help a small group to be more effective in the field of higher education continuing education.

In continuing higher education the basic administrative model of the larger institution structures some of the small group interactions. Continuing education can be located on a continuum of connectedness, with one end of the continuum being the model of a unit very connected to the institution of higher education (IHE). This means the regular campus academic departments hire all the adjuncts, supervise all course work for credit, and say yes or no to new program and location initiatives depending on the faculty support available and other commitments of faculty. This model has the lasting benefit of keeping the course work current and up-to-date to the same degree that the main campus course work is refreshed and relevant. Faculty do not administer the continuing education courses beyond this, however. The disadvantage of this model is that occasionally tenured professors will turn down opportunities for fairly frivolous reasons including time and trouble involved, or their car is too old to go that far, etc.

The model at the other end of the continuum of connectedness is the totally separate model, with courses, faculty, degrees, *and* administration completely separate which leads in some cases to splitting the unit off from the institution of higher education completely, to become a separate institution of higher education with a separate President. The benefit of this model is that the short term revenue expenditure and planning is much more efficient and is in the control of the continuing education unit. Courses can be kept relevant easily. The disadvantage of this model is that course quality can erode and highly technical degree programs are hard to offer and sustain over time.

CONTINUUM OF CONNECTEDNESS

<u>Least connected</u>   50-50*   <u>Most connected</u>

*   50-50 Means non-credit programs not connected at all, but credit programs are.

The *middle* of this connectedness continuum is filled with varying degrees of connectedness, including credit programs supervised by academic departments, and non-credit or conference programs not at all connected or supervised by the academic sector, or other variations. Different factors can be seen in small groups or teams, in the varying categories of Fiedler's small group theory, that are impacted by the amount of connectedness also.

Examples of Different Factors in Work Groups

Fiedler's variables can be seen in the examples that follow. The predictability this model gives works especially well in non-profit organizations and in higher education institutions.

Lack of Leader Position Power

Since higher education institutions have been characterized as "loosely coupled" (Lutz 1982, Weick 1976), which means that units do not have a direct effect on each other, neither for good nor for ill, many meetings and situations involving continuing education will have no one present that has (or has very much) "hiring and firing" power over the others present. Therefore, having a clear task and good leader-member relations are essential for effectiveness of the outcome. An example would be two leaders of units discussing, planning or meeting for a variety of continuing education reasons. Anything the continuing education leader and unit can do to clarify the task at hand, such as draft or write the proposal in question, submit multiple copies of printing deadlines and information session dates well in advance of due dates, and establishing a yearly ebb and flow of activities that are recognizable and fit faculty schedules help. Another example is setting up summer and fall information session dates in the same phone call in April. Since some faculty members will be tempted to use their veto power just to establish (or maintain) their status (Birnbaum, 1988), it is important to have a number of "clear task" projects going so that overloading the system reduces frivolous vetoes (Birnbaum, 1988 p. 171).

Institutions of higher education, hopefully, are collegial, so that good "leader-member" relations (e.g. collegiality), the other essential in effectiveness are possible. A diagram of this fairly frequent interaction with a continuing education unit would look like Figure 6.2.

Figure 6.2 Lack of Leader Position Power		
Leader *Member relations* +	Task *Structure* +	Hiring-Firing (Leader Position) *Power* 0

In a tightly coupled situation, such as when the continuing education unit hires some or all of its own faculty, the instances of this situation would be fewer.

Unclear Task

A different combination of factors can be seen in many continuing education marketing situations. This is frequently an "unclear task" although many efforts can be made to clarify it (see the Chapter on Marketing) with direct mail, advertising and more. The need to make choices of what programs to place in a new location can show the need for strong leader-member relations with academic departments and hiring-firing power with contractors, to have the unit make effective long range choices. (See the Chapter on Problem Solving for an analysis of possible market and content choices). An example of this can be seen in an unconnected continuing education model in a state university, which did hire its own faculty, but was unable (therefore) to offer or sustain a highly technical degree in wireless telecommunications and electrical engineering. This was badly needed by 50 companies in an area surrounding a satellite off-campus location. It was hard to hire adjuncts with enough expertise for an entire highly technical degree program. Five years later, this opportunity was wide open for a competing continuing education unit from a private institution, more tightly connected than the state university (but still with "loose coupling" so therefore the department might refuse to travel and provide this M.S. degree). Figure 6.3 diagrams the latter plus the marketing of the program – which is always an unclear task.

Figure 6.3 Unclear Task		
Leader *Member relations*	Task *Structure*	Hiring-Firing (Leader Position) *Power*
+	0	0

Leader-Member Relations

A third illustration might show poor leader-member relations between an academic vice-president and an academic department. The department was told to hire contract professors to fill two (formerly) tenured slots by the academic vice-president. Attempts to correct this approach failed (poor leader-member relations) and two contract professors were hired at somewhat higher pay then the beginning tenured slots would have carried. In two years these two left (for even better jobs) and the department was left unable to fill the two slots at the lower pay rate, but now a tenured slot again. The lack of leader-member relations plus a task (hiring) that looked clear but became unclear, caused this department to have to turn away not one, but two large contract programs that had been carefully developed from the proposal stage. These would have brought in $800,000 or more for the initial cohorts of students to the university, but the income was lost to this university, as was that from on-going cohorts of students. (See Figure 6.4). This example is missing two of the three variables needed for success and did NOT succeed.

Figure 6.4 Poor Interpersonal Relations		
Leader *Member relations*	Task *Structure*	Hiring-Firing (Leader Position) *Power*
0	+	0

More on "Loose Coupling" in Institutions of Higher Education

The characterization of "loose coupling" implies that coupled events and units are responsive to each other BUT that each maintains its own identity and separateness.

This can be seen with academic departments and also the continuing education unit; the library; the career counseling center, and other administrative institution units. The attachment between units in an institution of higher education may be infrequent, weak, unimportant, or slow to respond, partly due to the fact that they have little in common. Glassman (1973) rates the activities of the variables into two categories. One category has few variables in common and the other category is when they are weak or unimportant variables. An academic department that presents courses off-campus infrequently might be an example of this "little in common". If these infrequent classes are always small, this class activity would become unimportant as well as infrequent. The coupling concept relates further to the idea that activities in one or another unit can be expanded, minimized, or severed, within the organization without affecting other units at all or very much (Simon 1969). An example of this would be the closing of the classics department in a large university having little adverse effect on other departments, or other schools in the same university except for the effect on morale.

There may be also "loose coupling" between the intentions and the actions of two units such as a department planning to do a new degree program at a satellite location, participating in proposal writing and withdrawing after winning the award as "the distance is too great and two professors have old cars and too many consulting commitments."

Benefits of loose coupling (Weick, 1982) include allowing some elements of the organization to be able to persist, thus freeing the rest of the organization from the need to constantly adapt to new changes in the whole environment. Continuing education is frequently the place that new, relevant, market-request-driven courses are offered. Having many independent elements, only externally constrained, and NOT standardized, allows the continuing education unit to be more sensitive to the outside environment's requests for programs. Loose coupling allows for local adaptations, allowing one graduate education center to offer an array of programs particularly suited to its geographic location and different from those at another site. The system can retain a greater number of mutations and innovation solutions to problems, than a standardized approach would allow. It also allows a greater sense of efficacy and effectiveness for its participants and their (somewhat) autonomous units, than a tightly coupled system would. And, lastly, units in a loosely coupled system can be sealed off from other units, if there is a breakdown (or embarrassment) in one part of the system, such as wrong advertising copy or an incorrect description of a degree or program. In the early days, when institutions of higher education held "marketing" in low esteem, having a Continuing Education unit keeping the name of the university or college before the public, took advantage of this "sealed off" attribute of a loosely coupled system. (If they had a misstep, they could always be blamed as "separate").

Furthermore, a loosely coupled system can be relatively inexpensive to run, as there is a reduction in the sometimes expensive necessity for coordination. However coordination *is* important for smooth running, continuing education in higher education, so clarifying the task including courses, programs, degrees, formats, etc., as much as possible and having good collegial leader-member relations, is very important, especially in situations where there is no hiring-firing power.

Team Learning and Shared Vision

Now that some of the group dynamics of small groups have been analyzed and understood, a better understanding of "team learning" is possible. As a team becomes more aligned, a commonality of direction emerges, and individual energies harmonize, according to Peter Senge (1990). A commonality of purpose, a shared vision or philosophy, leads to an understanding of how to complement one another's efforts, and there is less wasted energy. A jazz ensemble or an orchestra is another example of when "the whole becomes greater than the sum of it's parts" (the definition of this synergy). However music ensembles may have leader position power and a clear task so thus can manage without much in the way of leader-member relations. Learning organizations that build team learning can work together to build energy and enthusiasm. But they require building organizations in which people continually expand their capabilities: to understand the complexity, to clarify vision, and to improved shared mental models (Senge), whether they are mental models for a balance of academic programs, or scenarios for the Division or for one education center (see Chapter 3 on Planning). A first step for team builders is to be responsible for learning, for adults, for students, and for one's own learning. Peter Senge sees leaders as designers, stewards and teachers and says that while learning disabilities are tragic in children they are fatal in organizations (1990).

Thoughts on Team Work

"There is nothing good or bad per se about a group. A group can be a roadblock to progress, enforcing 'group think' and conformity upon its members, paralyzing decision-making processes, and smothering individual initiative. Under other conditions, a group can be a powerful synergism of talents, strengthening its members, speeding up the decision-making process, and embracing individual and personal growth."

-Rensis Likert (1930-1981)
Director of the Institute of Social
Research, University of Michigan

Building and Articulating the Vision

No matter what role a continuing education entity has or plays in an institution of higher education, it can be a major contributor to the vision of the institution. Our great universities require care and attention and the reaching out to the major market of 'non-traditional' students' is bringing in new ideas, new possibilities and new challenges.

In articulating a vision there are two major components according to Jim Collins in *Built to Last* (1994). These are the *core ideology* and the *envisioned future*. Cornell University, for example, had as its *core ideology* for at least 100 years, that of the founder: "to build a university where any student can find learning in any subject." However the *envisioned future* allows room for "big, large, audacious goals" or BLAG or as Collins calls them 'big, hairy, audacious goals' which may be a bit undergraduate in flavor, but still suggests energy and transformation. Stanford University wanted to become "the Harvard of the west" in their vision in 1940's. Henry Ford gave a vivid and specific description of a vision when he said: "I will build a motor car for the great multitude . . . when I'm through . . . . the horse will have disappeared from our highways, the automobile will be taken for granted . . ." As we know, this has happened.

In an adaptation, continuing education might have a big, large, audacious goal of "education centers for the great multitude . . . . soon illiteracy will disappear from the nation. Higher education will be taken for granted in the information/knowledge age." Emotion and conviction are essential parts of a vivid description and these in turn attract and motivate others. Setting a large vision is a creative process. It creates a future, but it doesn't predict the future, as there can be no right answer with this 'unclear task'. This audacious vision may need new processes, mechanisms and strategies. And it may need an *analytic process* to review processes, structures, and strategies, thus uncovering misalignments.

By asking "what processes should we use to solve this problem?" one contributes to a strong, well-aligned continuing education entity within the institution of higher education. Few people can build a continuing education enterprise without vision. Institutions of higher education and non-profit organizations operate very successfully with large, audacious visions.

One Continuing Education Center in a somewhat rural area communicated the 'car or education for everyone' vision with a flyer, used widely, illustrating "A Degree Costs the Same as a New Car". See Figure 6A. By "meeting people where they are" one can communicate higher education goals. The center was in an area where cars were important but higher education had been non-existent for a radius of 85 miles except for the community college, used this flyer.

In assessing the Continuing Education Unit's team and "teamness" consider constructing three rating scales (Eitington 1984). With measures from 1 to 5, a list to assess "teamness" such as the following, can have each item rated on a 1 to 5 scale, and thus give a measure to work from for improvement.

Figure 6.5
Team Assessment Rating

(Please rank from 1 to 5)

___Cohesion	___Cooperation
___Pride	___Communication
___Decision Making	___Goal Setting
___Openness	___Creativity
___Trust	___Conflict
___Team self-assessment	___Support
___Team membership identification	___Mutual Respect
___Leadership	___Commitment
___Feedback to leader	___Atmosphere

A rating scale to assess team communication can be constructed with 10 or more statements about communication when it is at its best. See Figure 6.6.

Figure 6.6 A RATING SCALE TO ASSESS TEAM COMMUNICATION					
Criteria	StronglyAgree	Agree	Undecided	Disagree	Strongly Disagree
1. Team members listen to each other.					
2. The team leader listens to all group members.					
3. Everyone feels free to level and to be candid with everyone else.					
4. All team members "check things out" with all concerned before action is taken.					
5. Constructive feedback is given freely to group members to improve their functioning.					
6. Broad participation is strongly encouraged at all group meetings.					
7. No one uses disproportionate amount of the available "air time" at group meetings.					
8. People are available to secure information needed.					
9. Information is shared willingly and no one hoards information.					
10. Information of interest to team members, such as information on new policies, new projects, and pay, is not categorized as "secret".					
11. Information about one's performance is communicated regularly and candidly by the team leader so that there are no surprises at performance time.					
12. Team members are not afraid to give the boss the "bad news".					
13. We communicate well with other groups in organization.					

This also might be used as a rating scale to assess team problem solving and creativity and yield insights. These scales once developed and adapted for the Division, can be added to and distributed to staff for self-assessment. They can be used as a springboard for discussion at a staff meeting, and they can be especially useful as an occasion for praise and recognition of a staff that is really working well together.

Summary

A group exists when two or more people have a unifying relationship, such as common goals or physical proximity. When physical proximity is missing as in many national and international organizations, team building is even more important and frequent electronic communications plus telephone and fax communications become a must. Utilizing the characteristics of groups is an important skill of leadership and understanding their dynamics as described by Fiedler or other theorists can be useful.

Teamwork is as necessary in higher education as in other organizations, no matter how loosely coupled the teams are. While the teams will evolve and have an ebb and flow with academic departments in the higher education context, the continuing education unit needs to stay strong, as a working team. All three factors in the Fiedler model need to be present as often as possible: leader position power; clear (or structured) tasks; and leader-member relations. Since the task often will not be clear (for instance in marketing choices), it is well to be aware of these dynamics and put in the extra effort that is needed. Any activities that clarify the task will help. These might include having marketing text books or article copies in an electronic newsletter or on a unit resource shelf; advice from experts; or hiring particular expertise such as a graphics and marketing firm or a technology consultant.

Characteristics of groups include norms, a standard of behavior expected by group members, and roles which can consist of the total pattern of expected behavior or the behavior during a certain situation. An informal group is defined as two or more people associated with one another in ways different from the formal organizational structure.

Informal group leaders can be powerful and may be chosen by consensus, or to fill a leadership vacuum, but they are usually trusted. This is a good person to have on a leader's side at work, and to explain things to in the community. They are sometimes called "opinion leaders" in sociology. The synergism and energy that teams and small groups can provide are a beneficial force for accomplishing an organization's objectives.

Chapter 7

Motivating and Empowering Staff, Faculty and Students

The best Deans, Directors, and leaders of all kinds, agree on one thing: People support what they help to create (Senge, 1990). This includes the understanding and building of vision, goals and strategies. When people are involved in thinking through the vision, the goals, and the strategies, a task structure is more likely to evolve that will capitalize on the natural motivation inherent in all people, especially with the great variety of people found in continuing education (Johansson, 2004). Everyone is motivated all the time by something, so the Dean or Director's task is to set a supportive climate with high performance goals to try to access this natural motivation (Senge, 1990). This will promote a self-fulfilling prophecy that this is an excellent continuing education division where excellent people work. By encouraging people to take responsibility and by constantly checking one's own assumptions about people, being wary of multi-cultural or gender filters, a leader is well on the way to having a continuing education unit in which people motivate themselves. Two theories of motivation give new insights into what actions on behalf of employees in a service or education field might have desired effects. The first is two-factor or group motivation theory, developed by Herzberg (1959). The second one discussed here is Maslow's theory (1970), which can be called one-factor or individual motivation theory. Of the many theories of motivation, these two are particularly useful in administering continuing education programs in institutions of higher education.

Organizational Group Motivation Theory

"What would motivate my staff to really work towards our Continuing Education goal of able, satisfied, competent students and graduates in large numbers?" wonders a leader. "I wish I could pay them more money. Maybe I can give Sue a small raise – that's only a few dollars a week more. Then I think I'll ask Mary if she'd like to attend that all day conference next month. It has a moderate cost but it's only a one time cost." What will be the results of these two "trial balloons"? A staff member who got the raise asked for another raise in three months, but the staff member who received the training used new skills for several years.

In two factor motivation theory as outlined by Herzberg (1959) and diagrammed on the next page, two types of factors are needed to motivate employees. The first category of factors are the dissatisfaction or "hygiene" factors in the left hand column. The second category in the right hand column are called motivator factors. Many motivator factors are an inherent part of higher education work, such as a sense of achievement and the worth of the work. The story about Mary and Sue illustrates this theory, in part, with a raise (hygiene factor) only bringing Sue up to zero or "not dissatisfied" while the conference helped Mary's competency and growth.

Dissatisfaction or Hygiene Factors

The words "hygiene factors" used with dissatisfaction factors really mean the extrinsic or outside factors – the things in a continuing education division that a leader can do something about. They are group-oriented factors that are all around a person at work, and set the working atmosphere. Included are salary, working conditions, interpersonal relations, policy, hours, status, and security, as shown in Figure 7.1. Quality of supervision can be measured by observing whether the director follows staff around and is nosy, or whether the leader trusts the staff. Trust is also a major component of empowerment for employees (Peters, 1994; Covey, 2004). These factors are those usually chosen for improvement when a leader or manager wants to strengthen motivation in an organization. However, Herzberg found that even if all of these factors are excellent, this excellence will merely prevent an employee from being dissatisfied. On the diagram this is shown by the arrows bringing the employee from a minus position up to a zero position. He or she may not complain as much now but the individual is still not motivated to do his or her best work.

Many people think that when they want to motivate people, they should increase the pay, improve the hours, have more staff parties (improve interpersonal relations), or improve on some of the hygiene factors in the left hand column in Figure 7.1. In numerous studies it has been found, however, that all that improving the hygiene factors does is to keep people from being dissatisfied. It is important not to ignore the hygiene factors, however, because if a person is too dissatisfied he or she will not even be interested in the motivator factors. However, in any organization one or two of the hygiene factors may be beyond the administrator's control. In continuing education the hours and the wages are somewhat controlled by outside factors but the two factor group theory of motivation is particularly applicable in continuing education organizations, because all of the motivator factors can be developed within a given continuing education division or Center and cost nothing or very little.

Figure 7.1

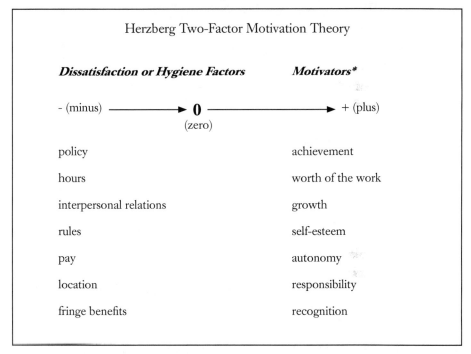

Herzberg Two-Factor Motivation Theory

Dissatisfaction or Hygiene Factors	*Motivators**
- (minus) ⟶ **0** ⟶ + (plus) (zero)	
policy	achievement
hours	worth of the work
interpersonal relations	growth
rules	self-esteem
pay	autonomy
location	responsibility
fringe benefits	recognition

*Factors to build into all jobs

Motivator Factors

The second type of factors needed, according to Herzberg, are the motivator factors described in the right hand column of Figure 7.1. In order to motivate people, leaders need to build-in motivators that are really internal. Feelings of job satisfaction and motivation are more likely to come from the work itself. These include a sense of achievement, a sense of responsibility, and a sense of the worth of the work itself. In continuing education there is a tremendous benefit gained from this factor because the work persons are doing with higher education continuing education is inherently worthwhile. Persons active in higher education helping students gain continuing education will have a part in shaping the future. It is important to remind staff and faculty of this, and to say "Thank you: this is *important* work. You are enhancing people's lives."

Being an educator can be a "psychologically draining" job – because faculty and staff are on duty long hours, and there may be crises. On the other hand, it is an important life's work because one is helping people improve their lives and develop their potential in ways that may have far-reaching consequences.

In any continuing education program or center this factor of the importance of working with people and helping them develop, is a built in motivator, inherent in the job itself. In contrast persons who work in most factories, turning three bolts all day long, or inserting three computer chips everyday, will have to be turned to other motivators as the work itself will never be as inherently important and as far reaching, as working with people (students) who are improving their lives. Factory owners know that they have this problem so they pay assembly line workers increasing wages and just assume that they will always have morale problems.

The **motivators** are some of the things that can be developed by any leader or manager, so that employees feel a real sense of satisfaction in their work, not just an absence of dissatisfaction. Other motivators include building self-esteem, encouraging people to grow and learn, giving them opportunities for professional growth and advancement, and giving people some autonomy. Giving people autonomy means allowing them to work on their own, whether they are an exempt or non-exempt employee or are faculty.

Studies have found that people will stay in work longer, if the work really satisfies (or motivates) them, even though it doesn't pay well. Some people say "if I only earned more I wouldn't care what I did" but studies have found that this is not true. Earning more in an unrewarding job may please a person for a year or two, but really satisfying life's work is one of the finest life-enhancing qualities one can seek.

Recognition is another important motivator for all ages, adults or children. Everyone likes to be recognized for something: for a bright smile, for a job well done, for having the most registrations, for bringing in a new contract program, or for their own unique qualities whether job related or not.

These motivating factors are the important variables that really cause people to be motivated and happy. Helping them keep themselves happy can be done using some of the newest positive methods to approach any task "at their best" and furthermore to build on their strengths and manage their weaknesses. When people approach any task at their best, their energy, excitement, creativity, resiliency and problem-solving skills expand. This is as opposed to pessimism which results in limited and reactive behaviors and a "survival in the present" orientation plus a focus on winning. Organizations operating with "strength-based management" move ahead towards their goals 1.9 times as fast as organizations without this approach (Gallup 2004).

While operating at their best three Continuing educators reflected back and reported these example from their own lives:

1) I moved a team of 27 from one university campus to another with the required culture change.
2) I created a 726 page training manual in six months in conjunction with a contract.
3) I found I did very well in "telephone meetings" and was praised (and enjoyed) being a good listener and a good synthesizer. These meetings added a much needed communications link.

Hygiene factors are important and lead to job commitment. These factors actually build job commitment. But if the motivating factors are also present it leads to job and *organizational* commitment. Organizational commitment is commitment to the goal of this particular program, which may be having the best quality continuing education program in town or developing happy competent, satisfied, graduates. The Continuing Education Division has some overriding goals beyond just keeping the Division barely going. The Center goal might be for the students to have a sense of pride in being enrolled in such a fine program. However, all of the staff needs to be committed to the Division's overriding goal of being the best continuing education division in town, or whatever goal is selected. Developing these motivator factors within the working conditions really helps to secure this needed commitment of staff and students.

It is interesting to take this list of motivators and brainstorm ways that more motivators can be written into the job description of a staff member, a faculty member, a Dean or a director or into the plans for an education center.

The following list of motivators to involve faculty more in a center, was developed by one "staff meeting" role play group in a motivation segment of a college credit workshop in higher education.

Brainstorming Ways to Involve Faculty and Recognize Staff, Based on Motivating Factors

Achievement and Recognition

1. Give a certificate of commendation (with a gold seal on it?) at a meeting to a faculty member for her or his *first* contribution to a center. Even a pen with your Center logo on it gets the point across.
2. Mention names of those faculty or staff who have helped in unusual ways in a newsletter.

3. Give "thank you" notes at the end of the semester to those faculty or staff who have helped in extra ways.
4. Feature a "Professor of the Month" on an electronic notice board or in the newsletter. Tell hobbies, interests, scholarly achievements and family news, if appropriate. List compliments given that person, or have adult students do this. Adjunct professors especially, get little recognition, other than an annual dinner or reception at some schools. They often serve a vital role in continuing education and these low cost motivators validate their efforts. Since adjunct salaries tend to be low, many individuals serve in this role because they love teaching, or love their subject, or because it balances their other work; but efforts to smooth their path and to help them to get to know the staff, the students and each other are appreciated.
5. Acknowledge and implement faculty member's ideas whenever possible. Validate their input at meetings for solutions that are useful.
6. Praise the faculty member in front of their adult students. Reinforce and complement faculty members' positive interactions with adult students.
7. Do paragraphs on one or two Adjunct Faculty and full-time Faculty per month in the Continuing Education Division eNewsletter. This also helps staff members answer prospective students' inquiries and questions from a more solid information base.
8. Involve adult students in writing paragraphs for the newsletter for recognition, or for thank-you notes.
9. Share information about other higher education institutions' practices of inviting adjunct faculty members to attend department or subject-area meetings and/or orientations. This is a form of academic recognition.
10. Encourage the academic vice-president and schools or departments to grant faculty status at the quarter- or half-time level to key adjunct professors.

The Worth of the Work

1. Send thank you notes to the staff and faculty for their efforts. Include current statistics, when possible, about the benefits of getting a college degree (at any level), and how their work is helping to enhance people's lives.
2. Have a faculty member be a guest speaker at staff meetings telling about his or her degree program, course content, and view of the trends for the future in that particular discipline. This helps staff members pick up new leads for new programs; helps them counsel students; and it helps in generating advertising copy that is timely, yet accurate.

3. Share good ideas on academic teaching, distribute the best ideas in the newsletter.

4. Praise faculty members in the newsletter or in person when they build a support network for each other. Include the department chairs or lead program professors in this praise, who put in hours organizing and coordinating, and often are unsung heroes and heroines.

Responsibility

1. Invite and train professional staff members to hold briefings and information sessions, hosting the faculty member, who covers degree and course information.

2. Train staff members who are creative to make suggestions for brochures and direct mail pieces, and to help in proof reading them. Try to have each item proof read at least four or more times. Hire a marketing firm if your staff is more the "accounting" personality types than the "creative" types. Thus one can build on their strengths and manage this weakness.

Advancement and Growth

1. Invite staff members to attend workshops and conferences.

2. Train staff members to advance to responsible positions and then allow them to attend selected conferences, or when appropriate, faculty meetings.

3. Share information with staff about adult stages of human development, adult supports needed at different life-stages, and adult learning at a staff meeting, perhaps as one of several "themes" covered at different meetings. Distribute a photocopied article on this topic ahead of the meeting.

4. Share information about resources in the community.

5. Encourage staff to read library books on different topics such as marketing, management, or higher education for adult students or adult learning in general, and then at a meeting vote on which books to give their "seal of approval." Have a staff library shelf. (This is especially good for books on marketing, as they inspire new ideas and insights).

6. Invite faculty members to attend Continuing Education Conferences.

7. Share adult student development and marketing demographics information frequently.

In looking for a job one interviewee uses this two factor motivation theory as a criterion for selecting a job. When she goes for an interview, she says to the other people working there "What is it you like about working here?" If they reply "the pay is regular," "the hours are good," (the hygiene factors), she doesn't take the job. If the employees reply, "they let you try out your own ideas," "they'll support you when you get going in an initiative", – those are motivators and she listens – even if the job in question pays a little less than the first job described.

It is important to spend more time thinking how to get more motivators into the higher education faculty and staff work settings, because, mostly, these motivators are free, or at least easily affordable. It is important to remember that the goal is job enrichment, not job enlargement, however. The pay-off in commitment and motivation is to get a good job done for the Continuing Education Division or Center and to get the "maximum effort" at least some of the time. (The minimum effort is the minimum an employee does to avoid getting fired. Of course tenured faculty have a different set of dynamics.) The goal is to help people realize their full potential.

If there is a secretary or staff member in the center or division who is very creative, give her more opportunity to do electronic notice boards, newsletter design, ad or brochure computer design, or to develop a marketing plan, or to use that talent of creativity in another way that helps him or her to grow. The organization has an obligation to recognize the potential in people and this leads to great pay-off for the organization. If the division or center believes in people, they will reward the unit by being motivated and by expending more effort on the unit or center than on something else. Many organizations are losing a lot in talent today because they do not motivate people with these motivators (Covey, 2004). This results in an economic loss as well as a loss in human happiness. The hygiene factors can recharge a person but with motivator factors he or she becomes his or her own generator.

This theory of motivation parallels what adult educators believe in: the importance of building a employee's self-esteem, and of helping an employee to reach his or her potential. Good theory about people can apply to any age or stage of adulthood. Adults respond to those who believe in them and who recognize their potential, just as younger students do. Adults like to be helped to create and achieve, to be responsible and to grow also. There is often an expectations gap between what a person does and what he or she is capable of.

Figure 7.2
Gap in Expectations

What one does———▶ What one is capable of, or what one is expected to do

The more the organization can help close that gap the more of a sense of commitment it will build in its employees towards the organization's goals.

People need to be trained to handle more *responsibility*, however, and they have to find satisfaction in it. People need to build competence and confidence, and have a sense of being able to grow. It is not wise to just require a lot of extra responsibility and say "Aren't you fulfilled?"

Ways to train people might include giving or delegating a small section of a market plan to another person to train them, for example, allowing a new program representative to accompany a more senior representative during some calls. A support staff member can be trained in the same partnership way on a regular basis, and with something specific to do. This builds a *sense of achievement* into an adult's job and also some responsibility.

Emphasizing the *value of the work* itself is one of the easiest things to reinforce but it is often not done. Remind people of the continuing education division's philosophy regularly: in a newsletter and on notice boards. Say "we believe in having an excellent program for adult students – respecting adult students and the learning that is occurring – helping them develop to their full potential' or whatever simply stated goals you may have. (The goals can vary every year, to keep interest in them high).

Recognition is also easy to give. For staff, have a "Highlighted Person of the Month" (or Week) bulletin Board. Show a picture of him or her and list his or her birthday, hobbies, names of any children, favorite jokes or pets. Faculty members see it as they come in and can better greet the staff member. Anything that gives the staff a lift, just naturally helps them to be nicer to the students and to prospective or inquiring students.

Deans and Directors need a lift too, and it is important for them to attend workshops, conferences, or courses to gain new ideas and to receive some recognition for what can be a lonely and isolated job. Since there are many problems a dean or director cannot complain about to his or her staff, it is important to go to a program where people have similar problems.

Growth can be provided by paying a staff or faculty member's way to a local or regional conference, or by offering regular staff and faculty training at the center. Often training for staff ends up educating the faculty member about more options and opportunities in the marketing arena. Even if only two or three people seem to be getting something out of training provided at a center, training on a regular basis is an opportunity for growth. College courses are in this category also. Tell the staff "we want you to grow professionally, so you can apply for an even better job in the future." People need to feel that they're getting something back from working with the organization. The most usual benefit in higher education is the tuition benefit package most institutions offer but often staff members may need to be encouraged to take advantage of this. It should not just be assumed that no staff development is needed because most of the staff are enrolled in courses. If they feel they are growing, that is one of the best things employment can do for people. In a field where people are asked to give all day, units and centers have to give staff something in return – refill them – so that they can be informative and responsive to the adult students. Studies on stress show that people can only give out so much. As a general rule the more that an administrator can support staff, help them feel self-esteem and a sense of personal worth, and help them feel that what they are doing is really worthwhile, then the more they will have a better sense of feeling good about themselves. The Leader can encourage staff to realize their importance to the continuing education unit, to the adult students, and to the faculty. People like to feel good about themselves. It is a real human need. Helping people feel good about themselves is something that is not very hard to do. There is a tendency that when an administrator feels discouraged he or she thinks "how come *they* get to feel good about themselves when I've got this budget problem?" However this is dead-end reasoning. If the unit can give staff something (recognition, self-esteem) it is likely that the fruits of this will eventually cheer up the leader, and perhaps even improve the budget, too. To build any kind of marketing program, morale build-up is an on-going need, because representatives of the institution are being asked to risk rejection for their efforts in the outside world every day.

Leaders can find out just how their staff feels and in what areas motivating factors might be increased by asking some questions. Now that higher education continuing education is becoming less of a monopoly, (with new schools, satellite centers, and distance learning options constantly entering the field), *maximizing* the way the institution of higher education's programs are presented by all concerned, will help the bottom line of the institution.

Figure 7.3
"Analysis of Staff Members Motivation
and Engagement" Questionnaire

Figure 7.3

FANTASTIC	PRETTY GOOD	JUST OKAY	NOT SO HOT

QUESTION:

1. How do you like the work you do?

Great, highly exciting, the work you always wanted to do	Better than Average Worthwhile	Average so-so	Routine, dull & meaningless
SCORE 3	SCORE 2	SCORE 1	SCORE 0

2. Does your work call for you to do jobs on your own? Do you know what's expected of you?

Always	Often	Sometimes	Never
SCORE 3	SCORE 2	SCORE 1	SCORE 0

3. How much control do you have over the way you do your work?

Do it my way	You think how to do it & get approval	You & Dir. decide together	You do as you're told
SCORE 3	SCORE 2	SCORE 1	SCORE 0

4. How much time and freedom does your work allow you?

Your time is your own, freedom to come & go to do the job as you see fit	Better than average many late nights	Some free time Work Saturdays	Constant surveillance
SCORE 1	SCORE 2	SCORE 1	SCORE 0

---

5. Have you received any acknowledgment for a job well done in the past year? In the last seven days?

Every time	Occasional pat on the back	Almost never	Don't know what you're talking about
SCORE 3	SCORE 2	SCORE 1	SCORE 0

---

6. Are you given opportunities to attend classes, conferences or other events in the areas of interest and specialization? Do others care about your development?

Regularly	Once in a while	Rarely	Never
SCORE	SCORE 2	SCORE 1	SCORE 0

---

7. Does your job encourage you to be competent in the areas of your choice and to achieve?

Too much	Yes, it's great	Often	Never
SCORE 1	SCORE 3	SCORE 2	SCORE 0

---

8.   What kind of guidance do you receive from your leader?

Well planned & helpful	Periods of no guidance	Occasional vague guidance	Poor, little or no individual guidance
SCORE 3	SCORE 2	SCORE 1	SCORE 0

9.   Does your leader and/or co-workers recognize your efforts when you pitch in and help?

Usually	Occasionally	Almost Never	What are you talking about?
SCORE 3	SCORE 2	SCORE 1	SCORE 0

10.   How do you feel about the progress you've made this year?

Am learning new and more challenging things	Have some new tasks	Routine learnings & tasks	Not going anywhere, same old thing
SCORE 3	SCORE 2	SCORE 1	SCORE 0

11.   Have you been given a raise in salary, promotion, or better work location this year?

Every 6 months	Once a year	Every 1 1/2 to 2 years	Never
SCORE 3	SCORE 2	SCORE 1	SCORE 0

12. What kind of relationship do you have with your leader? Does he or she care about you as a person?

Great, effective, really understands me	More often effective than not	Average	In-effective, so-so
SCORE 3	SCORE 2	SCORE 1	SCORE 0

13. To what extent do you participate in decision making?

My ideas are asked for & often used constructively	My ideas are asked for	Not involved in decision making but informed of what I need to know	Not informed of job-related matters
SCORE 3	SCORE 2	SCORE 1	SCORE 0

14. Do you have responsibility or authority over any others?

A lot	Somewhat	Very little	Not at all
SCORE 3	SCORE 2	SCORE 1	SCORE 0

15. How well do you get along with your co-workers? Are your associates committed to doing quality work? ____Yes, ____No

Great group, I like them	Some likeable	Pleasant but dull	Boring
SCORE 3	SCORE 2	SCORE 1	SCORE 0

16. All in all, how do you feel about your pay?

Top dollar	Generous	Average, ordinary	Plenty of room for improvement
SCORE 3	SCORE 2	SCORE 1	SCORE 0

---

17. Do you like where your job site is located?

Ideal	Sub-ideal	Too far, could be closer	Too far from everything
SCORE 3	SCORE 2	SCORE 1	SCORE 0

---

18. What kind of fringe benefits do you receive?

Vacation, tuition, medical coverage, pension	Most of these	Some of these	Few of these
SCORE 3	SCORE 2	SCORE 1	SCORE 0

---

19. Is your work setting _____? Are you given the materials and equipment you need to do your work?

Luxurious, lots of resources & equipment	Comfortable, nice place, sufficient resources & equipment	Run down, hot, stuffy	Dismal, sick building
SCORE 3	SCORE 2	SCORE 1	SCORE 0

20. Who evaluates your progress?

You evaluate your own with Dean/Dir.	Cooperate in evaluation & review	Given a chance to discuss evaluation given you	Given an evaluation
SCORE 3	SCORE 2	SCORE 1	SCORE 0

21. Do you feel _____

Secure	More secure than insecure	More insecure than secure	Don't know one day to the next
SCORE 3	SCORE 2	SCORE 1	SCORE 0

22. Do you have input into marketing plans, direct mail list selection, program development? Does the mission or purpose make you feel your job is important?

It's my main job	Once in a while	Occasionally (or as an afterthought)	Not at all
SCORE 3	SCORE 2	SCORE 1	SCORE 0

23. Do you feel an emotional high at work and/or feel invigorated when you reach the end of a long busy day?

Daily	Weekly	Monthly	Rarely
SCORE 3	SCORE 2	SCORE 1	SCORE 0

24. How often do you find yourself feeling positive anticipation about your work in non-work hours, or get so involved you loose track of time?

Daily	Weekly	Monthly	Rarely
SCORE 3	SCORE 2	SCORE 1	SCORE 0

25. What percentage of the work day do you spend your time doing things that you really like to do?

75%-100%	50%-74%	25%-49%	Less than 25%
SCORE 3	SCORE 2	SCORE 1	SCORE 0

Figure 7.3 A Key to Motivation Questionnaire

Total: 26 factors (9 hygiene and 17 motivators, #2 falls into both)

Questions:

Hygiene Factors	*Motivators*
Salary – #16	Autonomy – #2, 3, 4
Leader/Director – #12, 20	Worth of Work – #1
Co-Workers – #15	Recognition & Achievement #5, 9
Location – #17	Growth Needs – #6, 7, 8
Fringe Benefits – #18	Advancement – #10, 11
Working Conditions – #19	Responsibility – #13, 14, 22
Security – #2, 21	Engagement – #23, 24, 25

The "hygiene" factors are easy to complain about and when rated at 100% still only keep people from being dissatisfied. The "motivator" areas in the other questions are much more important for lasting success and an optimistic future outlook for the division of continuing education.

Numbers 2,5,6,7,12, and 19 are the most predictive of positive engagement at work. In the U.S. only 29% of the workforce are engaged positively, and 55% of the employees are *not engaged* and thus more likely to quit or have an accident (HBS Publishing Conference 2006).

Individual Motivation

Abraham Maslow (1970) is quite well known in the field of psychology and his work on the hierarchy of human needs is also used in management. The theory states that the bottom level of needs in the triangle or hierarchy must be met before an individual can or wants to move on to the next level. A person therefore is motivated by one factor: whether his or her needs on his or her level are met or not. The theory, in terms of motivation, assumes that meeting the person's needs on his/her level will *motivate* the person to go on to the next level. When the need is filled, the person is satisfied and ready to move. Maslow's theory of motivation looks at individuals, whereas Herzberg's theory looks at motivation within organizations and organizational groups. Maslow's theory is based on the assumption that those things absent will satisfy when they are present and is therefore called one-factor motivation.

Figure 7.4
Maslow's Hierarchy of Needs

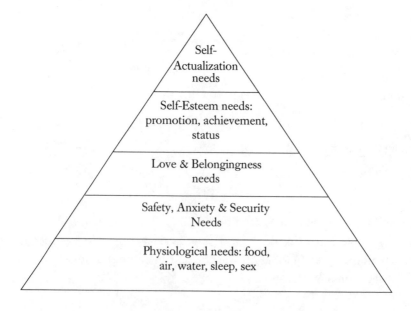

Figure 7.4A

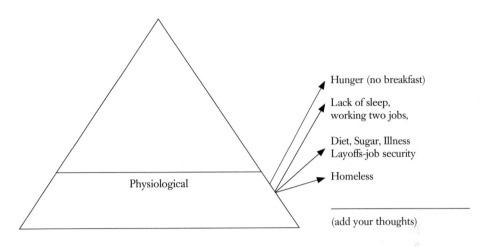

Physiological level

Figure 7.4A Lethargy Problem

What could cause a staff member to be a lethargic and unmotivated because of safety concerns, fear or anxiety?

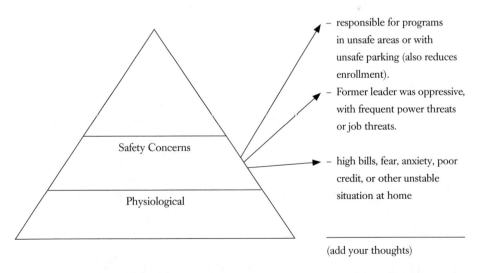

Figure 7.5
Lethargy Problem Considered from the Safety and Security Needs Perspective

What could cause an employee to be lethargic and unmotivated because of love and belongingness needs?

Figure 7.6
Lethargy Problem from the Love and Affection Needs Perspective

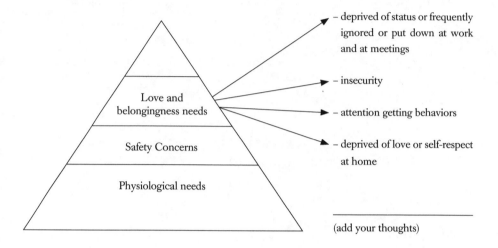

Love and belongingness needs

Safety Concerns

Physiological needs

– deprived of status or frequently ignored or put down at work and at meetings

– insecurity

– attention getting behaviors

– deprived of love or self-respect at home

(add your thoughts)

Physiological Needs. Humans tend to concentrate on meeting these needs before being concerned with higher level needs. When the needs at this level are partially satisfied, other needs emerge. The classic example of this is of the early missionaries attempting to preach to people that were starving. Starving people have to eat before they can hear any message being brought to them.

Safety and Security Needs, Anxiety. One can see the effect this has on a personality by observing elderly people who live in big cities, who worry about being mugged, and have twelve locks on their doors. This fear and worry (need) is so great, and with good cause, that the higher level needs do not concern them. If a continuing education center requires a public transportation ride into the inner city to take courses (due to expensive or inadequate parking), it might be time to consider some suburban satellite centers for safety reasons. An individual at a higher level may also experience this level after a traumatic experience such as an auto accident. The person might be quite fearful and worried about safety while driving or riding in a car for several months or years following the accident. It is important according to Maslow's theory to "meet people where they are."

Love and Belongingness Needs. Maslow believes that most of America is at this level. This need can be seen in adult students that seek companionship.

Self-Esteem Needs. If a person has a feeling of being cared about, is not really feeling unsafe, is not really hungry or in need of rest – then that person would not mind being Chair of a workgroup, task force or something similar, or gaining self-esteem in some way. A person with pressing needs in another area doesn't need or want status responsibilities on top of their other worries, however.

Maslow says to motivate people one needs to meet them on the level where they are and help move them forward to the next level. Leaders must be cautious, however, as it is difficult to be certain of correctly estimating the level of need.

Self-Actualization Needs. The highest level needs for development and self-actualization are satisfied only after needs at the four lower levels have been met. At this fifth level, the individual is concerned with the development of his or her potential. This person has peak experiences of insight or understanding. The person at this stage, which many people never reach, has a better perception of reality, accepts herself or himself and others, is more creative, and is better able to become completely human in the realization and development of his or her full potential. Truth, goodness, beauty, and meaningfulness are recognized and enjoyed by this person.

Some writers say that only older people can be at this level, people like Winston Churchill or Eleanor Roosevelt. This writer has found many positive people in continuing adult education that have periodically, tremendous moments of feeling really good about their work with adults of all ages. One example is one Director that had planned a good staff training program and can see that it has really helped the staff. It is important to take time to value this feeling as it is a "pay-off" of a kind for the effort expended. A dean or director might take a moment to think: "I worked hard on that, and it really seems to be clicking". Similarly, people must value the insights that come to them about what they might do next. One can write down these insights and review them until one is ready to put them onto a goals list – either long range or short range goals.

Practical Application of One-Factor Motivation

Since the previous section discussed practical ways of motivating faculty and some staff, the application here will only be to staff members' needs and staff members' motivation. The same process may be used for adult students.

The first step is to think of the different reasons a person could present a problem based on each level of Maslow's hierarchy of needs. For instance, an adult who seems unmotivated and lethargic could be reacting to any of the five levels of needs on the hierarchy. What would cause an adult to be a lethargic and unmotivated problem on the love and belongingness level? Idea: The 'Staff Member of the Month' activity is particularly good for the staff employee with this need. One education center placed a picture of the employee in the center of a poster, and all the employees wrote a compliment about Tom. These were written down all over the poster and given to the employee. He was proud enough to post it on his refrigerator at home. This is also self-worth and self esteem in action. this can also be accomplished less publicly with notes on group birthday cards to an individual.

The activity is good for all adults, because besides receiving their poster or card, they like to see nice things said about themselves. This has become rare in the mass-media culture of today in which the put-down-for-a-laugh has become so popular. Therefore this type of activity becomes doubly valuable and needed. Adults respond to esteem-building activities – especially if they add a light touch to the office.

What would cause an employee to be lethargic and unmotivated because of self- esteem needs?

Figure 7.7
Lethargy Problem
Considered from the Self-Esteem Needs Perspective

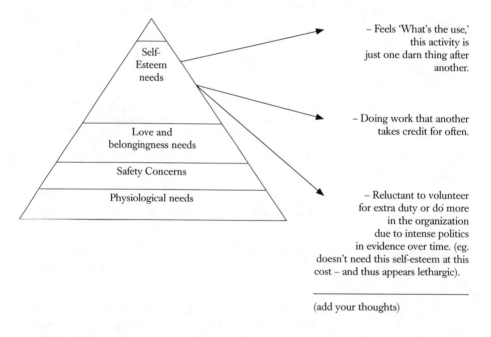

– Feels 'What's the use,' this activity is just one darn thing after another.

– Doing work that another takes credit for often.

– Reluctant to volunteer for extra duty or do more in the organization due to intense politics in evidence over time. (eg. doesn't need this self-esteem at this cost – and thus appears lethargic).

(add your thoughts)

From this exercise one can see that adults or (children) might act the same way for many different reasons. For example one staff member came to work and was sarcastic with almost everyone every morning. This person was feeling ignored and this turned out to be a belonging need.

The Dean or Director's analysis of what level the employee is on, needs to be on target. For the leader, seeking out more training can be helpful in sharpening one's analysis, as selecting a level is hard to do. One looks at the employee who is lethargic and unmotivated and realizes there could be a number of causes. If that person is really exhausted or hungry, more attention or expanded duties will not help him or her much.

If someone really needs something, solutions based on another level of need will not be effective motivators. For example a staff member who had grown up in a large family and never had a room of her own, was having problems over sharing an office with one or more other staff members. By giving her assigned desk and shelf space of her own, the leader really met a need of hers of having her 'stuff' protected; of having her own space. This solution met this employee's need better than perhaps sending her to a workshop on interpersonal office relationships might have.

A leader or manager can think about each employee, decide if they have a pressing need, identify it, and then try to work with that level. Adults can be operating on the level of physiological need also: coming to work without breakfast, too little sleep, or having a problem with alcohol or other substances.

Other problems or needs, that lead to applications of Maslow's theory to understand more about the level that an adult (faculty member, staff, or adult student) might be on, in addition to the *physiological level* mentioned above, might be:

Anxiety level	– worried about a health problem
	– worried about financial problems
	– spouse lost job
	– sudden divorce
	– spouse abuse
Love and Affection level	– single parent
	– conflict with spouse
Esteem level	– loss of job or spouse
	– passed over for promotion
Self-Actualization level	– not enough opportunities to use talents, skills and abilities

Figure 7.8 Lethargy Problem
Considered from the Self-Actualization Needs Perspective

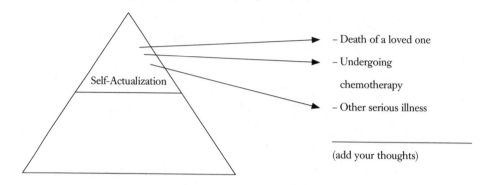

Obviously a Dean or Director or other leader's job is not designed to deal with many of these problems, but understanding their existence and helping find referrals to an appropriate community resource or resources, might be a first step. Encouraging adults involved in the unit to be supportive and kindly also builds a positive climate in the workplace.

Occasionally a leader or manager may have an employee who has such a strong need that they really cannot work in continuing education. One example is that of a support staff member, who had been wonderful answering prospective students questions on the telephone, but who was having tremendous problems at home with an alcoholic husband and an ensuing divorce. The Leader did not know all this, but all the rest of the staff noticed that the individual had started being rude and abrupt with telephone inquiries. The Leader realized that there was no way that she could meet the staff member's needs, that were extremely severe. The unit found another job for this employee in institutional research with less student interface for a year or two. Not all jobs require patience with people all day long. There are other jobs available for someone who cannot reasonably expect to change their behavior right at a given point.

Maslow's one factor theory encourages one to look carefully at an individual, try to identify their level (or one's own) correctly, and try to work towards solutions based on this level. It is helpful to draw out the hierarchy triangle chart, and brainstorm (even alone) some of the possible causes for a person's behavior at each level. This will help prevent identifying the wrong level, and then going down a blind alley.

Two other process theories about motivation, not often seen in continuing education but still observable, are an 'expectancy' theory and an 'equity' process theory. The expectancy theory states that persons fill positions because they *expect* better positions to evolve from them (e.g. Dean? Academic Vice-president? Alumni Development Director? Business School Professional Development Director?). The equity theory states that persons are in jobs because they see the jobs as 'fair' and 'equitable' (Hillriegel, 1997). One hears about this often in political campaigns. However the agonized comment of a government worker of 'That's not fair!' upon hearing a down-linked speech by a noted management guru about employees having 8 jobs and 5 careers in a lifetime demonstrates a trend away from 'cradle to grave' or 'career until pension' job likelihood.

Encouraging staff, faculty, and students to do their best, to reach for their full potential and to feel good about themselves is a valuable life's work. This encouragement will reap tremendous returns to the organization and persons who engage in it.

Supportive and Defensive Workplaces

Certain generic themes run throughout this chapter (and this book) which are known to facilitate any organization and are particularly appropriate in adult continuing education programs. These include the provision for a 'supportive workplace' rather than a 'defensive workplace' which allows for the openness, caring, and good morale so needed for all adults who work with students. In a supportive workplace there is empathy and a realistic concern for the self-esteem of all persons involved (students, staff, and faculty). Equality of all concerned to take part in problem solving regardless of rank or status is another hallmark of the workplace climate needed in an open, caring continuing education division. The climate needs to be focused on problems to solved rather than interpersonal fault finding, and on use of technical expertise and training to solve issues. The focus is on how to do it better, with concern for mutual learning and strategies-to-do-better. In short, a supportive climate would be :

1. descriptive (of behavior)
2. solution oriented
3. vision driven
4. empathetic
7. collegial (friendship among equals)
8. experimental

Therefore many of the chapters in addition to this one, mention involving many persons in the planning and implementation of programs for adult students. This is also the most professional approach as developed in the next chapters.

Summary

Both organizational and individual motivation are applicable in the continuing education workplace. This chapter has examined two major models of motivation. Herzberg, in two factor motivation theory, claims that motivators, such as job challenge and worth of the work, lead to job satisfaction, not to job dissatisfaction. However the hygiene factors, such as working conditions, only prevent job dissatisfaction and don't/can't lead to job satisfaction.

One factor motivation, as demonstrated here with Maslow's theory, assumes that needs motivate people and when a need is satisfied, it no longer motivates a person. This can be very helpful in understanding the behavior of individuals, but if the analysis targets the wrong level, it can be misleading. Knowing one's employees, and friendly one-to-one interaction, builds the trust to make this understanding clearer and more on target.

Assuming that motivation is 'built in' to the continuing education workplace can be a mistake. Professional interaction and inspiration may be available, but creativity and risk-taking need to be recognized and supported, with recognition and credit freely given. Frequent repetition of the vision is needed at every possible opportunity: every speech, every meeting, and every electronic newsletter, so that staff and others know that the leader is really serious about *this* idea (Kantor, 1983). Since the concepts of creativity, risk-taking, and of building on innovations already achieved, often are not the norm in higher education, extra effort needs to be made in these directions, coupled with adequate staff development. The rewards of these extra efforts will be seen in almost all the areas discussed in this book: planning, decision-making and especially in problem solving and marketing, which are discussed in the next chapters.

Chapter 8

Problem Solving:
Creative And Analytical

Continuing education is one of the fastest growing segments of education in North America and possibly in the world. In the last ten years, individuals and organizations are turning to institutions of higher education in increasing numbers to build their futures and change their lives. Continuing Education is being called upon to educate diverse audiences and solve new problems in a society that is being reshaped by technology plus economic and social changes, both local and global.

Employers and policy makers look to continuing education to supply the structure that can provide ongoing learning to the workforce. Furthermore the emerging global economy is inviting continuing education to reach out to international audiences, while also creating demands for local service to the workforce and to local cultural publics. The Internet and digital communications are bringing global students to continuing education, yet the traditional face-to-face setting remains an important need. Continuing education is often asked to serve many audiences because of its proactive orientation, innovative strategies and flexibility. Continuing Educators are often the first in the institution of higher education to recognize and respond to local community problems and the needs of new professions.

To keep creativity and problem solving fresh this chapter presents a variety of strategies to be used to address changes in society, especially as continuing education moves more into the mainstream of institutions of higher education. A Dean's or Director's problems in continuing education in higher education are often a group of sub-problems or activities. Breaking down these problems into parts can be helpful, but a Dean or Director also needs a feel for the total situation. It is helpful to state the problem in as open-ended a way as possible. Then a selection can be made from any or all problem solving techniques appropriate.

STEPS IN PROBLEM SOLVING

Ask: Is It Within the Problem Solver's Sphere of Influence?

An initial question to ask is whether the problem is within the director's sphere of influence. If it is, then individual techniques may well be enough to solve the problem (See Figure 8.1). If it is not within the director/administrator's sphere of influence, then group techniques are a must. It is helpful to identify key persons and involve them in the group techniques. Aids to decision making such as the decision tree in chapter 5, brainstorming, and synectics are group techniques to be discussed later in this chapter.

Figure 8.1
Creative and Analytical Individual and Group Problem Solving Techniques

Individual ——————————————— Either ———— Group—————

Creative	Analytic	Creative
1. Morphological Analysis and Attribute Lists	1. Check Lists and Attributes Lists	1. Brainstorming
2. Redefining the Problem	2. Decision Trees and Other Aids	2. Synectics
3. Reversals	3. Six-Question Approach	
4. How Is It Done In Nature?	4. Computer Aided Projections and Scenarios	
5. Boundary Examinations		
6. Drawing a Model		
7. Wishful Thinking Big Dream, Inspired Approach		
8. Analogy and Metaphor		
9. Questioning		
10. Ten Ways This Can Be Done		

Ask: Are Time and Change Important?

Problems can further be divided into those for which time and change are important and those for which time and change are less important. Planning a new schedule for next year would fall into the second category as more static (not changing rapidly, less time pressure) and meeting a proposal deadline this month would fall into the first as more dynamic (with high time pressure and possible change). Obviously, there will also be situations that include *both* categories, that is time and change.

INDIVIDUAL TECHNIQUES

Many individual creative techniques listed here can also be used for group problem solving. An administrator can 'walk through' the technique alone first, or gather group ideas first. Individual analytical techniques are quite familiar.

Individual Analytical Techniques

Checklists are a familiar problem solving aid, as is the listing of 'pros' and 'cons' for a specific decision or problem solution that is basically analytical. Weighing ideas on a scale of 1 to 10 (that is, marking them 'plus one' to 'plus ten' or 'minus one' to 'minus ten'), according to one's feelings or some particular criteria, as they appear on a checklist of pros and cons, also helps clarify priorities. This is an individual analytical technique. An attribute list, as described in the next section, can also be an analytical technique. The decision tree used in Chapter 5 is also analytical in nature and can be used by individuals or by a group.

Another individual analytical technique could be called the 'Six-Question Approach.' To demonstrate this, one can use the example of a need to purchase an LCD projector, V Tel/Polycom two-way compressed video equipment or some other non-routine large purchase. First, gather catalogues (or other reference materials appropriate to a given problem). These resource materials serve to help 'warm-up' the group and help as a springboard into the discussion. Then ask these six questions:

> What is it?
> What must it do?
> What *does* it do?
> What does it cost?
> What else might do the job?
> What will that cost?

Thinking through these questions individually sharpens one's thinking and clarifies the issues involved.

Computer-Aided Problem Solving

Another aid to individual (and group) decision making and analytical problem solving is planning made possible by the one or more computer software programs. Three types of software, that are useful for continuing education provide for: planning (that is software to aid projections, long range plans, cash flow and budgets); communications and printing; and record keeping. The planning type of program can also be used for simulations as a director develops the five possible plans discussed in Chapter 4: for things as expected; for situations that are a little better; a little worse; much better; and much worse. Simulating the numbers, budgets, and other factors in a one-year, five-year and ten-year plan can help a Dean or Director have a 'dry run' or pilot program view of a likely scenario. These are subject to error, as the future *is* uncertain and computers are famous for only projecting the known or linear possibilities that have been entered into the computer. However, uncovering hidden possibilities or problems that can be predicted is worth the effort involved (Senge, 1990).

Individual Creative Techniques

Morphological Analysis. Morphological analysis is an example of a technique that can be done individually or with a group. Morphological analysis is a comprehensive way to list and examine all of the possible combinations for solutions to a problem. The steps are:

1) define the problem broadly
2) list the interdependent variables
3) enter the variables on the horizontal axis of a chart
4) select the most promising alternatives and list them on the vertical axis of the chart.

The object is to review all possible combinations as in Figure 8.2, where the broad problem was: how to expand a center's services in order to increase income. Many creative techniques can be done by an individual and or by a group.

Figure 8.2
Morphological Analysis:
How to Expand and Increase Income and Services

Variables	Old Population	Some New Population	New Population
Old Product	Existing Center for Continuing Education	Advertise a variety of off-campus sites in High Schools or Corporate locations	New Continuing Education Center across town: Build, rent, buy?
Some New Product	Offer new masters degree programs – not offered off-campus before – along with established degrees & programs	Advertise to new populations such as teachers or engineers vs. corporate business employees, if one of these new groups had not been reached recently	Advertise *only* to new population, e.g. employees of a Government Agency or a Corporation
New Product	Offer all new Masters degree programs. Rotate existing ones to a new center	Offer mostly new masters degrees to old and new populations	Offer all new programs at an all new center location across town (This is the most difficult.)

It can be seen that a gradual progression can be made through the chart with goals and objectives for future years. Floor space and expertise might be problems in the example in Figure 8.2. Acquiring the space and building solid relationships with a less active (or new) academic department might take some time. By building on old strengths of either the population served at present or the product, that is the program for adult students under discussion, an education organization doesn't get too far out on a limb in trying new things. It has been found that to *start* with a new service for a new population is the least feasible and most difficult of these alternatives. It is easier to start with a familiar service to a new population or a new service to a familiar population. For instance, if you haven't been providing engineering programs at a distance, don't open a new center (new population) with two thirds new engineering programs. Each discipline has it's own parameters, and market, so a familiar academic content area, such as providing teacher education or information systems/information technology courses should make up more than half of the new center's array of programs.

How to decide which new programs are needed and should be offered? A Curriculum Advisory Committee for each discipline area is a great place to start and also helps keep current programs updated. Community opinion leaders in that specialty should join professors on such committees.

This morphological analysis can also be done with a group in a brainstorming session to gain more ideas and add details to concepts already suggested. A staff training session might be greatly enlivened by such as exercise. In general, the whole process is designed to generate ideas. The combining and recombining of functions and possible alternatives provides numerous opportunities to look at a problem and come up with fresh, novel solutions rather than looking along old lines with old habits.

Attribute Lists

A specialized form of morphological analysis is the *attribute list*. By listing attributes of the functions desired (or not desired) on one side of a matrix and possible forms across the other side of a matrix, form and function are separated and new insights emerge. Each function can be considered as it would appear in each form. Also, elements within the function can be considered.

An example of an attribute list of this type used to better understand a difficult administrative personnel problem involving a grievance filed, is as follows in Figure 8.3:

Figure 8.3
Attribute List

Dimensions of the Problem	Elements Within the Dimension
Rudeness	Administrative Assistant rude to Professionals, Faculty, Visitors
Incompetence	Late Work, Lost Work, Surliness about Complaints
Programs Threatened	Income and Prestige Loss, Relationship with surrounding Community Threatened

Wants All Requests to be Made in Writing	Delays Work, Creates Rigidity, Violates Norms of Integrity
Sexism, Racism, Grievance Filed by Person with Attributes Listed Above (Citing Sexism and Racism as Reasons for the Behavior Described above)	Involves Legal Language and Delays, Learning About Parameters Involved, Can Work to the Benefit of Management or the Employee

This problem was resolved when the person took three months medical leave without pay and actually took a new job. It was found that her references had not been checked when she was hired and that she had shown this behavior in the past. Her grievances against a large number of people in the organization (17 out of 23) were found to be unsubstantiated.

Attribute lists are also intended to generate ideas about a service, situation or product. First, the list is generated and then analyzed for which items would improve the situation, service or whatever is produced (satisfied, competent students in the case of continuing higher education programs).

For example with this kind of attribute list, an individual or a group (staff or faculty) may want to improve offerings from an academic department to better fit the market requests. A list of attributes or features can be developed:

Possible Content	*Market Fit*	*Market Requests*
Project Management	X	X
Information Systems	X	X
Construction Management	X	X(certain areas)
Artificial Intelligence	X	O
Organizational Behavior	X	X
Industrial Statistics	X	O
Management for Scientists & Engineers	O	X
Entrepreneurship	O	X
Finance and Economic Analysis	X	X
Calculus	X	O
(0 = not offered)		

Checklists can be developed under these items and then forced relationships developed next or later. When done with a group, the leader or facilitator can introduce a new word or words and then the group can brainstorm new ideas around it, before coming back to the main task. In this case, 'New uses of Computers' or 'New Software' generate thoughts of introducing laptops with LCD projectors for all the instructors at off-campus sites to facilitate courses that have no computers or lab available to them. Students are then required to have access to a computer at home or at work. Other analogies for other lists can help enhance this problem solving method, as an interim step in the main problem solving task. A word like 'Computer' causes forced relationships and new ideas in one direction. Words like 'mission and goals in re-aligning processes' bring in a whole new group of relationships and ideas in another direction.

Problem Redefinition

In creative problem solving, whether done by an individual or a group, *re-definition of the problem* may be needed. There are many re-definitional techniques, and only few will be reviewed in this chapter. Since personnel managing programs for adult students are often quite creative, applying these skills to administration can be very useful. The book *Applied Imagination* by Alex Osborne is filled with springboards for additional ideas.

Questioning is always a favorite technique:

> What would happen if I made it (the Center; the Program, etc.) larger? If I made it smaller? What would happen if we turned it upside down? (e.g. ran it all weekend instead of all week?) Put it on top floor instead of the bottom floor?) These are called Reversals. Rearrange it in another way? What would happen if we made it larger, so it would be more useful? Reach towns within 100 miles instead of 50 miles with a hybrid combination of alternating live classes, and distance technology such as web-based or compressed video classes?

Restating the problem with key beginning phrases is helpful:

> What would I do if I had three wishes?
> 'You could also define the problem as . . . '
> 'The main point of the problem is . . . '

'The problem, put in another way is like . . . '
'Another, even stranger way of looking at it, is . . . '
'The worst thing that could happen is . . . ' (another reversal approach)

Another question approach that is also creative is the 'List Ten Ways This can be Done' approach (or ten ways this might *look*, or similar phrasing for ten aspects of a problem). One can also ask 'How is it done in nature?', sometimes called the Bionic approach. An example would be: If a mighty oak grows from a little acorn, maybe a system of higher education programs or centers can be grown from an acorn of an idea or an offshoot of one Center.

Systems Thinking and 'Shifting the Burden'

In redefining problems it is important to worry about the 'quick fixes' that work, as they can postpone the need for a fundamental solution. One university, for example, had a problem with their Engineering Management graduate degree registrations being low. A quick fix was to advertise more and to wider audiences, but the fundamental solution of overhauling and updating the curriculum (and the title) plus offering the program in consolidated off-campus education centers had actually been put into place. Basic fundamental solutions often are slow to show an effect and there is a 'delay.' A fresh spurt of direct mail and advertising might then 'take up the slack' until the refreshed course content and new locations can 'catch on' and reach into and past the awareness stage to the Registration step.

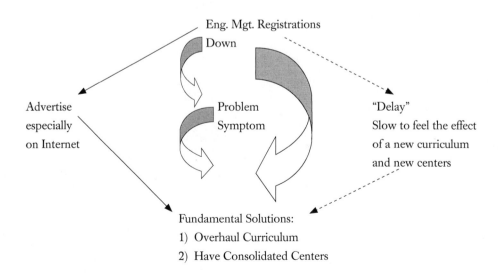

Eng. Mgt. Registrations Down

Advertise especially on Internet

Problem Symptom

"Delay"
Slow to feel the effect of a new curriculum and new centers

Fundamental Solutions:
1) Overhaul Curriculum
2) Have Consolidated Centers

With a fundamental solution, the problem will go away. This is unlikely with the 'quick fix' in which the problem keeps reappearing. In fact, problems that are reappearing are usually an indicator that a more fundamental solution is needed. In systems thinking being 'glad that the hole in your boat isn't in the end you're sitting in' is shown up as being a 'short term' gladness.

To understand completely and to help redefine problems, the 'root problem' thinking tool is often useful. In discussing whether information systems courses required computer labs at a distant site, the following root diagram from synectics was useful.

Figure 8.5
Root Figure

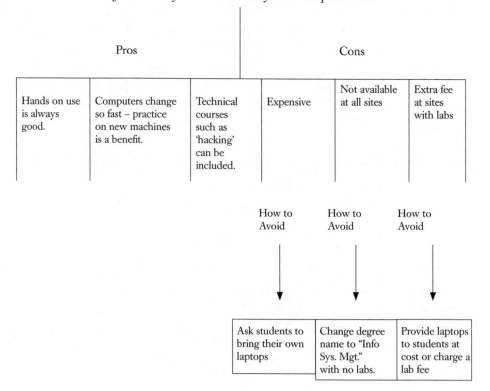

Idea and Problem as Stated or Redefined:
Information Systems Courses may need Computer Labs

Pros			Cons		
Hands on use is always good.	Computers change so fast – practice on new machines is a benefit.	Technical courses such as 'hacking' can be included.	Expensive	Not available at all sites	Extra fee at sites with labs
			How to Avoid	How to Avoid	How to Avoid
			Ask students to bring their own laptops	Change degree name to "Info Sys. Mgt." with no labs.	Provide laptops to students at cost or charge a lab fee

Boundary Examinations

Boundary examinations, another technique, are done by first writing the problem out. Then underlining the nouns and verbs, and with a dictionary find three substitutes for each noun and verb. This produces new ways to see what the problem is and thus can yield new solutions. For example:

Problem: Angry students take up too much of the receptionist's

| – upset | – adults | – use/discuss | – counselor's |
| – frustrated | – customers | – talk | – administrator's/deans |

time at the beginning of evening class *times*.

– hours	– mid-morning
– minutes	– lunch time
– attention	– evening

Solutions that pop up from this boundary examination, include finding out *all* the reasons students are upset; having time for students at lunch time; or offering evening information sessions to offer admission requirements and logistics to help students with frustrations in enrolling and attending classes. These concerns might include parking and library issues or strategies for their degree applications, as well as understanding conflicts with their jobs or families.

Wishful Thinking

Wishful thinking, another creative technique, can make a valuable contribution to formal problem solving needs. To get started, try completing the sentence: 'If I could break all the constraints I would . . . . ' For example, in budgeting seminars the advice is always given to design an ideal budget for what is really needed and wanted, and then work backwards to what can be afforded, rather than to start with the present dollar amount available. Often one of the dreams may be the latest topic in style for corporate grants or corporate contract courses. One education center posted a long sheet of shelf paper inside the Director's office door. As people had good ideas, they jotted them on this 'wish list.' When requests for education or training proposals came out from the state or federal government, they checked the list to find the topics that matched. One year 'Environmental Engineering' and 'Information Assurance' as degree options in ROTC programs were featured, as these are specific needs for the U.S. Department of Defense. (Another request might be for Management Information Systems or Enterprise IT Architecture in graduate, undergraduate and non-credit formats.)

Many kinds of restraints can be ignored in wishful thinking. The size of the building, the salary of workers, or the education or training budget in an organization are only a few examples. This device sets up new thinking patterns. The next phase is to return to the practical with statements such as: 'I can't really do that, but I can . . .'

Analogies and Metaphors

Analogies and metaphors are often found in childhood storybooks, analogies and metaphors, can also be used in administration. An analogy is a direct comparison with a similar thing, object or idea. In contrast, a metaphor is a reference to one thing, object or idea to suggest a reference to another concept such as 'the ship of state' or referring to an old age as 'the evening of life.' Both are useful in problem solving to generate data and to produce ideas or solutions about a problem. Metaphors are more powerful because they demand a greater change of perspective, but both help participants see new principles. For example, in the evening (as in the 'evening of life'), the light softens, the birds sing and things quiet down. Other metaphors include 'quiet leadership,' 'bear hug,' 'paper shuffler' or even 'brainstorming.'

Discussion involving analogies can be a useful lead-in to a group creative problem solving session using brainstorming or synectics. A current discussion using analogies in adult education is the concept that continuing education serves as a support system in helping the faculty develop the student, according to the student's goals. An architect also designs according to the client's goals. An opposing view is that of the staff person as a lackey fetching and carrying as requested. Both analogies bring in a whole new cluster of concepts and make a good springboard for discussion at either a staff or faculty meeting, as to what role an education center supports. Another analogy is that the Dean or Director is like a 'supportive parent' as both Director or faculty member are concerned with the growth of those for whom he or she has responsibility. Direct analogy can be used by using 'as if.' For example, suggest staff think of rude faculty members 'as if' they had a terrible tragedy in the recent past. This builds compassion and patience before the faculty member even starts talking. A metaphor small business owners use frequently to describe their feelings about their enterprise is that of 'having a child watching it grow.' They mention the great joy of creating something where there had been nothing.

Several approaches suggest *drawing a model* of the problem showing the relationships involved, drawn out in boxes or circles, much like the models for scenarios in Chapter 4 on planning. One can then add to this systematic outline of the problem or situation boxes connected by broken lines showing what lies outside the problem but is closely related to it. This can uncover possible causes of a problem and encourage decision making or planning (See Figure 8.6)

Figure 8.6
Factors Outside the Situation Model

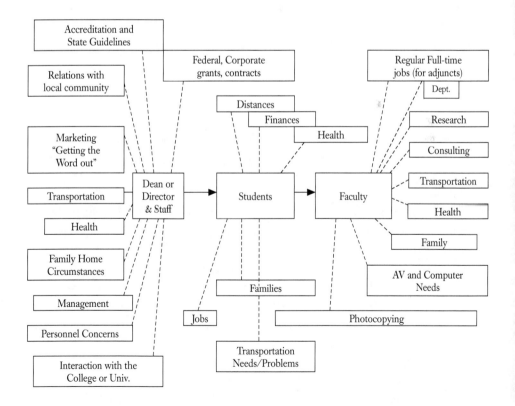

Group Techniques

Analytical techniques, such as creating a checklist, or listing pros and cons can also be done effectively in a group. Decision aids can be individual or group processed. More suggestions can be found in the chapter on Decision Making. Just addressing the questions:

> What is the problem?
> Who needs to involved?
> What more do we need to know?
> What would be an ideal solution?
> What would be the first step?

begins to get answers (written on a whiteboard or flip chart) from group discussion that 'break open' the problem.

Creative group techniques that will be discussed include brainstorming and synectics. Brainstorming produces a large number of ideas but not necessarily a deep level of new insights. Synectics, unlike brainstorming, requires that someone play the role of the client with the problem, and produces fewer, but more in-depth, solutions.

Brainstorming

Brainstorming works best when there has been some sort of warm-up, whether at a staff or faculty meeting on a certain topic, which can be just a detailed description of the issues to be considered. The questions ('What is the problem? etc.') listed previously provide a group warm-up for many problems. The group can then go on to brainstorming possible first steps. Another warm-up that is individual, is to ask each person to write down three, five or ten or more ideas on the topic or possible solutions, before the group time begins. This "Brainstorm Writing" has actually been found to provide a group with more and better ideas than a group provides without this as a first step (Johansson, 2004).

Brainstorming is divided into two parts. The idea-generation part is first, and there are some set rules for it. These are: 1) that all ideas are given equal respect; 2) there is no criticism of any suggestion no matter how wild: and 3) that all ideas are written down on a whiteboard or flip chart that can be seen by the group. This allows people to see the ideas and build on other members' suggestions. Reverse brainstorming can be used also, as in: 'What are all the possibilities of what could go wrong?' (or whatever the reverse side of the question might be).

Writing the ideas also sets the stage for the second part of brainstorming when the ideas are ranked or given priority. One approach to the ranking is to give every group member 3 to 7 votes (depending on the total number of ideas that will be ranked). Allowing 3 to 7 votes rather than just one, demonstrates greater nuances within a solution. As voting occurs, a natural ranking appears. If the client or person with the problem is present, it always needs to be stated that the client may choose among all the solutions generated by the group and need not follow the group's ranking. The client, after all, knows the problem most intimately and may have received new insights from the idea-generation section, that he or she prefers to use.

Synectics

The Synectics is a group problem solving technique that requires a leader to serve as a facilitator and requires that there be a client (who can be assigned) who has the ultimate say as to whether a solution will work or not and who 'owns' the problem. The client also can say what could correct the factor that blocks the solution's usability. The group acts as a 'think tank' for the client. Synectics is a Greek word that means joining together different and apparently irrelevant elements. While the client is the evaluator in this technique, others can see the ideas generated and written on a flip chart or board and use them in their own way.

After a suitable warm-up for the group, staff or faculty, which describes the situation, the facilitator writes out the problem, as defined in an open-ended way for all to see. Then solutions are generated by the group and written below the problem in columns (See Figure 8.7). Then the client is asked to respond to the solutions and give them a plus or minus sign. A paraphrase of the comment about why a solution would not work is written on the visual aid, if the solution is given a minus sign. The minus responses are then addressed with 'How to Avoid' questions, and new solutions are generated, as in Figure 8.7 which addresses the broad current problem of 'How to Have a University policy on Continuing Education Centers for a higher education administration graduate class. This topic is a good springboard for discussion for a professional association meeting or other similar groups.

Figure 8.7
Synectic Problem Solving Example:
How to have a University Policy on
Continuing Education Centers

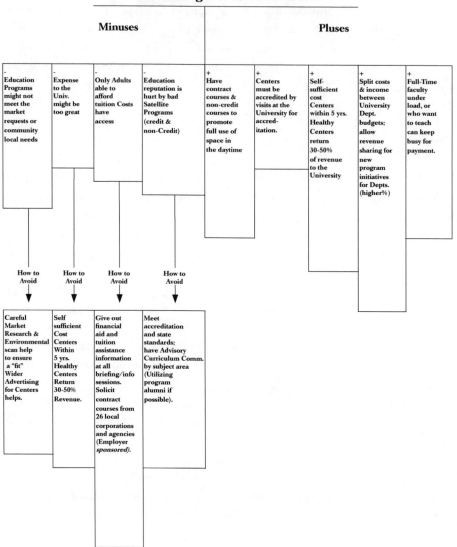

Summary

Since problem solving is a continuing component of administering and managing programs for adult students, using creativity as applied to problem solving can give one a lift as well as uncover new ideas. Educators (and hopefully, administrators) know that creativity builds self-esteem. It also builds adults' self-esteem and feelings of competence. Reading through this chapter and trying some of the ideas, starting with a small sphere of influence, perhaps before branching on to a larger sphere, can give one that extra supply of energy that is needed in work with people.

Decision making, as opposed to problem solving, is usually future oriented and concerned with future consequences and the probability of success. Some management experts see problem solving as often looking back. That is, when a problem is solved, a decision is no longer needed as things are restored to 'normal' or a 'steady state.' Decisions, however, lead to change and changed circumstances, so that problem solving is again needed. As Deans and Directors see change as opportunity, and practice problem solving techniques alone and with their groups, ahead of time or on small problems, they are better equipped to make decisions that focus on the future and a new optimal stage for their continuing higher education programs and centers.

Several analytical approaches can be used in the prediction of success. These can include: 1) Asking 'What will guarantee success?' and 'What will guarantee failure?'; 2) Listing in two columns 'Our Expectations' and 'Our Concerns' to facilitate analysis; and 3) Listing 'Anticipated Risks' and 'Ways of Overcoming Risks' in two columns in a device similar to synectics. It would be ignoring the 'real world' not to think through some of the negative questions that are likely to be asked, so sharpening the issues and facilitating the analysis with questions such as these, helps prepare the administrator and/or staff for their new, more excellent stage or plan.

Some last Do's and Don'ts might include:

- Try to identify the real problem, not just symptoms of the problem.
- Identify the 'owner' of the problem if possible. If the wrong group is asked to solve the problem, it can produce resentment, non-cooperation and even charges of meddling.
- Try to identify all the possible alternatives, as high quality problem solving and decision making require a good look at the choices.
- Develop a written plan for implementation. No solution is better than the plan to activate it. This means getting consensus on who does what, how, and when.

❑ Monitor the implementation. Appoint a monitor, coordinator or trouble-shooter who can use time and staffing charts developed jointly. These can be developed roughly with flip charts at consensus meetings and later refined. This avoids bottlenecks, frustrations, finger-pointing and slippage's.

The best problem solving supports and facilitates decision making, and helps programs move to a more optimal stage or condition. Using problem solving techniques helps the Dean or Director and the group move through each of the stages:

- idea generation,
- decision,
- course of action,
- alternatives,
- planning,
- implementation,
- operation, and
- evaluation.

A trained facilitator can even be brought in for help with big problems or big decisions affecting a large percent of the program's resources.

Chapter 9

Marketing in Continuing Education in Higher Education

Since marketing relates to exchanging something of value between two parties, the exchange must be seen as a process, not as an event. Good marketing tries to build up long-term, trusting relationships with valued student/customers. Institutions of higher education have accomplished this for many years by promising and delivering high quality, good service and fair prices to their students over time. Tuition has been subsidized in many ways to keep prices/tuition fair and education accessible to all. Relationship marketing, as relating to the student/customer is called, cuts down on the costs of transactions in both time and money, as interactions become routinized rather than negotiated each time (Kotler, 1994). That is, once a student enrolls in a degree program there is a routine for registering and paying for each course. This savings in marketing time and expense long has been taken for granted by institutions of higher education. In times of scarce dollars, further cutting into this "pared down", yet traditional, approach to "routinized relational" marketing (meaning routine relationships) will do more harm than good to revenues. In fact *spending* some budget dollars on improved registration and accounts payable systems will yield dividends. In today's world with so many institutions of higher education having online registration, those that don't or that have poor registration systems, stand out.

The concept of exchange leads to a broader concept of the "market" of potential students. A new definition would be "all potential students sharing a particular need or want who might be willing and able to engage in classes and learning to satisfy that need or want" adapted from Kotler, 1994. This doesn't mention *where* the students are (are satellite courses an option?); *how old* the students are (traditional students or working adults or seniors?); or other variables such as time of classes (evening, weekend?) which have traditionally been included in the view of institutions of higher education as to how, why and where they provide education services. In a time of declining outside and government financial supports, broader thinking about potential students can begin to bridge the gap appearing in the budgets of many institutions of higher education.

The Marketing Concept most useful to institutions of higher education (IHEs) would be:

Figure 9.1

Starting point	Focus	Means	Ends
Target Market	Customer Needs	Coordinated Marketing	Profits/Surplus through satisfaction and return

This might be contrasted with the old "industrial" selling concept of:

Factory	Products courses) (IHE)	Selling and Promoting	Surplus/Profits through Sales volume

Many institutions of higher education's have long eschewed "marketing" concepts as "commercial", but this way of thinking, or not thinking, about student/customer satisfaction is on the way out and could positively or negatively affect some large institutions of higher education including community colleges and state universities.

If the previously mentioned customer/student focused approach seems attractive, it is important to understand **what** the customers/students need. They may have stated needs, real needs, unstated needs, "delight" needs, and secret needs according to marketing literature. This complex state of the human psyche requires that institutions of higher education must select aspects of their courses and education services that will have the most relevance for the students and help students to see how to get what they want. This is especially important for small private institutions with little or no public funding. Student counseling at intake and even career counseling has long been part of most institutions of higher education's tradition, but this concept has implications for getting to know about potential students also: their likes, needs, dislikes and past behavior. This can include a variety of measures that can be surveyed in an existing group of students in a field such as information systems, and then the information can be used to mail materials to potential students. A once-a-year survey that will clean up the mailing list while asking adult students such questions as "what magazines do you read?" and "what professional associations do you belong to?" begins to collect data. This data can be used to point to what mailing lists from journals or professional associations for that particular discipline's potential students should be purchased.

Coordinated marketing may mean a new "student/customer" orientation for the whole institution as these concepts are becoming the norm for businesses and much of higher education nationwide. Students, especially adult students, expect the courtesy and ease in making a purchase for the amount of tuition money involved, that they would expect to pay for any transaction of over $100.00 or more.

Many organizations do not grasp the customer service/marketing concept until they see a "sales" decline; slow growth; change in buying (enrollment) patterns; increasing competition; or increasing marketing expenses without notable improvement.

Organizational Resistance

Many institutions of higher education, not unlike other institutions and bureaucracies, have shown resistance, and slow learning (followed by fast forgetting after a success), to concepts of marketing and to departments tasked to do it. Marketing can be seen as a less than equal function of the institution as in "A" in Figure 9.2 or as more central as in "B", or in "C" as an integrating opportunity for the institution to focus on its teaching mission.

Figure 9.2
Marketing as a Function of the Institution

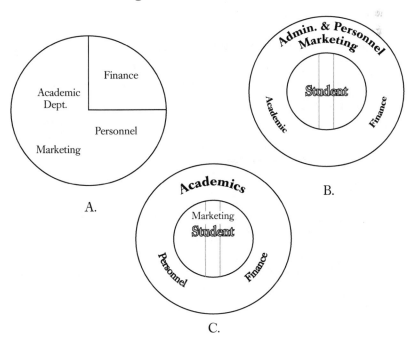

Marketing can be seen as a less than equal function of the institution, or marketing may be seen as related to the student of any age, as the controlling variable, or marketing may be seen as the integrative function around the student as the central orientation of the institution of higher education as in "C". Other models with marketing as the largest or even the central function of the institution are almost never seen in institutions of higher education, but exist in the corporate marketing literature. However marketing is viewed, and these models only scratch the surface, most institutions of higher education and organizations manage to get some marketing going. They may attend seminars or hire outside marketing talent and introduce marketing planning and control systems. However, in the wake of marketing success, there is a strong tendency to forget the marketing principles of *continuing* to *know* the target markets/potential students: communicating with the market including adult students in many ways; and responding better to the market's, especially the adult students', wants and needs (Kotler and Fox, 1985).

Communication and Change

"Communication is essential for social change" according to writers in the communications field. The communicating of innovations draws on long traditions of diffusion of innovations from anthropology, from early and rural sociology, and up through communication and marketing today. When individuals or the society changes, for example the society moving into the information age and/or living longer lives, there are three sequential steps:

1) The invention or innovation for example in higher education this would be the college or university's new courses, new degree programs or new sites as may be related to learnings needed for the information age;

2) the diffusion of information about it – today called communication and marketing, and

3) the consequences, e.g. better jobs for graduates, better processes for organizations and corporations using information technology, etc. Sociologists and anthropologists have long held that change occurs when a new idea is used or not used, and that social change is therefore an effect of communication (Rogers and Shoemaker, 1971). While it is not the purpose of this book to discuss all the larger societal ramifications of this concept, it does give a firm foundation to the goals and budgets for marketing in Continuing Education in colleges and universities. One must also pay careful attention to the message, the audiences targeted and the messengers. Everyone on the staff needs to be able to tell what Continuing Education

does. Each can draft their own examples for answers to questions and scripts can even be provided to communicate the vision with consistent, formalized statements.

Diffusion of Innovations

The diffusion process, often the title for marketing in non-profit and health organizations, includes four steps which are also found in marketing:

1) awareness
2) knowledge
3) persuasion
4) adoption

These four steps are applied to continuing education in Chapter 4 on Planning, as: *awareness* of the programs; enough *knowledge* about the programs often through direct mail brochures, to enroll; *persuasion* opportunities, such as attending information sessions and counseling telephone calls or interviews; and *adoption* or enrollment in courses (see figure 4.3 in Chapter 4).

In discussing innovations, which could be descriptions of new courses or refreshed old-course content, as well as new degree formats and new location sites, there are five attributes to consider:

Relative Advantage
Compatibility
Complexity
Trial-Ability
Observability

The *relative advantages* are much akin to the features and benefits listed in marketing texts and might include convenience, attractiveness of format, smallness of classes, superiority of faculty, and quotes from distinguished alumni. These are much the same as possible features and benefits of all higher education. These advantages as compared to or related to short term, non-credit training might be stressed, as non-credit in some disciplines seems to compete with credit courses. The *compatibility* refers to how evening, weekend and satellite programs fit into the lives of their students: obviously the rise in enrollments in such programs is related to their timing and location being more appropriate and convenient for adult students. Anything that describes compatibility in terms of existing values or activities of the targeted student population, will help. These might include nearness to public transportation, accessible and free parking, weekend classes and weekend computer lab hours.

The *complexity* of how to begin higher education programs needs to be reviewed and simplified. Do students stand in line for two hours in the snow to register or do they have on line and/or touch-tone telephone registration hours from 6:00 a.m. to 9:00 p.m. or Internet 24/7? Do students have to wait in long lines at the book store or can books be ordered online or by phone, charged to a credit card and delivered to their home by delivery service? Needlessly complex registration activities can be simplified, and this will greatly enhance adult enrollments and, thus income, and also the service provided. One school even waived the degree application fee for online applications as it saved *the institution* money. The students' use of libraries and of the Internet and search services can be enhanced by freely and routinely giving out the ID codes, library card codes, or software needed for Internet access from home or workplace personal computers.

Trial-ability of a new degree program can be greatly increased by allowing one two or three courses to be taken by students in a "non-degree" or "non-matriculated" (trial) status. Individual school faculties within a university may allow transfer in of a variety of non-degree/non-matriculated courses (not non-credit) from their own programs, or transferred from other institutions (2 to 4 at the most usually, for the graduate level). Faculty group cultural norms will determine how these courses are to be viewed: from important evidence of work done, to unimportant evidence – as graduate enrollees traditionally receive high grades – , and varying views in between these two extremes. For example, some assess the total applicant, and others look only at the undergraduate grade point average (G.P.A.).

Observability means the inquiring students can observe something about the degree and center location, possibly by attending Information Sessions, or Open Houses on upcoming semesters, held *in* the center or class location. Briefing attendees also observe each other taking in the information and get a sense of who else might be in their classes. *Observability* gives students a chance to see other potential students and ask questions about how they would handle and enjoy being in a class. Furthermore, they see other students in classes and are reminded that as adults they look familiar (compatible) to them.

Adopter Categories

Adopter categories, a term used in communications and in marketing, follow the bell curve (see figure 9.3). At the leading edge are the "Innovators" (2.5%) who are venturesome types of people, eager to try new ideas – especially modern ones, and are willing to try something first in their circle of friends. The "Early Adopters" follow and this group (13.5%) and often includes opinion leaders. The "Early Majority" are more deliberate thinkers and represent 34% of the adopter group. They may deliberate for some time before they start a course or program. They represent one standard deviation above the norm, and early adopters are two standard deviations above the norm, as frequently cited in the marketing literature.

Figure 9.3
Adopter Categories on the Innovation Adoption Continuum (Bell Curve)

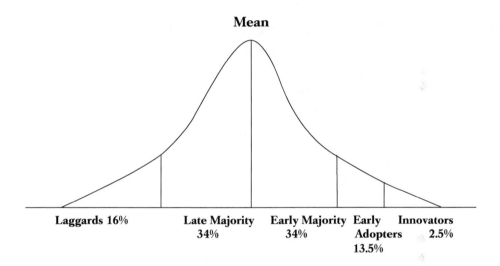

The "Late Majority" follows, another large group, one standard deviation below the norm, also 34%, who are people who won't try something unless a friend has tried it and reports back. They are skeptical types of people and probably won't start unless economic necessity or increasing social pressures require it. Lastly are the "Laggards", the last 16% who really do not try new things, such as college courses, unless nearly all their friends have enrolled already. Communication research generalizes about these types and summarizes the findings under 1) socioeconomic status, 2) personality variables, and 3) communication behavior. Obviously a different part of the marketing strategy for a discipline can be aimed at each adopter group. For example, the phrase or slogan "Be the first in your group to try _____" would reach innovators, but would not reach the same group as "the information age is here *now*. NOW is the time to tune-up your skills," which might reach the early or late majority, depending on the locale. Another ad for this group had a picture of a dinosaur and said "Don't be one."

Don't be one . . . .

12 Departments at the Town College Campus will help you move forward.

Don't live in prehistoric times. Higher education can help you build your future. The Town College Campus has the programs and degrees you need.

- **Prestigious Degrees**
- **Convenient Location**
- **Right here, right now in Southern Town**

Come to the Open House
Thursday, June 18 4-7pm
44219 Town Rd., State, US
Town College
www.TC.edu/ 201-797-2800

Direct Marketing

Direct marketing and public relations are tools of importance in marketing planning of all kinds, and are especially useful in continuing education in higher education. In developing a Marketing Plan having a clear mission statement is a first step (Galbraith, 2001). Ask:

- What is our purpose?
- Who are our students/stakeholders?
- What do we have that is valuable to our students/stakeholders?
- What *should* our purpose be?
- What will our purpose be in the future?

Direct marketing is an interactive system of marketing, which uses one or more media such as direct mail, catalogs or schedules, telemarketing, electronic web sites and shopping, and more, to effect a measurable response from the consumer directly. In other words programs are not marketed *only* at and for the main campus location. In continuing education this accountability measure might be of the number of responses or inquiries generated and captured by a direct mail campaign or an Internet Home Page. The advantages of direct marketing are selectivity, personalization, better timing, continuity, high readability, testability and privacy (Kotler, 1994). Since higher education is a targeted market in terms of seeking those interested in getting a college degree or an advanced degree, but also is a market of those possible adult students who want quite a bit of information to make an expensive investment, information might include the mission and objectives of the program, course descriptions for a particular discipline, the degree structure and schedule, format, and cost considerations. Direct mail is an ideal vehicle with which to convey this information, and, of course, there is no competition within the same direct mail piece. Newspaper and radio advertising enhance the impact of a direct mail campaign by a factor of four (Elliott, 1982) but these media do run ads from competing colleges and universities, and they cannot convey the amount of information that a single direct mail piece can. Print ads can drive people to the website for more information. Ads are also useful for "reminders" about information sessions, Open Houses and registration dates, or other short pieces of information.

A "VIP" letter (for Very Important Persons or opinion leaders), in advance of a direct mail campaign, sent to opinion leaders and heads of corporations or agencies in a particular discipline, can further enhance the impact of a direct mail campaign. While the cost per thousand people reached in a direct mail campaign is higher than a mass media campaign, the higher target-market selectivity reaches much better prospects for a particular student population match to a program. Some research shows that 55% or more of marketing for continuing education through direct mail is the correct per cent for the higher education "marketing mix" of approaches to marketing always mentioning the website prominently. This is due to the narrowness of the target markets and also because of the amount of information that can be sent in a direct mail piece (Elliott, 1982).

Since direct mail campaigns can be effective, but are costly, higher education continuing education administrators need access to good advice, marketing textbooks, and perhaps to join the Direct Marketing Association, so as to have continuing input of new ideas and applications or use of direct mail pieces. Becoming knowledgeable and purchasing direct mailing lists for your area to reach those whom you haven't reached in the past can also be important. Hiring a marketing firm or individual can be useful but the "style" of the University must be represented properly and not down-graded to a lawn mower-selling-approach which can cause internal institutional repercussions.

The response rate to direct mail advertising, which, normally at 2% to 3% rated "good," understates the long-term impact of the campaign. This is especially true in higher education and can be more easily understood when reviewed against the time lag for the adopter categories. Colleges and Universities *always* have another semester. Regardless of problems, late schedules, snow and ice, students KNOW this educational service will continue and be there for them when they decide to go. The only exception perhaps is in the case of very small, underfunded, private colleges, as some of those may close. Direct mail has a high readership thus producing a high awareness of the content of a program or programs over time. A percentage of readers form an intention-to-buy-at-a-later date, which should not be underestimated, especially in higher education.

Direct Mail, e-Mail, and Direct Marketing Strategy

Continuing educators need to analyze the characteristics of present students and possible future students in a particular discipline. Who would be the most able, willing and ready to enroll in the future? Who would benefit greatly and improve their career path with this program or degree? A once a year "audit survey" of addresses, tastes, employment and even of books and magazines read, or professional or organizational memberships, is invaluable and also keeps the in-house mailing list current. In addition to surveys, student comments, personal interviews, and employee enrollee's comments can help planners learn more about potential adult students. This is called the "target market." Once it is defined, perhaps by sending this "audit" questionnaire by e-mail to current students, and then using what is learned to clarify the list acquisition and management steps. The e-mail responses will give a better knowledge base for future students. The direct mail and e-mail lists compiled "in-house" by the continuing education staff, made up of current students, current inquiries, and opinion leaders, are typically the best lists (Copeland, 2007, Kotler, 1994). Additional lists can be purchased from list brokers, but small segments of these lists should be pilot-tested before a large mass mailing or a large e-mail initiative is done, to know their worth. A 35% return from an expensive list might be a better buy than a 3% return from an inexpensive mailing list. These lists reach a valuable group that is frequently missed: those who have not been involved with these continuing education programs before.

Challenges for mass e-mails include measuring the impact on enrollments. It is best to only use e-mail for reminders for Information Sessions and Registration as spam was considered "annoying" by 77% of a large survey (Copeland, 2007).

What is sent in a direct mail campaign is of key importance. Five components in a direct mail piece are as follows: 1) *the envelope* which could be the regular, dignified, institution of higher education's usual logo and style of envelope, as a too "jazzy" or slick an envelope usually represents the wrong "style" for a higher education institution (and reminds people again of lawn mower sales); 2) the *letter enclosed* should have the how, what, why, when, and where, and some narrative as to what benefits the receiver will gain from attending an information session and/or taking this course or degree. A relevant "P.S." on the letter increases response rate. 3) A *flyer* or *brochure*, in color, with a 4) *response coupon*, which together with the brochure should tell details, course descriptions, the degree structure when appropriate, and even have testimonials from students and opinion leaders; and 5) *a postage-free reply envelope or the coupon postcard* already mentioned, as a tear-off on the flyer or brochure, also boosts response rates.

A great advantage of direct mail is that it allows early testing of the elements of the mailing piece in the real, prospective adult student population market, which can save costly mistakes. Watch for differences produced by copy, features and benefits listed, tuition prices, the media used and mailing lists selected. These are best observed when only one major component is changed per mailing, such as using the same brochure design and mailing list, but with a new tuition rate.

By adding up the planned direct mail campaign costs, based on a conservative figure of 2% return, the administrator can figure out in advance the break-even rate needed to advance a given program when balanced against projected tuition income for this 2% that are enrolling. In this analysis, it is important to figure the additional future enrollments, needed to finish a degree program (but decreased somewhat for attrition), into the response rate numbers, and income. These future enrollments are called "customer lifetime value" and this value is usually high in higher education. Projected income for a campaign can be: 1) conservatively based on last year's similar initiative; 2) somewhat more aggressively based on last year's enrollment numbers plus a percentage of new students, or 3) aggressively based on all new student projected return.

Eventually integrated direct mail processes and "database(d) marketing" will be key in all higher education institutions willing to be involved in continuing education according to marketing companies. A Time-Line in figure 9.4 shows a possible sequencing of a VIP letter followed by a direct mail campaign for a new semester of adult continuing education. The sequence shown depicts a 10 week cycle leading up to a 12-14 week semester. A mailing of a VIP letter-with-one-circular or brochure is followed in two to four weeks by an extensive direct mailing, featuring dates for information sessions in letters and circulars describing courses and degrees. Radio, newspaper and Internet/on-line services and advertisements can further reinforce the dates in reader's minds. Follow-up phone calls, (or blast group facsimiles), can be made to remind students of acceptances for briefing dates and to do advance counseling regarding the program(s), if appropriate.

Figure 9.4
Time Table for Direct Marketing

Week	1	2	3	4	5	6	7	8	9	10	11	12-14
1. Send VIP letters and brochures to opinion leaders and to newspapers, radio, and TV (for public service PSAs	X											
2. Send direct mail and brochures to identified target lists	-	-	X									
3. PSA spots or radio & web & TV ads running	-	-	-	-	-	X						
4. Information sessions/Open House held, reminder and counseling telephone calls made	-	-	-	-	-	-	-	X	X	X		
5. Registration										X	X	
6. Statistical analysis is done, comparing direct mail factors and information session attendance with number of enrolled students											X	
7. End of term – students get degrees, certificates and do final assessment evaluations of courses												X

- - - - - - - - - - - - - = preparation time

Next in the Time Line, as depicted in figure 9.4, the information sessions are held with opportunities for Program Chairs or Lead Professors and Deans, to describe course content, faculty and student characteristics, admissions procedures, and to answer questions from the group and from individuals. Evaluation forms with a name and address block are turned in after each session. Registration by telephone or mail follows, the semester begins, and ends, and the all important course evaluations are done. Insights from these evaluations, in addition to improving the courses and programs, can be used in future advertising.

Questions adapted from the Malcolm Baldridge National Quality Awards criteria for addressing customer/student focus and satisfaction follow. Questions like these account for 25% of the points in the Baldridge Awards criteria. Much of the information needed for understanding the market of adult students must come from measuring results and tracking trends. Expensive marketing without this analysis and input can be far less effective (Hodlin, 1996). Adult student satisfaction is one of the best indicators of an institution's prosperity.

Questions to ask about the evaluation process are:

- How does the institution evaluate and improve its processes for determining adult student requirements and expectations?
- What are the institution's processes for determining current and near term requirements and expectations of adult students?
- How does the institution provide effective management of its responses and follow-ups with adult students (or any students)?
- How does the institution provide easy access for students specifically for the purposes of seeking information or assistance and/or to comment or complain? 'Frequently Asked Questions' and 'Contact Us' pages on the website increasingly help this access.
- How does the institution ensure prompt and effective resolution of complaints, including recovery of student confidence?
- How does the institution learn from complaints and ensure students receive information needed to eliminate the causes of complaints?
- How does the institution follow-up with students regarding courses, services, and recent transaction to determine satisfaction, to resolve problems, to build relationships, and to gather information for improvement?
- How does the institution evaluate and improve its overall adult student relationship management?
- How does the institution determine adult student satisfaction and satisfaction relative to competitor institutions?

The Four "P"s of Marketing

Product, price, place and packaging are the famous four "P"s of marketing taught in business schools. Higher education continuing education is able to impact *place and packaging*, including format and advertising, more easily than *price* or in this case tuition which is usually set by the Board of Trustees, or *product* / course content. Having said that, creativity in the areas of impact can lead to enormously attractive innovations and therefore increase enrollments. Would a summer condensed "Institute" for 2, 4, or 6 courses be possible for a highly distinctive topic or degree such as security management for the information age? Would a weekend or Saturday program be attractive?

Packaging and format can include variety in class scheduling which helps adult students, and helps multiply the use of existing classroom space. Other factors that can be included in *"packaging"* include *self-service,* such as registration online or by telephone, on-line access to libraries, or online or telephone ordering of books by course number, and, of course, advertising.

Other areas of impact to increase effectiveness of marketing might include consideration of *consumer affluence,* which can mean that students are willing to pay more for convenience, dependability and prestige; *name and image* recognition for the total institution of higher education; and *innovation opportunity* which means marketing should stress to the student in advertising and direct mail, the large benefits of this location, this schedule, this format, this topic or degree program or otherwise spell out the opportunity this new innovation is creating for them in today's knowledge-based economy.

Students need to learn about the aspects of the program that will mean the most to them. Messages should have meaning and relevance to them. Students also need to be shown how to get what they want, which requires the staff to know as much as possible about the students' and the potential students' wants and needs: their likes, needs, dislikes and past behavior. All of this shows "caring" and helps to reduce the usual 5 or 6 contacts needed to create an actual registration. These contacts can be by mail, with advertising or by personal contact.

Place refers to the site of your courses off-campus, at contract sites, in your own facilities, in rented space, or online at home or at work. Care should be taken in establishing long term arrangements with new sites, for example in high schools or government agencies. For a large set of programs, building or renovating space for classrooms provides the greatest long term benefit and the least possibility of unwanted disruption.

Price as mentioned earlier, usually refers to the tuition set by the Board of Trustees, but variations for contract course group rates or a percentage off for distant locations, can usually be arranged. Many institutions provide a discount rate for school-teachers or other special groups.

Product, which is course content and quality in this discussion, is the most important element, and should always receive priority in logistical concerns. Facilitating instructional materials and equipment to enable high quality teaching and learning is important, as this is the core benefit or essential service for which the student is paying tuition. The generic or expected attributes of any college level course or degree program, are the absolute minimum of service that can be provided. Coasting on a monopoly situation as the only institution of higher education in the area, due to state or federal funding, can be short-lived as the "niche" that is safe for institutions. Distance learning, competing institutions opening new satellite centers, and, of course, the giant training industry have made serious inroads on the market for the provision of education to adult students. However with the information age ever requiring new skills and more substantial knowledge information backgrounds, the "augmented" offerings of additional services and benefits that institutions of higher education can offer, and the "potential" offerings of possible new features and services that might be eventually be added (Kotler, 1995), the possibility for prosperity and community service are large indeed for higher education. A 2006 Survey showed 16% of universities in communities larger than three million, with revenues of more than $100 million a year. Those in communities of 1 to 3 million had 5% with revenues of this amount (UCEA, 2006).

Figure 9.5 shows how the four "P"s" of marketing can be adapted in planning for a second (or alternative) education center, with similar but different educational needs. These needs determine the "product". Packaging and format, whether evening, daytime, or weekend, and price, are important. The "right angle" problem solving device is used, to show that the thinking done for one center can be a springboard for another.

Figure 9.5
Right Angle Transfer of Start-Up Planning (and Marketing)
Site A to Site B: Product, Place, Format

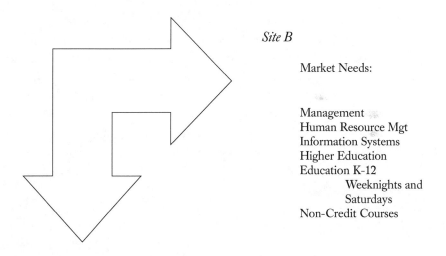

Site B

Market Needs:

Management
Human Resource Mgt
Information Systems
Higher Education
Education K-12
       Weeknights and
       Saturdays
Non-Credit Courses

Site A:

Public Policy, M.A.
EE/CS (Electrical Engineering/Computer Science)
Engineering Management
Human resource Management
   (Government agency contract on weekdays)
Non-Credit Courses

Public Relations

The process of promoting the image of the continuing education organization of the institution of higher education includes activities, techniques, and strategies that educate "the public" about the organization. Often the Continuing Education leader is the primary promoter, image shaper, opinion influencer, lobbyist and public relations director for the continuing education organization. Stakeholders and students need to know why they should invest their time, money and effort in this or that program of study. Letters to the editor, press releases, attendance at community or voluntary and political events all can serve to enhance the image of a continuing education organization. Even the website for your institution of higher education and its link to your offerings are part of the public relations image the continuing education group or division projects. The mission of the continuing education organization, and the future life and career benefits to students, should always be in the forefront of public relations strategies (Galbraith, 2001).

Summary

In summarizing, marketing, direct mail, and all kinds of diffusion for innovations includes innovative approaches like e-mail, text messaging and podcasts, and are all useful to institutions of higher education. When marketing is seen as an *exchange* of information between the institution of higher education and the student, the concept of potential students can be widened considerably. The more each knows about the other, the more likely it is that a favorable match-up (or enrollment) can be made. Lastly, organizational resistance to marketing is not limited only to institutions of higher education but can be found in many organizations and bureaucracies. Arguments that have proven effective for the use of marketing include:

- The university/college's assets are of little use without students;
- The key task institutions of higher education is to attract and retain students, although research and service remain part of the mission;
- Student satisfaction is affected by the performance of a variety of other departments;
- Marketing needs to influence these other departments, such as the library, student accounts, registration, etc. to cooperate in delivering student satisfaction.

Marketing and public relations are essential to adult and continuing education organizations (Galbraith, 1997) as adults are used to making their selections with knowledge about a program and services. The importance of the Educational Administrator/leader becoming informed about marketing and public relations, and being involved in their planning and implementation becomes evident. Electronic marketing may lead to the need to build new metrics for tracking and measuring impacts, but the current generation is very tuned to these approaches. Being sure to add contact information to the website, is an easy but helpful first step, for example.

Education traditionally increases in enrollments in a recession. As the global society moves into the information or knowledge age, appropriate communication and marketing of the education provided by institutions of higher education should help to ensure these institutions' continuing prosperity, when coupled with good management. A focus on the external customer or student, needs to be deployed internally through the layers and departments of the institution also, no matter how loosely coupled they may be. Otherwise, the internal needs which receive focus may not be in phase with student needs and may create non-value added work in the institution. Student satisfaction is one of the best indicators of the institution's prosperity. When employees are empowered to help students, they became involved and committed. A staff that has become an "office of enrollment prevention" can do real harm. The staff are capable of helping students only when provided with right information. This requires teamwork and practice. Successful leaders in any type of organization provide the resources their people need to serve the customers /students well.

Chapter 10

Planning, Implementing and Evaluating Non-Credit Programs

Non-credit programs are traditionally more flexible, more market responsive and sometimes more relevant than credit programs. They are certainly profitable on the whole, and many institutions of higher education have added non-credit or training divisions in one guise or another. The variety of titles of those in charge of continuing education whether for credit, non-credit or for both combined under one director is interesting to note, and demonstrates a wide-spectrum of perceptions: Dean, Director, Associate Vice Chancellor for Extended Studies and Public Service, Associate Vice-President for Academic Development and Continuing Education, and even Vice President for Student Services and Economic Development. These titles show the rising importance of planning and administering programs for adults.

Changes in demographics, in the economy, and in the nature of work are altering the way public and private sector organizations provide training, and also the ways in which higher education delivers its programs and services to agencies, business and industry. The education and training of adults has become highly important according to the U.S. Department of Labor and the American Society for Training and Development, as population trends are creating democratic changes in the composition of the workforce. Workers will change careers three to five times, and jobs five to eight times, in their life times. Two thirds of the people working now will be working in five years. Over half of the new jobs of the future will require postsecondary education and training. An emerging service economy will provide jobs for 88% of the workforce in the next 5 years. Over the next 10 years, 75 percent of the workforce will need significant re-training. These and other trends of change are announced frequently in the media and in research.

How much an institution of higher education wants to play a significant role in the area of workforce development varies, but this is an area high in possibilities and opportunities, especially in the non-credit arena. Some institutions divide their non-credit programs into various categories for ease of administration such as: 1) Management technology such as computer courses, and small business and entrepreneurship courses; 2) Work preparation such as real estate licensure, nurses aide training, or apprenticeship or other contract programs developed in partnership with local industry; 3) life-long learning, such as oil painting, music appreciation, or languages. Some of these are "pre-employment" preparation as well as on-the-job training. Usually a category also exists such as number 3) life long learning or life enhancement. Many institutions have found "Alumni Universities" filled with this category of short, one-week summer classes to be very profitable for all ages of Alumni including senior citizens. An active and well-run children's program is often partnered with these alumni "college camps."

Certificate programs of 5 to 8 courses in an organized format are also a viable non-credit option. These can range from financial planner certification to landscape design to publication specialist. Information systems, complex software, and client/server requirements lend themselves to training courses of this type. Training opportunities for mid-level professionals continue to be an unmet need appropriate for higher education, non-credit courses. Some have even been called "graduate level non-credit" courses.

Adult Learners

No consideration of non-credit education or training would be complete without considering the contribution of Malcom Knowles (1989, 1987, 1979). He developed a framework for learning situations with the complexity of the learning task on the vertical axis of a graph and the level of the learners learning ability on the horizontal level of a graph. Level of learning ability included previous exposure to the subject matter, readiness to learn, motivation, general intelligence and other factors. He then placed learning theorists on the continuum in the graph, with behavioral teaching methods for the lower levels of task and ability at one end. If the learning task was complex, such as gaining knowledge and understanding of theory behind the applications, then the cognitive theorist's teaching approach was appropriate for a highly complex task and a high level of learning ability (as in management classes), therefore self-directed learning and projects, and the humanistic theorists approach are appropriate. This was all put forth in his foundational book *The Adult Learner: A Neglected Species* (1973). Adult learners, with their myriad experiences and varied backgrounds do make a real contribution to the classroom and this group had indeed been neglected. He came up with a number of corollaries to his framework including the concept that people feel a commitment to a decision in proportion to the extent that they feel they have participated in making it; that creative leaders stimulate and reward creativity; that creative leaders are committed to a process of continuous change and are skillful in managing change; and that creative leaders encourage people to be self-directing (Knowles, 1989). Some of these theories are foundations to other chapters in this book in discussing administration of continuing education in ways that can release human energy and group synergism.

Applying these concepts to student learning for adults releases additional insights. Learning takes place when the student perceives the subject matter as relevant to his or her own purposes; when the student is responsible for participation in the learning process; and when self-evaluation is primary and evaluation by others is of secondary importance. Continual learning and an openness to experience and change, Knowles believes, are the most socially useful things to learn in the modern world (1989). Some adjunct faculty staff development in these and other aspects of adult learning may be necessary to undergird a new continuing education program in an institution of higher education.

Long Range Forecasts, Goals, Objectives and Activities

As colleges and universities review their roles and philosophies in relation to non-credit programming, it is likely to become apparent that non-credit programs are a viable option for additional income producing activities while providing much needed additional educational services to a particular geographic area. Long range forecasts taken from major trends, such as those discussed in Chapter I, can be spelled out with implications for a non-credit unit of an institution. As a follow-up, goals and then more specific objectives and activities can be developed. For example, since an increased demand for service and technical professions and occupations is a trend, an increase in career and job-related education might be one goal. The work-related needs for the following levels can help expand an institution's non-credit role:

a)   entry level training
b)   retraining
c)   cross training
d)   upgrading
e)   job transitioning

If the population is mobile in an institution's surrounding geographic area for a state or county publicly supported institution, or in a wider area for other institutions, then education and re-education about the non-credit division or unit's programs and services will be needed. This is also called marketing. A marketing plan needs to be developed and implemented (as discussed in Chapter 9) which is a complement to the institution's overall plan. The non-credit unit must establish additional relationships with employers in surrounding agencies, industries and businesses concerning the education and training needs for their personnel. This can be done at greater distances, if distance or online learning is an option for off-campus credit and non-credit courses. One institution even had CD and DVD courses with Internet chat rooms and discussion groups for students on several continents.

If the citizenry in the area is well-educated and interested in education, utilizing the talents and expertise of members of the community to enhance the non-credit education program is always a good idea. All of the planning should be done against a backdrop of continuing assessment of the educational needs of the population served. Once a year planning is a must, with more frequent adaptations to keep offerings current and relevant. The service area might be a county for a community college and a metropolitan area or the nation for a larger four-year institution.

Another major long range forecast based on a trend might be that the potential student population will be more diverse and embrace a broad expanse of age, race, ethnic origins, languages and entry-level skills. Implications would be that the unit must then assess the needs of its changing population, identify available resources, and implement, where feasible, offerings to meet those needs. Activities might include ESL classes, test preparation classes, more activities and classes for senior citizens, and even alumni discounts for senior citizens, to name a few of the hundreds of options possible. The unit may focus on these special needs but must maintain a comprehensive program to attract all students and to aid them in fulfilling their educational needs. Ongoing examination and evaluation of program, services and staff plus revising where necessary, will be needed to meet the changing student population requirements. This may mean broadening the base of instructional programs and the expertise of faculty members so that it can respond to changing student demands for non-credit curricula.

Accessibility to the Division or Unit's instructional sites for potential adult students becomes more important, as does alternative types of scheduling and planning that consume less commuter time and energy. These are both goals that need to be developed for part-time students (both credit and non-credit). With career mobility as a current trend, students will place more emphasis on course content as opposed to degree preparation as reasons for enrolling in programs. Furthermore, alternative methods of instructional delivery will continue to need development, such as compressed video, satellite, and online delivery for non-credit as well as credit programs.

Increased competition for enrollments is also a trend both for credit and for non-credit students. The more than 50 billion dollar training industry attests to this in the non-credit arena, but as institutions shorten the response time from initial request to course delivery (for a long time, a main complaint from industry), the institution of higher education non-credit units are competing with an edge towards higher quality. Non-credit courses, of course, should be self-funding, or be discontinued.

Computer technology, interest in information technology and management implications in the work environment for business processes continues to develop rapidly. As individuals own one or more computers, and the management of whole enterprises is more streamlined, short courses at all levels will be welcome. Implications will be for new courses, computer labs, requiring laptops for classes, and many other approaches. These can be developed from the forecast and trend in computers and information technology.

While these are external forecasts, as they are outside the institution of higher education, internal forecasts and their implications can also be developed on a one-two-or three-year planning cycle. Predictions or forecasts about new technology being used internally, new education centers being opened, and new marketing plans, for instance, will all be useful when followed by spelling out the implication and the activities needed. This can be done as a group or by individuals. The ongoing planning, implementing, operating and evaluating of non-credit courses and programs keeps them fresh and relevant, and also income-producing for the host institution. A marketing plan will be needed.

The marketing plan also:

- Identifies marketing opportunities
- Stimulates thinking to make new uses of the institution's resources
- Assigns responsibilities and schedules work
- Coordinates and unifies efforts
- Facilitates control and evaluation of results of all activities
- Creates awareness of obstacles to overcome
- Provides a valid marketing information source for current and future reference
- Facilitates progressive advancement toward the unit's or division's goals

Therefore the marketing plan, based on long range forecasts and goals, should be *simple, clear, practical, flexible* (i.e. adaptable to change), *complete* and *workable.*

Future of Non-Credit and Certificate Programs

Completion of non-credit short courses, or longer non-credit courses and certificate programs, raises the quality of an individual's work life and increases professional ability needed to contribute to his or her field of work and to the community at large. Helping individuals prepare themselves for rapid success in their efforts to enter, upgrade, or transition in the workplace through non-credit programs seems to have a very bright future for institutions of higher education, as this is another quite do-able form of education service.

Contract Courses

Contract courses or on-site courses that are non-credit, allow employers to pay for a group of students on one billing, often at a group discount. The course(s) can then be somewhat tailored for the employer's need or a new course can be designed. Special employer needs can be addressed in other ways also such as an open-enrollment certificate program in Basic Literacy, or any number of other topics, with the courses that make up the certificate, selected by the employer or the military service. Some employers provide a "graduation" at which to present the certificate, some do not.

Quality Concerns

While non-credit programs are more flexible, more responsive, and even sometimes more relevant than credit programs, the maintaining of high quality content must be a first concern. Without the "quality engine" of academic departments and curriculum review committees, the issue of quality must be addressed directly. Having a "Board of Advisors" (formal or informal) by topic area, helps temper this concern, somewhat, and regular course evaluations are a must.

Summary

Non-credit continuing education can provide a useful service to an institution of higher education by bringing in input about important potential student market needs, and by pilot testing some of them. Units that provide non-credit services also often develop a welcome surplus of funds for the general fund of the institution, but this always should be done against the backdrop of the following ten activities:

1. Assessing needs
2. Planning
3. Organizing
4. Developing cooperative relationships
5. Marketing/Promoting
6. Implementing
7. Evaluating

8. Reporting
9. Projecting
10. Budgeting

As horizons open for high quality institutions of higher education services, both credit and non-credit, to those who need it and can afford it or find funding for this "investment", the mission of teaching, service and even for research, will also broaden and deepen for these participating institutions of higher education.

Bibiliography

Introduction

Abecassis, Alan (1996) Interview *Chief Information Officer of the French Ministry*, March 28, Washington, D.C.

Ackoff, R.L. (1970). *A Concept of Corporate Planning*. New York: Wiley.

Birnbaum, Robert (1988). *How Colleges Work*. San Francisco, Ca: Jossey-Bass Publishers.

National Information Infrastructure Awards Contest (1996). "Beyond the Barriers" Panel Presentation, March 19. U.S. Postal Service: Washington, D. C.

Cosmos, Spencer (1984). Personal interview with Dean of Continuing Education. January 20, Catholic University, Washington, D.C.

Harden, Blaine (2003). "Brain-Gain Cities Attract Educated Young" in *The Washington Post*, November 9, pp. 1, 14-15.

Hrabowski, Freeman, A. (2003). "Building A University in a Changing World" in *Continuing Higher Education Review*, Vol. 67, Fall, 7-18.

Jacks, L. (1930). *Journal of Adult Education* (2) p. 123.

Kantor, Rosabeth Moss (1983) *The Change Masters: Innovations for Productivity in the American Corporation*, New York: Simon and Schuster.

Knowles, Malcolm (1978). *The Adult Learner: A Neglected Species*, 2nd edition. Houston, Tx.: Gulf Publishing Co.

Kayser, E. L.(1970). *Bricks Without Straw*. New York: Appleton-Century-Crofts.

Likert, Rensis (1961). *The Human Organization*, New York: McGraw Hill.

Lynch, William (1994). "Distance Learning" speech given at Training Offices Conference, October 11, 1994, Washington, D.C.

Meredith, J. R., and Mantel, S. J. (1995). *Project Management: A Managerial Approach*. New York: John Wiley & Sons.

Naisbitt, John and Aburdene, P. (1990) *Megatrends 2,000*. New York: Random House, Inc.

Peters, Ed "The Virtual Data Warehouse and Middleware" 1996. Data Management Association Conference (April 3,) Rosslyn, Va.

Rand, Cynthia (1995) Speech given at Association Federal Information Resource Management Seminar, October, Washington, D.C.

Senge, Peter (1990) *The Fifth Discipline*. New York: Doubleday

Trachtenberg, S.J. (1996) George Washington University Management Forum, Feb. 14. "The Role of the CIO" (1996) Fose-Affirm Panel, Fose Conference, (April 2-4) Washington, D.C.

U.S. Department of Labor, Bureau of Labor Statistics (1989, November). New Labor Force Projections Spanning 1988-2000, *Monthly Labor Review*, 112(11), 3-11.

Vaill, Peter (1989). *Managing as a Performing Art: New Ideas for a World of Chaotic Change*. San Francisco: Jossey Bass, 1989.

Vaill, Peter (1996) "Managing a Changing Environment." Speech given at the Management Forum, April 3, Washington, D.C.

Wee, Eric L. (1996) "More College Students Live, Then Learn." *The Washington Post*. March 5.

Whitaker, Roger (1995). "Position Paper on Distance Learning" Division of University Programs Meeting, March 24, Washington, D.C.

Chapter I Futures

Billmyer, K. (2007). "Translating Institutional Renewal into Action." Presentation given at the University Continuing Education Association (UCEA) conference, April 13. Vancouver, B.C. Canada.

Bryson, J. M., (1988). *Strategic Planning for Profit and Non-Profit Organizations*. San Francisco, CA: Jossey-Bass.

Cetron, M. J. and O. Davies (2003). "Trends shaping the Future: Technological, Workplace, Management, and Institutional Trends" in *The Futurist*, Vol. 37 (2) pp. 30-43.

Galbraith, M. W. et al (1997). *Administration of Successful Programs for Adults*. Malabar, FL: Krieger Publishing.

Gardner, John W. (1963, reissued 1995). *Self Renewal: the Individual and the Innovative Society*. W.W. Norton.

_____ (2003). "The World is Your Classroom: Lessons in Self-Renewal" in *The Futurist* Vol. 36 (3) pp. 52-53.

Simerly, R. G. (1995). *Strategic Planning and Leadership in Continuing Education*. San Francisco, CA: Jossey-Bass.

"Using Information Technology to Improve Government Services to Citizens" (2007). Panel presentation at the Association for Federal Information Resource Management (AFFIRM), April 11, Washington, D.C.

Chapter II Challenges

Abecassis, Alan (1996) Interview *Chief Information Officer of the French Ministry*, March 28, Washington, D.C.

Ackoff, R.L. (1970). *A Concept of Corporate Planning.* New York: Wiley.

Birnbaum, Robert (1988). *How Colleges Work.* San Francisco, Ca: Jossey-Bass Publishers.

National Information Infrastructure Awards Contest (1996). "Beyond the Barriers" Panel Presentation, March 19. U.S. Postal Service: Washington, D. C.

Chicago Tribune (1996). February 11.

Collins, J. (2001). *Good to Great: Why Some Companies Make the Leap . . . and Others Don't.* New York: Harper Collins.

Collins, J. and Porras, J., (2002). *Built to Last.* New York: Harper Collins.

Cosmos, Spencer (1984). Personal interview with Dean of Continuing Education. January 20, Catholic University, Washington, D.C.

Jacks, L. (1930). *Journal of Adult Education* (2) p. 123.

Kantor, Rosabeth Moss (1983) *The Change Masters: Innovations for Productivity in the American Corporation*, New York: Simon and Schuster.

Knowles, Malcolm (1978). *The Adult Learner: A Neglected Species,* 2nd edition. Houston, Tx.: Gulf Pub. Co.

Kayser, E. L.(1970). *Bricks Without Straw.* New York: Appleton-Century-Crofts.

Kohl, Kay (2003). "The State of Continuing Education Today." Speech given at the Regional University Continuing Education Association Conference, Washington, D.C., October 9.

Likert, Rensis (1961). *The Human Organization*, New York: McGraw Hill.

Lynch, William (1994). "Distance Learning" speech given at Training Offices Conference, October 11, 1994, Washington, D.C.

Naisbitt, John and Aburdene, P. (1990) *Megatrends 2,000.* New York: Random House, Inc.

Peters, Ed. "The Virtual Data Warehouse and Middleware" 1996. Data Management Association Conference (April 3,) Rosslyn, Va.

Rand, Cynthia (1995) Speech given at Association Federal Information Resource Management Seminar, October, Washington, D.C.

Senge, Peter (1990) *The Fifth Discipline.* New York: Doubleday

Trachtenberg, S.J. (1996) George Washington University Management Forum, Feb. 14. "The Role of the CIO" (1996) Fose-Affirm Panel, Fose Conference, (April 2-4) Washington, D.C.

U.S. Department of Labor, Bureau of Labor Statistics (1989, November). New Labor Force Projections Spanning 1988-2000, *Monthly Labor Review*, 112(11), 3-11.

Vaill, Peter (1989). *Managing as a Performing Art: New Ideas for a World of Chaotic Change*. San Francisco: Jossey Bass, 1989.

Vaill, Peter (1996) "Managing a Changing Environment." Speech given at the Management forum, April 3, Washington, D.C.

Wee, Eric L. (1996) "More College Students Live, Then Learn." The Washington Post. March 5.

Whitaker, Roger (1995). "Position Paper on Distance Learning" Division of University Programs Meeting, March 24, Washington, D.C.

Whitaker, Roger (2003). "Why be Bold?" Speech given at the Regional University Continuing Education Association Conference, Washington, D.C., October 8.

Chapter III Leadership

Ackoff, R.L. (1970). *A Concept of Corporate Planning*. Philadelphia: John Wiley & Sons, Inc.

Allen, R.W., Madison, D.L., Porter, L.W., Renwick, P.A., and Mayes, B.T., (1979). "Organizational Politics: Tactics and Characteristics of Its Actors," *California Management Review*, Fall, Vol. 22, No. 4, pp. 77-83.

Baldridge, J. V., Curtis, D. V., Ecker, G., and Riley, G. L. (1978). *Policy Making and Effective Leadership: A National Study of Academic Management*. San Francisco: Jossey-Bass.

Banfield, E.C., (1961). *Political Influence*. New York: The Free Press.

Bass, B. (1981). *Stodgill's Handbook of Leadership*. New York: The Free Press.

Birnbaum, R. (1983). *Maintaining Diversity in Higher Education*. San Francisco: Jossey-Bass.

Birnbaum, R.(1988). *How Colleges Work: The Cybernetics of Academic Organization and Leadership*. San Francisco: Jossey-Bass.

Blake, R.R., et al., (1964). "Breakthrough in Organizational Development" *Harvard Business Review*, Nov.-Dec.

Blau, P.M. (1964). *Exchange and Power in Social Life*. New York: John Wiley & Sons, Inc.

Boyatzis, R. (1982). *The Competent Manager*. New York: John Wiley & Sons, Inc.

Brearley, A. (1976). "The Changing Role of the Chief Executive." *Journal of General Management*, 3(4), pp. 62-71.

Bryson, J. M. (1988). *Strategic Planning for Public and Non-Profit Organizations*. San Francisco, CA: Jossey-Bass.

Business Week. (1980). "CBS: When Being No. 1 Isn't Enough," May 26, pp. 128-132.

_____. (1981). "Still Another Master," August 17, pp. 80-86.

_____. (1980). "When A New Product Strategy Wasn't Enough," February 18.

Beach, D.S. (1975). *Managing People At Work: Readings in Personnel.* New York: John Wiley & Sons.

Collins, J. (2001). *Good to Great: Why Some Companies Make the Leap . . . and Others Don't.* New York: Harper Collins.

Drucker, P. (1974). *Management.* New York: Harper & Row.

_____. (1967). *The Effective Executive.* New York: Harper & Row.

Fiedler, F.E. (1967). *A Theory of Leadership Effectiveness.* New York: McGraw-Hill.

_____. (1971). *Leadership.* New York: General Learning Press.

French, J. R., Jr., and Raven, B. (1996) "The Bases of Social Power". In Matteson, M. T. and Ivanevich, J. M., Eds., *Management and Organizational Behavior Classics.* Irwin: Boston, MA.

Galbraith, M. W. et al (1997). *Administration of Successful Programs for Adults.* Malabar, FL: Krieger Publishing.

Gardner, J. W. (1990). *On Leadership.* New York: The Free Press.

Herzberg, F., Mausner, B., and Snyderman, B. (1959). *The Motivation to Work.* New York: John Wiley & Sons, Inc.

Jacobs, T.O. (1971). *Leadership and Exchange in Formal Organizations.* Alexandria VA.: Human Resources Research Organizations.

Kotter, J. P. (1999). *What Leaders Really Do.* Harvard Business School Press.

Kotter, J. P. (1996). *Leading Change.* Boston, MA: Harvard Business School Press.

Kotter, J. P. (1990). *Force for Change: How Leadership Differs from Management.* New York: Free Press.

Kotter, J.P. (1979). "Managing External Dependence." *Academy of Management.* Review 1979, Vol. 4, No. 1, pp. 87-92.

_____. (1978). *Organizational Dynamics: Diagnosis and Intervention.* Reading, MA.: Addison-Wesley.

_____. (1977). "Power, Dependence, and Effective Management." *Harvard Business Review,* July/August, pp. 125-136.

_____. (1979). *Power in Management.* AMACOM.

_____. (1982). *The General Managers.* New York: The Free Press.

_____. (1973). "The Psychological Contract: Managing the Joining Up Process." *California Management Review,* Vol.15, No.3, pp. 91-99.

_____, Faux, V.A., and McArthur, C.C. (1979). *Self-Assessment and Career Development.* Englewood Cliffs, NJ: Prentice-Hall, Inc.

Labovitz, G. and V. Rosansky. (1997). *The Power of Alignment.* New York: John Wiley & Sons, Inc.

Likert, R. (1961). *New Patterns of Management.* New York: McGraw-Hill.

Likert, R. (1996) "Human Organizational Measurements: Key to Financial Success". In Matteson, M.T., and Ivanevich, J. M., Eds., *Management and Organizational Behavior Classics*. Irwin: Boston, MA.

_____. (1967). *The Human Organization*. New York: McGraw-Hill.

Lorsch, J., Allen, S.A., (1973). *Managing Diversity and Interdependence*. Cambridge, MA.: Harvard University Press.

McClelland, D.C. (1975). *Power: The Inner Experience*. New York: Irvington Publishers.

_____. (1970). "Two Faces of Power." *Journal of International Affairs.*, Vol. 24, No.1, pp. 29-47.

McGregor, D. (1960). *The Human Side of Enterprise*. New York: McGraw-Hill Book Co.

Miles, R.H. (1980). *Macro Organizational Behavior*. Santa Monica, CA.: Goodyear Publishing.

Nichel, W.G. (1982). *Marketing Principles*. 2nd Ed., Englewood Cliffs, NJ.: Prentice-Hall.

Pascale, R.T. and Athos, A.G. (1981). *The Art of Japanese Management*. Simon and Schuster.

Peters, T. (1978). "Symbols, Patterns, and Settings." *Organizational Dynamics*. Fall, pp. 3-23.

Pettigrew, A. (1973). *The Politics of Organizational Decision Making*. London: Tavistock.

Pfeffer, J. (1981). *Power in Organizations*. Marshfield, MA.: Pitman Publishing.

Presthus, R. (1962). *The Organizational Society*. New York, NY.: Vintage Books.

Rickarts, T. (1975). *Problem Solving Through Creative Analysis*. Epping, England: Gower Press Limited.

Rumelt, R.P. (1974). *Strategy, Structure, and Economic Performance*. Cambridge, MA.: Harvard University Press.

Richman, B. M., and Farmer, R. N.(1974). *Leadership, Goals, and Power in Higher Education: A Contingency and Open-Systems Approach to Effective Management*. San Francisco: Jossey-Bass.

Salancik, G. R., and Pfeffer, J. (1974). "The Bases and Use of Power in Organizational Decision Making: The Case of a University." *Administrative Science Quarterly. 19*, 453-473.

Salancik, G. & Pfeffer, J. (1977). "Who Gets Power and How They Hold On To It: A Strategic Contingency Model of Power." *Organizational Dynamics*, Winter, pp. 3-21

Sayles, L. (1964). *Managerial Behavior*. New York, NY.: McGraw-Hill.

Simerly, R. G. (1987). *Strategic Planning and Leadership in Continuing Education*. San Francisco, CA: Jossey-Bass.

Sonnenfeld, J. & Kotter, J.P. (1982). "The Maturation of Career Theory." *Human Relation*, Vol. 35, No. 1, pp. 19-46.

Tannenbaum, R., & Schmidt, W.H. (1973). "How To Choose A Leadership Pattern." *Harvard Business Review.* May-June.

"The 100 Most Effective College Leaders, Named in a Survey of Their Peers." *Chronicle of Higher Education*, Nov. 5, 1986, p. 13.

UNESCO (2003). "Learning from Experience and Moving Ahead." New York: Author.

Vroom, V.H. and Yetton, P.W. (1973) *Leadership and Decision-making.* Pittsburgh, PA: University of Pittsburgh Pres.

Weick, K.E. (1983). "Managerial Thought in the Context of Action." In S. Srivastva and Associates, *The Executive Mind: New Insights on Managerial Thought and Action.* San Francisco: Jossey-Bass.

Yukl, G. A. (1981). *Leadership in Organizations.* Englewood Cliffs, N. J.: Prentice-Hall.

Chapter IV Planning

Ackoff, R.L. (1970). *A Concept of Corporate Planning.* Philadelphia: John Wiley & Sons, Inc.

Allen, R.W., Madison, D.L., Porter, L.W., Renwick, P.A., and Mayes, B.T., (1979). "Organizational Politics: Tactics and Characteristics of Its Actors," *California Management Review*, Fall, Vol. 22, No. 4, pp. 77-83.

Baldridge, J. V., Curtis, D. V., Ecker, G., and Riley, G. L. (1978). *Policy Making and Effective Leadership: A National Study of Academic Management.* San Francisco: Jossey-Bass.

Banfield, E.C., (1961). *Political Influence.* New York: The Free Press.

Bass, B. (1981). *Stodgill's Handbook of Leadership.* New York: The Free Press.

Beach, D.S. (1975). *Managing People At Work: Readings in Personnel.* New York: John Wiley & Sons, Inc.

Birnbaum, R. (1983). *Maintaining Diversity in Higher Education.* San Francisco: Jossey-Bass.

Birnbaum, R.(1988). *How Colleges Work: The Cybernetics of Academic Organization and Leadership.* San Francisco: Jossey-Bass.

Blake, R.R., et al., (1964). "Breakthrough in Organizational Development" *Harvard Business Review*, Nov.-Dec.

Blau, P.M. (1964). *Exchange and Power in Social Life.* New York: John Wiley & Sons, Inc.

Boyatzis, R. (1982). *The Competent Manager.* New York: John Wiley & Sons, Inc.

Brearley, A. (1976). "The Changing Role of the Chief Executive." *Journal of General Management*, 3(4), pp. 62-71.

Bryson, J. M. (1988). *Strategic Planning for Public and Non-Profit Organizations.* San Francisco, CA: Jossey-Bass.

Business Week. (1980). "CBS: When Being No. 1 Isn't Enough," May 26, pp. 128-132.

_____. (1981). "Still Another Master," August 17, pp. 80-86.

_____. (1980). "When A New Product Strategy Wasn't Enough," February 18.

Drucker, P. (1974). *Management.* New York: Harper & Row.

_____. (1967). *The Effective Executive.* New York: Harper & Row.

Fiedler, F.E. (1967). *A Theory of Leadership Effectiveness.* New York: McGraw-Hill.

_____. (1971). *Leadership.* New York: General Learning Press.

French, J. R., Jr., and Raven, B. (1996) "The Bases of Social Power". In Matteson, M. T. and Galbraith, M. W. et al (1997). *Administration of Successful Programs for Adults.* Malabar, FL: Krieger Publishing.

Ivanevich, J. M., Eds., *Management and Organizational Behavior Classics.* Irwin: Boston, MA.

Herzberg, F., Mausner, B., and Snyderman, B. (1959). *The Motivation to Work.* New York: John Wiley & Sons, Inc.

Jacobs, T.O. (1971). *Leadership and Exchange in Formal Organizations.* Alexandria VA.: Human Resources Research Organizations.

Kotter, J. P. (1999). *What Leaders Really Do.* Boston, MA: Harvard Business School Press.

Kotter, J. P. (1996). *Leading Change.* Boston, MA: Harvard Business School Press.

Kotter, J. P. (1990). *Force for Change: How Leadership Differs from Management.* New York: Free Press.

Kotter, J.P. (1979). "Managing External Dependence." *Academy of Management.* Review 1979, Vol. 4, No. 1, pp. 87-92.

_____. (1978). *Organizational Dynamics: Diagnosis and Intervention.* Reading, MA.: Addison-Wesley.

_____. (1977). "Power, Dependence, and Effective Management." *Harvard Business Review,* July/August, pp. 125-136.

_____. (1979). *Power in Management.* AMACOM.

_____. (1982). *The General Managers.* New York: The Free Press.

_____. (1973). "The Psychological Contract: Managing the Joining Up Process." *California Management Review,* Vol.15, No.3, pp. 91-99.

_____, Faux, V.A., and McArthur, C.C. (1979). *Self-Assessment and Career Development.* Englewood Cliffs, NJ: Prentice-Hall, Inc.

Likert, R. (1961). *New Patterns of Management.* New York: McGraw-Hill.

Likert, R. (1996) "Human Organizational Measurements: Key to Financial Success". In Matteson, M.T., and Ivanevich, J. M., Eds., *Management and Organizational Behavior Classics.* Irwin: Boston, MA.

_____. (1967). *The Human Organization*. New York: McGraw-Hill.

Lorsch, J., Allen, S.A., (1973). *Managing Diversity and Interdependence*. Cambridge, MA.: Harvard University Press.

McClelland, D.C. (1975). *Power: The Inner Experience*. New York: Irvington Publishers.

_____. (1970). "Two Faces of Power." *Journal of International Affairs.*, Vol. 24, No.1, pp. 29-47.

McCune, S. D. (1986). *Guide to Strategic Planning for Educators*. Alexandria, VA: Association for Supervision and Curriculum Development.

McGregor, D. (1960). *The Human Side of Enterprise*. New York: McGraw-Hill Book Co.

Miles, R.H. (1980). *Macro Organizational Behavior*. Santa Monica, CA.: Goodyear Publishing.

Nelson, J. B. (1986). "Planning: Establishing Program Goals and Strategies" in A. W. Rowland (Ed.), *Handbook of Institutional Advancement* (pp. 44-56). San Francisco, CA: Jossey-Bass.

Nichel, W.G. (1982). *Marketing Principles*. 2nd Ed., Englewood Cliffs, NJ.: Prentice-Hall.

Pascale, R.T. and Athos, A.G. (1981). *The Art of Japanese Management*. Simon and Schuster.

Peters, T. (1978). "Symbols, Patterns, and Settings." *Organizational Dynamics*. Fall, pp. 3-23.

Pettigrew, A. (1973). *The Politics of Organizational Decision Making*. London: Tavistock.

Pfeffer, J. (1981). *Power in Organizations*. Marshfield, MA.: Pitman Publishing.

Presthus, R. (1962). *The Organizational Society*. New York, NY: Vintage Books.

Rickarts, T. (1975). *Problem Solving Through Creative Analysis*. Epping, England: Gower Press Limited.

Rumelt, R.P. (1974). *Strategy, Structure, and Economic Performance*. Cambridge, MA.: Harvard University Press.

Richman, B. M., and Farmer, R. N.(1974). *Leadership, Goals, and Power in Higher Education: A Contingency and Open-Systems Approach to Effective Management*. San Francisco: Jossey-Bass.

Salancik, G. R., and Pfeffer, J. (1974). "The Bases and Use of Power in Organizational Decision Making: The Case of a University." *Administrative Science Quarterly*. 19, 453-473.

Salancik, G. & Pfeffer, J. (1977). "Who Gets Power and How They Hold On To It: A Strategic Contingency Model of Power." *Organizational Dynamics*, Winter, pp. 3-21.

Sayles, L. (1964). *Managerial Behavior*. New York, NY.: McGraw-Hill.

Simerly, R. G. (1987). *Strategic Planning and Leadership in Continuing Education*. San Francisco, CA: Jossey-Bass.

Sonnenfeld, J. & Kotter, J.P. (1982). "The Maturation of Career Theory." *Human Relation*, Vol. 35, No. 1, pp. 19-46.

Tannenbaum, R., & Schmidt, W.H. (1973). "How To Choose A Leadership Pattern." *Harvard Business Review*. May-June.

"The 100 Most Effective College Leaders, Named in a Survey of Their Peers." *Chronicle of Higher Education*, Nov. 5, 1986, p. 13.

Vroom, V.H. and Yetton, P.W. (1973). *Leadership and Interpersonal Behavior*. New York, NY: Holt, Rinehart and Winston.

Weick, K.E. (1983). "Managerial Thought in the Context of Action." In S. Srivastva and Associates, *The Executive Mind: New Insights on Managerial Thought and Action*. San Francisco: Jossey-Bass.

Yukl, G. A. (1981). *Leadership in Organizations*. Englewood Cliffs, N. J.: Prentice-Hall.

Chapter V Decision-Making

Alber, H.H. (1961). *Organized Executive Action: Decision Making, Communication, and Leadership*. New York, NY: Wiley.

Anderson, J.G. (1968). *Bureaucracy in Education*. Baltimore: Johns Hopkins Press.

Argyris, C. (1985). *Strategy, Change and Defensive Routines*. Boston, MA: Pittman.

Beach, D.S. (1975). *Managing People at Work*. New York, NY: John Wiley and Sons.

Blake, R.R., and Mouton, J.S. (1962). *Intergroup Relations and Leadership*. New York, NY.

Bodily, S. (2007, March 12). What's Luck Got to Do with It? *Washington Technology*, p. 34.

Dale, E. *Management: Theory and Practice*. New York: McGraw Hill.

Drucker, P.F. (1967). *The Effective Executive*. New York: Harper and Row.

Fiedler, F.E. (1958). *Leader Attitude and Group Effectiveness*. Urbana, IL: University of Illinois Press.

Fishburn, P.C. (1973). *The Theory of Social Choice*. Princeton, NJ: Princeton University Press.

Goldman, T.A. (1967). *Cost Effectiveness and Analysis: New Approaches in Decision Making*. New York, NY: Praeger.

Horowitz, I. (1970). *Decision-Making and the Theory of the Firm*. New York: Holt, Rinehart and Winston.

Lakein, A. (1973). *How to Get Control of Your Time and Your Life*. New York: Signet.

Millett, J.D. (1968). *Decision Making and Administration in Higher Education*. Kent, OH: Kent State University Press.

Paine, F.T. (1975). *Organizational Strategy and Policy*. Philadelphia, PA: Saundus.

Schoemaker, P. J. H. and Russo, J. E. (1993, Fall). A Pyramid of Decision Approaches. *California Management Review*, pp. 9-31.

Senge, P. (1990). *The Fifth Discipline: The Art and Practice of the Learning Organization*. New York, NY: Doubleday.

Strata, R. (1989). "Organizational Learning-The Key to Management Innovation." *Sloan Management Review*, Spring.

Shirley, R.C. (1976). *Strategy and Policy Formation: A Multi-functional orientation*. New York, NY: Wiley and Sons.

Stodgill, R.M. (1974). *Handbook of Leadership*. New York, NY: The Free Press.

Vroom, V.H. (1967). *Methods of Organizational Research*. Pittsburgh: University of Pittsburgh Press.

Chapter VI Team Building and Small Group Interactions

Arragon, R.F. (1941). *The Technique of Group Discussion*. Portland, OR.

Argyris, C. (1962). *Interpersonal Competence and Organizational Effectiveness*. Homewood, Illinois: Dorsey Press.

_____. (1985). *Strategy, Change and Defensive Routines*. Boston, MA: Pittman.

Beach, D. S. (1980). *Managing People at Work: Readings in Personnel*. New York: Wiley.

Birnbaum, Robert (1988). *How Colleges Work: The Cybernetics of Academic Organization and Leadership*. San Francisco, CA: Jossey-Bass.

Bonner, H. (1968). *Group Dynamics: Principles and Applications*. New York: Harper and Row.

Cartwright, D., ed. (1968). *Group Dynamics, Research and Theory*. New York: Harper and Row.

Collins, J. and Porras, J., (2002). *Built to Last*. New York: Harper Collins.

Covey, Stephen, R. (1992). *Principle Centered Leadership*. New York: Simon and Schuster.

Drexler, A. and Sibbet, D.(1995). *Team Performance Model*. Rockbridge Baths, VA : Grove Consultants International.

Eitington, J. E. (1984). *The Winning Trainer*. Houston, Texas: Gulf Publishing House.

Fiedler, F.E. (1967). *A Theory of Leadership Effectiveness*. New York: McGraw Hill.

Fiedler, F. E. (1995). "How do You Make Leaders More Effective? New Answers to an Old Puzzle" in Eds. Pierce, J. J., and Newsroom, J. W. *Leaders and the Leadership Process*. Boston, Mass: Irwin/Austen Press, pp. 107-111.

Glassman, R. B. (1973). "Persistence and Loose Coupling in Living Systems" *Behavioral Science*, 18, 83-98.

Goldberg, S. C. "Influence and Leadership as a Function of Group Structure", *Journal of Abnormal and Social Psychology*, Vol. 51, mo. 1, pp. 119-122.

Hackman, J. R.(1976) "Group Influences on Individuals." In M. Dunnette (ed.) *Handbook of Industrial and Organizational Psychology*. Chicago: Rand McNally, pp. 1455-1525.

Hertzberg, F. (1996). "New Approaches in Management Organization and Job Design" in Matteson, M. T. and Ivanevich, J. M. *Management and Organizational Classics*. Boston, Mass: Irwin.

Hollander, E. P. "Conformity, Status, and Idiosyncrasy Credit." *Psychological Review*, 1958, 65, 117-27.

Jacobs, T. O. (1970). *Leadership and Exchange in Formal Organizations*. Alexandria, Virginia: Human Resources Research Organization.

Jaffee, C. L. & Lucas, R. L. (1969). "Effect of Rates of Talking and Correctness of Decisions on Leader Choice in Small Groups", *Journal of Social Psychology*. Vol. 79, 1969, pp. 247-254.

Kiefer, C. & Stroh, P. (1984). "A New Paradigm for Developing Organizations" in J. Adams, Ed. *Transforming Work*, Alexandria, VA: Miles Riler Press.

Lutz, F. W. (1982). "Tightening Up Loose Coupling in Organizations of Higher Education". *Administrative Science Quarterly*. 27, 6, 653-669.

Schon, D. (1983). *The Reflective Practitioner: How Professionals Think in Action*. New York, NY: Basic Books.

Senge, P.M. (1990). *The Fifth Discipline: The Art and Practice of the Learning Organization*. New York, NY: Doubleday.

Strata, R. (1989). "Organizational Learning-The Key to Management Innovation.", *Sloan Management Review*. Spring, pp. 63-64.

Tuckman, B. (1955). "Development Sequence in Small Groups," *Psychological Bulletin*, (23) May.

Weick, K. E. (1976). "Educational Organizations as Loosely Coupled Systems" *Administrative Science Quarterly*, 21, 1-19.

Weisbord, M. R. (1987). "Transforming Teamwork: Work Relationships in a Fast-Changing World" in *Productive Workspaces*. San Francisco, Ca: Jossey-Bass, 296-310.

Chapter VII Motivation

Adler, N.J. (1991). *International Dimensions of Organizational Behavior*. Boston, MA: PWS-Kent Publishing Co. Barley, J.E. (Sept. 1986). "Personnel Scheduling with Flex-shift: A Win-Win Scenario." *Personnel*. 63.

Bass, B.M. (1985). *Leadership and Performance Beyond Expectations*. New York, NY: The Free Press.

Bass, B.M. and R.M. Stogdill. (1989). *The Handbook of Leadership*. 3rd Ed. New York, NY: The Free Press.

Beach, D.S. (1975). "Managing People at Work" *Readings in Personnel*, New York, NY: John Wiley Sons.

Bennis, W. (1989). *Why Leader's Can't Lead: The Unconscious Conspiracy*. San Francisco, CA: Jossey Bass.

Bennis, W. and Nanus, B. (1985). *Leaders*. New York, NY: Harper and Row.

Birch, D. and J. Veroff (1968). *Motivation: A Study of Action*. California: Brooks/Cole Publishing Co.

Blake, R. and Mouton, J.S. (1964). *The Managerial Grid*. Houston, TX: Gulf Publishing.

Cone, W.F. (1974). *Supervising Employees Effectively*. Don Mills, Ontario: Addison-Wesley Publishing Co.

Conger, J.A. (1989). *The Charismatic Leader: Behind the Mystique of Exceptional Leadership*. San Francisco, CA: Jossey Bass.

Cook, C.W. (April, 1980). "Guidelines for Managing Motivation." *Business Horizons*. 23.

Covey, Stephen (2004). *The 8ᵗʰ Habit*. New York, NY: Free Press.

Drucker, P.F. (1977). *People and Performance: The Best of Peter Drucker on Management*. New York, NY: Harper's College Press.

Driver, M.J. (1979). "Individual Decision Making and Creativity" in S. Kerr Ed., *Organizational Behavior*, Columbus, OH: Grid Publishing.

Eysenck, H.J. (1964). *Experiments in Motivation*. New York, NY: Macmillan Co.

Fredrickson, B. L. and Branigan, C. (2005). "Positive Emotions Broaden the Scope of Attention and Thought-action Repertoires." *Cognition and Emotion*, 19, 313-332.

Fredrickson, B. L., and Losada, M. (2005). Positive Affect and the Complex Dynamics of Human Flourishing." American Psychologist. 678-686.

Fuller, J.L. (1962). *Motivation a Biological Perspective*. New York, NY: Random House.

Gallup. (October 2004). *Managing the Human Difference*. International Positive Psychology Conference. Washington, D.C., USA.

Gordon, G. (2002). Beware the remedial Approach to Teaching. Gallup Management Journal [Electronic Version]. Document available at http://www.gallup.com/poll/content/?ci'6673. Accessed February 12, 2007.

Gellerman, S.W. (1963). *Motivation and Productivity*. New York, NY: American Management Association.

Hamachek, D.E. (1968). *Motivation in Teaching and Learning*. Washington, D.C.: National Education Association.

Hammer, W.C. (1979). "Motivation Theories and Work Applications" in S. Kerr Ed., *Organizational Behavior*, Columbus, OH: Grid Publishing.

Hannaford, E. (1967). *Supervisor's Guide to Human Relations*. Chicago, Il: National Safety Council.

Harvis, P.R. and R.T. Moran (1990). *Managing Cultural Differences.* Houston, TX: Gulf Publishing.

Hersey, P. and K. H. Blanchard, K.H. (1988). *Management of Organizational Behavior: Utilizing Human Resources.* Englewood Cliffs, NJ: Prentice Hall.

Johansson, Franz (2004). *The Medici Effect.* Boston, MA: Harvard Business School Press.

Jones, C. C. (1981). *Motivation.* Rocvkville, MD: ECEA Institute.

Herzberg, F.P., Mausner, B. and Snyderman, B. (1959). *The Motivation To Work.* New York, NY: Wiley. Addison Wesley.

Klein, S.M. and R.R. Ritti (1984). *Understanding Organizational Behavior.* Boston: Kent Publishing Co.

Kotter, J. (1988). *The Leadership Factor.* New York, NY: Free Press.

Lawler, E.E. (1973). *Motivation In Work Organizations.* Monterey, CA: Brooks/Cole Publishing Co.

Mason, R.H., and R.S. Spick. (1987). *Management: an International Perspective.* Homewood, Il: Richard Irwin, Inc.

Maslow, A.H. (1970). *Motivation and Personality.* (second edition), New York, NY: Harper and Row.

McClelland, D.C. and D.H. Burnham. (March, 1976). "Power is the Great Motivator." *Harvard Business Review,* 54.

McGregor, D. (1960). *The Human Side of Enterprise.* New York, NY: McGraw-Hill.

Murray, E.J. (1964). *Motivation and Emotion.* New Jersey: Prentice Hall.

"Putting Strenths-Based Mangement to Work" (2006). Harvard Business School Publishing Conference, Chicago.

Quick, J.C. (July, 1979). "Dyadic Goal Setting Within Organizations: Role-making and Motivational Considerations." *Academy of Management Review,* 4.

Rosenthal, R. (September, 1973). "The Pygmalion Effect Lives." *Psychology Today.*

Seligman, M.E.P., (1998). *Learned Optimism.* New York: Free Press.

Seligman, M.E.P., (2002). *Authentic Happiness.* New York: Free Press.

Senge, P.M. (1990). *The Fifth Discipline: The Art and Practice of the Learning Organization.* New York, NY: Doubleday.

Stahl, M.J. (Winter, 1983). "Achievement Power and Managerial Motivation: Selecting Managerial Talent With the Job Choice Exercise." *Personnel Psychology.*

Terry, G.R. (1974). *Supervisory Management.* Homewood, IL: Richard Irwin, Inc.

Wagel, W.H. (April, 1986). "Opening the Door to Employee Participation." *Personnel,* 63.

Williams, S. and Davis, J. (2006). "Strengths – Based Management for Continuing Education." Presentation given at UCEA conference, October 5, Annapolis, MD.

Chapter VIII Problem Solving

Ackoff, Russell L. *The Art of Problem Solving.* New York: John Wiley & Sons, Inc., 1988.

Blake, Robert R. and Jane S. Mouton. *Building a Dynamic Corporation Through Grid Organization Development.* Massachusetts: Addison-Wesley,1969.

Cartwright, Dorwin and Alvin Zander. *Group Dynamics.* New York: Harper and Row, 1960.

Chase, Stuart and Marion Tyler Chase. *Roads to Agreement.* New York: Harper and Row, 1980.

Cummings, Paul W. *Open Management.* New York: American Management Associations, 1980.

Drucker, Peter F. *The Practice of Management.* New York: Harper and Row, 1954.

Drucker, Peter F. "Peter Drucker on the Manager and the Organization," (1977), *Bulletin on Training,* (March-April), p. 4.

Dyer William G. 'When is a Problem a Problem?' *The Personnel Administrator,* 1978, pp. 66-71.

Eitington, J.E. *The Winning Trainer.* Texas: Gulf Publishing Co., 1984.

Fisher, B. Aubrey. *Small Group Decision Making: Communication and the Group Process.* New York: McGraw Hill, 1974.

Gannon, Martin J. *Management: An Organizational Perspective.* Boston: Little, Brown and Company, 1978.

Harrison, E. Frank. *The Managerial Decision-Making Process.* Boston: Houghton Mifflin, 1975.

Johansson, F. (2004). *The Medici Effect.* Boston: Harvard Business School Press.

Lee, Irving J. *How to Talk with People.* New York: Harper and Row, 1952.

Likert, Rensis. *New Patterns of Management.* New York: McGraw-Hill, 1961.

Likert, Rensis. *The Human Organization: Its Management and Value.* New York: McGraw-Hill, 1968.

Marrow, Alfred J. *The Failure of Success.* New York: American Management Association, Inc., 1972.

McGregor, Douglas. *The Human Side of Enterprises.* New York: McGraw-Hill Book Co., 1960.

Miller, David and Martin Starr. *The Structure of Human Decisions.* New Jersey: Prentice-Hall, 1968.

Murnighan, J. Keith. 'Group Decision Making: What Strategies Should You Use?' *Management Review,* pp. 55-62, Feb., 1981.

Osborn, Alex. *Applied Imagination.* New York: Charles Scribner's Sons,1960.

Parnes, S.J., Noller, R.B., and Biondi. A.M. *Guide to Creative Action* and *Creative Actionbook*. New York: Charles Scribner's Sons, 1977, 1976.

Rawlinson, J. Geffrey. *Creative Thinking and Brainstorming*. New York: John Wiley & Sons, 1981.

Simon Herbert. *Administrative Behavior*. New York: The Free Press, 1976.

Ulschak, Francis L., Nathanson, L. and P.G. Gillan. *Small Group Problem Solving: An Aid to Organizational Effectiveness*. Reading, Mass.: Addison-Wesley, 1981.

VanDersal, William R. *The Successful Supervisor in Government and Business*. New York: Harper & Row, 1974.

Walker, D.E. (1979). *The Effective Administrator: A Practical Approach to Problem Solving, Decision making and Campus Leadership*. San Francisco: Jossey-Bass.

Chapter IX Marketing

Abraham, Magid M. and Leonard M. Lodish (1990). "Getting the Most Out of Advertising and Promotion," *Harvard Business Review*, May-June, pp 50-60.

Akao, Yoji (1990). *Quality Function Deployment: Integrating Customer Requirements into Product Design*. Cambridge, Mass.: Productivity Press.

Blattberg, Robert C. and John Deighton (1991). "Interactive Marketing: Exploiting the Age of Addressability." *Sloan Management Review,* Fall, pp 5-14.

Bossert, James L. (1991). *Quality Function Deployment: A Practitioner's Approach*. New York, NY: ASQC Quality Press, Marcel Dekker, Inc.

Copeland, J. T. (2007). "Interactive Marketing". Presentation given at University Continuing Education Association Conference (UCEA), April 12, Vancouver, British Columbia, Canada.

Dutka, Alan (1994). *AMA Handbook for Customer Satisfaction*. Lincolnwood, Ill: NTC Business Books.

Elliott, Ralph D. (1982). *How to Build and Maintain a High Quality Mailing List*. Learning Resources Network: Manhattan, Kansas.

George, S. And Weimerskirch, J. (1994). *Total Quality Management*. New York: John Wiley & Sons, Inc.

Galbraith, M. W. et al (1997, 2001). *Administration of Successful Programs for Adults*. Malabar, FL: Krieger Publishing.

Hayes, Bob E. (1992). *Measuring Customer Satisfaction*. Milwaukee, Wisconsin: ASQC Quality Press.

Hodlin, Steven F. (1996). "Stay Customer Focused to Ensure Long-Term Success". Presentation given at the Quality Network Seminar, Suburban Maryland High Technology Education Council, May 15, Rockville, MD.

Hopkins, Tom (1982). *How to Master The Art of Selling*. New York: Warner Books.

Houston, Franklin S. (1986). "The Marketing Concept: What It Is and What It Is Not." *Journal of Marketing*, April, pp 81-87.

Juran, J. M.(1989*). Juran on Leadership for Quality*. New York: The Free Press.

Kotler, P. and Fox K. (1985). *Strategic Marketing for Educational Institutions*. Englewood Cliffs, NJ: Prentice-Hall.

Kotler, Philip, and Alan R. Andreasen (1991). *Strategic Marketing for Nonprofit Organizations*, 4th ed., Englewood Cliffs, N.J.: Prentice-Hall.

Kotler, Philip (1994). *Marketing Management: Analysis Planning, Implementation and Control*. Prentice-Hall: Englewood Cliffs, NJ.

Nash, Edward (1986). *Direct Marketing*. New York: McGraw Hill.

National Institute of Standards and Technology (1996). *Malcolm Baldridge Quality Award Criteria*. Gaithersburg, MD: National Institute of Standards.

Ogilvy, David (1988). *Confessions of an Advertising Man*. New York: Atheneum.

Pride, W.M. and O.C. Ferrell (1987). *Marketing: Basic Concepts and Decisions*. Boston: Houghton Mifflin Co.

Rogers, E.M. and F.F. Shoemaker (1971). *Communication of Innovations*. New York: MacMillan.

Sarbanes, The Honorable Paul S. (1996). *U. S. Senate Productivity Award*. Washington, D. C.: U. S. Senate.

Stone, Robert (1993). *Successful Direct Marketing Methods*. Chicago: NTC Books.

Whiteley, Richard C. (1991). *The Customer Driven Company: Moving From Talk to Action*. Boston, MA: Addison-Wesley Publishing Co, Inc.

Chapter X Non-Credit Programs

Apps, J.W. (1981) *The Adult Learner on Campus*. Chicago: Follett.

Arends, R.I. and Arends, J.H. (1977) *Systems Change Strategies in Educational Settings*. New York: Herman Science Press.

Boone, E.J., Shearon, R.W., White, E.E. and Associates (1980). *Serving Personal and Community Needs through Adult Education*. San Francisco: Jossey Bass.

Brookfield, S.D. (1986). *Understanding and Facilitating Adult Learning*. San Francisco: Jossey-Bass.

Cross, K.P. (1981). *Adults as Learners*. San Francisco, Jossey-Bass.

Gross, R. (1977) *The Lifelong Learner*. New York: Simon and Schuster.

Gross, R. (1982). *Invitation to Lifelong Learning*. Chicago; Follett.

Knowles, Malcolm S. (1980) *The Modern Practice of Adult Education* (Rev. ed.) New York: Cambridge Book Co.

Knowles, M.S. (1984). *The Adult Learner: A Neglected Species*. Houston: Gulf Publishing Co.

Knox, A.B. (1986) *Helping Adults Learn.* San Francisco: Jossey-Bass.

Lopos, G. (1988) Holt, M.E., Bohlander, R.E. and Wells, J.H. (eds.) *Peterson's Guide to Certificate Programs at American College and Universities.* Princeton, NJ; Peterson's Guides.

Smith, A.O. (1991) An Institutional History of certificate Programs at George Washington University in *Perspectives on Educational Certificate Programs: New Directions for Adult and Continuing education*, No 52, Winter 1991, San Francisco, Jossey-Bass.

Smith, R.M. (1982) Learning How to Learn. Chicago: Follett.

Wee, Eric L. (1996) "More College Students Live, Then Learn." *The Washington Post.* March 5.

Appendices

Appendix A

Alternative Sample
Off-Campus Programs Mission Statement

The University's Graduate and professional degree programs are designed to accommodate working professional who wish to continue their development through part-time study. Such programs constitute a sizable portion of the University's offerings on campus. In addition, the university offers degree programs identical in quality to the on campus programs at off campus centers. Non-credit courses, seminars, conferences, and institutes offered by the various academic units of the University also meet the needs of working professionals for continuing education.

The University's location is critical to the character of the institution. This city offers unique intellectual and cultural resources for study and extra-curricular activity. The University seeks to relate these rich resources to its academic activities and to include among its offerings curricula and opportunities for research and public service specifically related to the metropolitan, national, and international aspects of the city.

Appendix B

Code of Ethics of the Association for Continuing Higher Education (ACHE)

CODE OF ETHICS The Association for Continuing Higher Education (ACHE) is an international institution based organization of colleges, university and individuals dedicated to the promotion of lifelong learning and excellence in continuing higher education. The Association is composed of a diverse group of education professionals from a cross section of the higher education community. In their various professional roles, members of the Association strive to serve their learners, their institutions and their own professional community, while advocating continuing higher education as a means of enhancing and improving society. With utmost regard for their profession, these members acknowledge their responsibilities to the ACHE community in particular, and to society in general and accept this Code of Ethics as a set of principles to guide them in their professional practice. In pursuing the mission and goals of the Association, continuing higher education practitioners:

- Deliver programs of measurable, high quality.
- Provide fair and equal services to all, regardless of race, color, religion, gender, age, sexual orientation, marital status, national origin or disability.
- Avoid conflicts of interest or the appearance of conflicts of interest in all aspects of their work.
- Ensure the confidentiality of learners and clients in areas where privacy is expected or required.
- Inform faculty and administrators of the unique and diverse needs of adult learners, and the best practices available for their success in a course or program.

- Articulate to the institution any impact that policies and procedures will have on the institution, the community and the learner.
- Present advertising information that is clear, truthful and descriptive of the real services and programming.

Provide programs that are fiscally responsible to the institution, the community and participant. http://www.acheinc.org/codeofethics.pdf

Appendix C

Papers from the 22nd ICDE
World Conference 2007 in Brazil

These papers show the wide variety of interest in continuing and distance education world wide.

Conference theme, representation and papers:

The main theme of the conference was: **"Quality in online, Flexible and Distance Education"**.

This theme was addressed through different streams:

1. The Value of distance and ICT based education: with focus on the political and philosophical aspects, from a national or international perspective: why and where does it make sense to use distance education.
2. Promoting Educational Quality: focus on pedagogical, technological and organizational aspects.
3. Institutional Quality Issues: from a management perspective, focusing on change management, project management and long term sustainability: what should be done and how.
4. Research and New Developments.

Geographic Representation:

The 22nd conference has attracted 1500 prominent scholars, researchers, public officers, CEOs and decision-makers from 73 countries of the world, covering all the continents:

Africa

Angola; Botswana; Ghana; Guinea Bissau; Mozambique; Niue; South Africa and Uganda

Asia

China; India; Indonesia; Japan, Saudi Arabia; Korea; Malaysia; Pasquotank; and Singapore

Europe

Austria; Belgium; Bulgaria, Czech Republic; Denmark; England; Estonia; Finland; France; Germany; Hungary; Ireland; Italy; Norway: Portugal Romania, Russia; Scotland, Slovak Republic, Spain; Sweden; Switzerland and The Netherlands.

Latin America

Argentina; Brazil; Costa Rica; Colombia, Ecuador; Mexico; Perú; Puerto Rico; Dominican Republic; and Venezuela

North America

United States of America and Canada

Oceania

Australia and New Zealand

This broad representation enabled the participants to learn more about different peculiarities and challenges based on cultural varieties in the field of e-learning in different countries and, as a result, to generate solutions for the problems of globalization and opening education to larger circles of population worldwide.

Besides English, the second working language at the conference was Portuguese, which contributed to the attraction of a high number of professionals from Latin America.

The Program Committee received over 650 papers, and accepted for presentation at the conference over 500 papers. Being Brazil, one of the world largest countries with a population of over 160 million people, the host country had a massive presence: almost half of the papers presented at the ICDE conference came from Brazilian distance education professionals.

Argentina

- Maldonado, Ángela; Giandini, Viviana; Caterbetti, Norma; Salerno, Mirta; Sanz, Cecilia; Zangara Alejandra; Gonzalez Alejandro, Universidad Nacional de La Plata, **"A Proposal to Shorten Distances between High School and University" Incorporating a Virtual Educative Environment"**
- Sanz, Cecilia; Zangara, Alejandra; Gonzalez, Alejandro Héctor, UNLP, **"Teaching Competence Development within the framework of the quality of a Distance Education System. The case of the National University of La Plata"**

Australia

- Naidu, Som, The University of Melbourne, **"The Missing Link in Promoting Quality Education: Exploring the role of pedagogical design in promoting quality in teaching and learning"**

Austria

- Ross, David, University of Southern Queensland, Mcmullen, Fiona, Lanstar Pty Ltd, **"Living English Simulation Game for Non-native English speakers a New Method to learn Spoken English"**

Botswana

- Oladokun, Olugbade Samuel, University of Botswana, **"Equity-Based Library and Information Service in Distance Learning Environment: Myth or Reality?"**

Brazil

- Aguiar, Vilma, Faculdade Internacional de Curitiba; **"The Quality in Distance Learning Education: The Construction of an Institutional Model"**
- Almeida, Érico Galdino; Corrêa, Silvia Fernanda; Jordão, Teresa Cristina, Senac São Paulo, **"The Use of LMS Potentialized by the Integration of Customizable Tools: The Development of Building Blocks"**

– Almeida, Rodrigo de Maio; Colugnati, Fernando A. Basile; Barretto, Saulo F. Almeida, IPTI – Instituto de Pesquisas em Tecnologia da Informação, Oliveira, Henrique J. Quintino, UMC – Universidade de Mogi das Cruzes, **"User Authentication in E-Learning Environments Using Keystroke Dynamic Analysis"**

– Almeida, Roseane, FATEC Internacional, **"Tutor's Role in Promoting Quality in Distance Education"**

– Alves de Santana Regis, Maria Claudia, Escola do Futuro da Universidade de São Paulo, **"Atividades Virtuais Síncronas e Assíncronas: Projeto Telemar Educação. Synchronous and Asynchronous Virtual Activities: Telemar Project"**

– Azevedo, Wilson, Aquifolium Educacional; Silva, Jose Manuel, SENAC/RJ; **"And How Hear We Every Man In Our Own Tongue, Wherein We Were Born? (Acts 2:8) Asyncrhonous Translated Online Courses and Seminars for a Globalized Education"**

– Backes, Luciana; Schlemmer, Eliane, Universidade do Vale do Rio dos Sinos, **"Construction of Virtual Realities in Teacher Training: Configuration of Cohabiting Spaces"**

– Barreto, Cristine Costa; Bielschowsky, Carlos Eduardo, CEDERJ, **"Instructional Design: planning and development of learning material for CEDERJ"**

– Baruque, Lúcia Blondet, Fundação Cecierj, Consórcio CEDERJ, Melo, Rubens Nascimento, PUC – Rio, **"A Reference Model for e-Learning Governance"**

– Beiler, Adriana; Franciosi, Beatriz R. T., PUCRS, **"The Conversational Network and Learning Environments Mediated by Technologies of Information and Communication"**

– Bignetti Bechara, João José; Haguenauer, Cristina, LATEC/UFRJ, **"Learning in Virtual Environments and the Experience of the Information and Communication Technology Research Laboratory of the Federal University of Rio De Janeiro"**

– Birman, Eliane, Roberto Marinho Foundation, **"The Construction of the Multicurso Cooperative Learning Net: A Story Written by Many Hands"**

– Brandão Neves, Cristiane dos Reis; Manssensini, Ariana Ramos, SENAI – Departamento Regional de Goiás, **"The experience of SENAI – Departamento Regional de Goiás in offering computer-assisted technical education"**

– Bueno de Camargo Cortelazzo, Iolanda, FACINTER/UNINTER; **"Teachers Formation at Distance: Quality in Teaching and Learning"**

– Buschle, Cristala Athanázio, Universidade Da Região De Joinville-UNIVILLE, **"Efl on Line Learning Course: A Case Study at Univille"**

- Caleffi, Paula; Garrido, Susane, UNISINOS, **"Model of Management for Institutional Initiatives in Online Education"**
- Canabrava, Bruna W.; Geiger, Noni, Universidade do Estado do Rio de Janeiro, **"NOH, a Web-Based System for Science Education"**
- Capello, Claudia; Longo, Carlos; Rego, Marta; Freitas, João Carlos, FGV, **"Technology and communicability in e-learning: tutoring and the instruments of the virtual environment at FGV Online"**
- Cardoso, Isa Mara, Fundação Dom Cabral, **"Andragogy in Virtual Learning Environments"**
- Cardoso, Regina Machado Araújo, Federacy of the Industries of the State of the Bahia, **"Intellectual Property Dissemination: A Distance Education proposal"**
- Carrancho da Silva, Regina, Universidade do Estado do Rio de Janeiro – UERJ, **"Building up Social Representations for WEB-Based Learning Environments"**
- Castellani, A. M., Lazilha, F., Amadei, J. L., Cesumar – Pr, Iwama, J. A., Farmacêutica, **"Project of Qualification of Agents of Health in the Orientation of Domiciliary Medicine Use for home carer: a long-distance Experience"**
- Colugnati, Fernando A.B.; Barretto, Saulo F.A., IPTI – Instituto de Pesquisas em Tecnologia da Informação, **"Surveying relationship between participation and test grades in learning management systems: a proposal for on-line student assessment method"**
- Comassetto, Liamara Scortegagna, Contestado University UnC, **"Applicability of Necessities of Pedagogical Drawing in Virtual Platform: Quality in Distance Education On-Line"**
- Doin de Almeida, Rosângela, Instituto de Geociências e Ciências Exatas – UNESP; Ramos, Cristhiane S., RMIT University, Melbourne (Australia); Cartwright, William, RMIT University, Melbourne (Australia); **"Internet Atlases for Primary Education: Issues in Atlas Use"**
- Faria, Elaine Turk; Cruz, Maria Waleska; Franciosi, Beatriz R. T., PUCRS. **"Virtual Interactivity and Pedagogical Mediation: A Possible and Necessary Relation"**
- Faria, Mônica Alves; Faculdades Docturn, Silva, Regina Coeli, Universidade Salgado de Oliveira, **"Technological Innovation in School and Gender"**
- Ferreira, Zuleika Nunes; Mendonça, Gilda Aquino de Araújo, Centro Federal de Educação Tecnológica de Goiás, **"Quality Function Deployment (Qfd) Applied in Distance Education"**

– Filippo, Denise; Barreto, Celso Gomes; Fuks, Hugo; Pereira de Lucena, Carlos José, Catholical University of Rio de Janeiro, **"Collaboration in Learning with Mobile Devices: Tools for Forum Coordination"**

– Foguel, Flávio Henrique dos Santos, Centro Universitário Nove de Julho – UNINOVE, Rosini, Alessandro Marco, Pontifícia Universidade Católica de São Paulo, **"Cluster Development in Brazil: The Contribution of Distance Education and Technological Professional Education"**

– Freire, Jerônimo, Instituto Natalense de Educação Superior – INAES, Mascarenhas de Andrade, Arnon Alberto, UFRN – PPGED, Cavalcante, Gilmara A., Faculdade de Ciências Empresariais e Estudos Costeiros de Natal – FACEN, **"How will be the University of the Future? A case study in the State University of Bahia – UNEB"**

– Freire, June Lessa, Faculdades São José, **"Challenge Methodology – A Methodology Based on Challenge Pedagogy"**

– Galembeck, Eduardo, Instituto de Biologia – Unicamp; **"Collaborative Science Library: A Peer Reviewed Digital Library on Science"**

– Gomes Carvalho, Ana Beatriz, Universidade Estadual da Paraíba, **"The Impact of the Distance Graduate Education in the Teacher's Formation of the Northeast Interior: Ways for an Education of Quality"**

– Gomes de Oliveira, Eloiza da Silva; de Abreu Costa, Marly; Villardi, Raquel; Pereira, Aline; Azeredo, Rachel A., Universidade do Estado do Rio de Janeiro, **"To Teach and to Learn out of the Classroom. The Internet as a Form of Didactic Strategy"**

– Greggersen, Gabriele, Faculdade Teológica Sul Americana (FTSA), **"Educação Teológica à Distância: do Brasil para o mundo. Theological Distance Education: From Brazil To The World"**

– Gregório, Miguel Angel; Marechal, Bernard Marie; Rausch Bello, Pedro Henrique, UFRJ, Nunes, Lizardo I I. C. M., CEDERJ/CECIERJ, **"Alternative Strategies for College Physics Education"**

– Grzybowski, Lourdes; Bernstein, Any; Costa, Giovânia; Hansen, Karla; da Silva, Leonardo S. Q.; Duque, Mônica; Dansa, Salmo, Fundação Cecierj/Consórcio Cederj, **"An overview of the first five years of the Portal da Educação Pública"**

– Guarezi, Rita de Cássia; Rodrigues, Mônica Guarezi, Instituto de Estudos Avançados, Grüdtner, Sônia I; Alves, Daniela Ferreira, Universidade Federal de Santa Catarina, **"Pedagogical System and Quality Guarantee in Distance Education E-Learning"**

– Guedes Monteiro, Ana Beatriz Lima; Tostes Leite, Maria Serrate, Sistema FIRJAN – SESI-RJ / SENAI-RJ, **"The Metamorphosis of the Instructors"**

- Haguenauer, Cristina, Moulin, Nelly, Carvalho, Fabrícia, Laboratório de Pesquisa em Tecnologias da Informação e da Comunicação, LATEC/UFRJ, **"Study on the Efficiency of Professional Training Programs Using Distance Education and Developed at the Federal University of Rio de Janeiro"**
- Hardy de Gómez, Irene, Fundación Cisneros, **"Program Upgrading Teachers in Education"**
- Locatelli, Ederson Luiz; Rocha da Silva, Alexandre, Universidade do Vale do Rio dos Sinos, **"Semiotics and Education: signs as devices in the production of knowledge"**
- Lopes, Maria Angela Soares; Matos, Márcia Maria; Malvestiti, Mirela L., Universidade de Brasília, Sebrae, **"Business Education of Quality: focus on the development of competencies"**
- Lopez Moreno, Esteban; Cascon, Vera; Bernstein, Any; Faria, Isabella Ribeiro; Brider, Inah; Jacobina, Maria da Penha Macedo, CEDERJ/CECIERJ, **"Improvement of Chemistry Education in Rio de Janeiro State, Brazil"**
- Lucena, Marisa; Lerner, Miriam; Chibante, Lucia; Moreira, Vania, Padre Leonel Franca Foundation / PUC-Rio, **"KFamily Project: Interactions between Young and Senior Citizens Mediated through Computers and the Internet"**
- Lucena, Marisa; Lerner, Miriam; Fernandes, Maria Cristina Pfeiffer, Padre Leonel Franca Foundation / PUC-Rio, Wagner, Rosina D.F., Education Department / PUC-Rio, **"The Partnership between the Education Department of PUC-Rio and the KBr/Kidlink Research Group to Incorporate Teachers in the Virtual World"**
- Lustosa, Volney, Instituto São Boaventura de Educação Continuada; Costa e Silva, Ana Paula, Universidade Católica de Brasília; Figueiredo, Rejane, Universidade Católica de Brasília; **"Application of Goal Question Metric Paradigm to Quality Evaluation in Learning Management Systems for Distance Learning"**
- Macedo, Margarete Valverde, Universidade Federal do Rio de Janeiro, Oya Masuda, Masako, Universidade Federal do Rio de Janeiro and Fundação CECIERJ, **"Report on the Attendance of Biology Students in Elective Tutorial Sessions in a "Semi-Presencial" Course in CEDERJ"**
- Maia, Marta de Campos; Meirelles, Fernando de Souza, Fundação Getulio Vargas – Escola de Administração de Empresas de São Paulo, **"Information and Communication Technology and Distance Education in Brazil"**
- Marlene Benchimol, CEDERJ-Centro de Ensino a Distância do Estado do Rio de Janeiro-RJ-Brazil, **"Teaching Biology: a new Approach"**
- Martelli, Ivana; Almas de Carvalho, Rose Mary, Universidade Católica de Goiás, **"Courses with Distance learning methodologies: a study for quality implementation"**

- Martinez, Joanir Fernandes; Martinez, Benedito Lafuente, Instituto Nacional de Educação à Distância – INED, **"Distance Education Close to the Student"**
- Matos, Hamilton; Mustaro, Pollyana Notargiacomo, Universidade Presbiteriana Mackenzie, **"Instructional design approach for creating learning objects using flash technology"**
- Mattar Neto, João Augusto; Rodrigues Maia, Carmem Silva, Universidade Anhembi Morumbi, **"Short Circuit: How an orkut-based environment is improving the communication between the different levels of a Higher Education Institution"**
- Mendonça Cardador, Débora, Freire, June Lessa, **"SENAI/CETIQT, Distance-Delivered Portuguese Levelling Course: A Research Application of the Challenge Methodology"**
- Montanheiro, Eder; Wuo, Wagner; Coutinho, Kaline Rabelo; Bonvent, Jean Jacques; Shida, Cláudio Saburo, Universidade de Mogi das Cruzes, **"Construction of a virtual teaching/learning environment to promote quality of the earth sciences undergraduate courses"**
- Monteiro de Oliveira, Luiz Rogério, Faculdade de Direito da Universidade de São Paulo; Carolei, Paula, SITE Educacional/Faculdade de Educação da Universidade de São Paulo; **"Copyright Problems in the Instructional Designer's Work"**
- Moresco, Silvia F. S., Doctoral Student in the Education Post Graduate Program – UFRGS; Behar, Patricia Alejandra, Computer Science PHD, by Computer Science Post Graduate Course – UFRGS; **"Blogs: an Interactive Educational Space for the Learning of Physics and Chemistry"**
- Murashima, Mary Kimiko G.; Rabelo, Sandro Alan Ramos; Longo, Carlos Roberto Juliano; Capello, Cláudia; Silveira, Elizabeth; Pimenta, Sophia R.; Freitas, João Carlos, FGV, **"The Place of Books on the Virtual Shelf – Creation and Customization of FGV Online Virtual Library"**
- Nascimento, Ronaldo José, Universidade Estadual de Londrina; Chanan, Douglas dos Santos, Universidade Estadual de Londrina; Chanan, Aline de Abreu Curunzi, Universidade Estadual de Londrina; Marchessou, François, Université de Poitiers; **"Information and Communication Technology (ICT) in Physical Education Classes in High School in Londrina-Paraná-Brazil"**
- Nogueira, Mário Lúcio L.; Gomes de Oliveira, Eloiza da Silva; Santos, Lázaro; Pereira, Aline; Nunes, Raquel S., Universidade do Estado do Rio de Janeiro, **"Teacher's Education for Future: a Brazilian Experience"**
- Oliveira, Paulo C., Nakayama, Marina K., Pilla, Bianca S., Universidade Federal do Rio Grande do Sul, **"Evaluation of Distance Learning Programs and the**

Criteria of Excellence of the National Quality Award: an Exploratory Study in Brazil"

- Quartiero, Elisa M., State University of Santa Catarina (UDESC); Zen Cerny, Roseli, Federal University at Santa Catarina (UFSC); Barbosa Mendes, Elise, Federal University at Uberlândia (UFU); **"The Places and Senses of Teacher Development: Study About a Physics Course of the Distance Learning Kind"**

- Paz-Klava, Carolina R.; Lopez, Karla A., TAM Brazilian Airlines, **"Content Development and e-Learning inside TAM Airlines. Some Considerations on an Emerging Experience"**

- Peretti, André P., UNOPAR – Universidade Norte do Paraná; Assis, Elisa M., UNOPAR – Universidade Norte do Paraná; Batista, Cleide V. M., UNOPAR – Universidade Norte do Paraná; Kfouri, Samira F., UNOPAR – Universidade Norte do Paraná; Rampazzo, Sandra R. R., UNOPAR – Universidade Norte do Paraná; **"The Construction of a Curriculum for Technological Courses in the Modality of DL"**

- Petrowa Esteves, Antonia, Universidade Federal do Estado do Rio de Janeiro – UNIRIO, **"Evaluation of the Effectiveness of Pedagogy Distance Course for the Early Years of Elementary School: an experience at UNIRIO/CEDERJ"**

- Pinto Figueiredo, Letícia; Vinicius Hurtado, Gabriel; Holms, Gilberto Augusto Tomaz de Aquino; Garcia, Dorotéa Vilanova,Universidade Santa Cecília, **"Gibrincar"**

- Pinto, Sônia M. C., Universidade do Estado da Bahia, Minho, Marcelle R S, Serviço Nacional de Aprendizagem Industrial, **"Multimedia Distance Education Course "Conquering My Future": An Experience of Digital Inclusion"**

- Queiroz, Tereza, Consórcio Cederj, **"Printing Didatic Material Production Department and the Quality in Distance Education"**

- Quirino, E.M.; Paraguaçu, F., Universidade Federal de Alagoas (UFAL), G.M.C.SOUZA, Universidade Estadual de Ciências da Saúde de Alagoas (UNCISAL), **"Recommender System to Diagnosis of Stroke"**

- Ramos Massensini, Ariana, SENAI – Serviço Nacional de Aprendizagem Industrial Departamento Regional de Goiás; Reis Brandão Neves, Cristiane do, SENAI – Serviço Nacional de Aprendizagem Industrial Departamento Regional de Goiás; **"The Role of Managerial Support as Mediator in the Buildup of Knowledge: A Case Study of SENAI – Departamento Regional De Goias"**

- Reichert, Clovis Leopoldo; Sander Costa, Janete; Axt, Margarete, Programa de Pós-Graduação em Informática na Educação – PPGIE-UFRGS, **"Dialogues and Authorship Processes in Distance Education Web Conference Environments"**

- Rezende, Flávia Amaral, Universidade Cidade de São Paulo, **"The Mediator Designer as a Quality Component in a Constructionist Learning Environment under High Interaction Approach"**
- Rizzon, Gisele, Universidade de Caxias do Sul, **"Metacognition as Constituted Way of Meaningful Learning in Distance Learning"**
- Rodrigues de Lemos, Maria de Fátima; Reichert, Clovis Leopoldo; Gambetta Schirmbeck, Fernando Ricardo, National Service for Industrial Apprenticeship – SENAI/RS, **"The Use of Competence Methodology in Distance Education Course Elaboration"**
- Rodrigues, Sonia, Centro de Educação Superior a Distância do Estado do Rio de Janeiro, **"The contribution of games for content setting and for improving virtual communities interaction in Distance Education"**
- Romiszowski, Hermelina Pastor, Tecnology-based Training Systems (TTS), **"Quality in Online Distance Education: The Dynamics of the Relationship between Learning, Evaluation and Instructional Design"**
- Ropoli, Edilene A., State University of Campinas – UNICAMP, **"Significant Learning and the Contribution to the Distance Learning"**
- Salvador, Daniel F.; Maia, Cristina de O.; Velloso, Andrea; Maia, Daniel F.; Giannella, Taís R., CEDERJ/CECIERJ, Lannes, Denise, UFRJ/CCS/IBqM, **"A performance Evaluation of Sciences and Biology Teaching Improvement Courses using on-line Distance-education, in the State of Rio de Janeiro"**
- Scavazza, Beatriz, Plonski, Guilherme Ary, Fundação Carlos Alberto Vanzolini, **"A Methodological Framework for Complex Teacher Development Programs"**
- Silva, Luís Rogério da, Universidade Paulista, Gonçalves, Eliane, Pontifícia Universidade Católica de São Paulo, **"Optimization of the online Notice Board to Guarantee Interaction in Distance Education"**
- Silva, Simone de Paula, Fundação CECIERJ/Consórcio CEDERJ, **"Strategies for the Web-Based Instructional Design in Distance Education"**
- Souza e Silva, Edmundo de; Meri Leão, Rosa Maria; Santos, Anna D., Federal University of Rio de Janeiro, Machado Netto, Bernardo C.; Azevedo, Jorge Allyson, Fundação CECIERJ, **"Multimedia Supporting Tools for the CEDERJ Distance Learning Initiative applied to the Computer Systems Course"**
- Spinelli de Carvalho, Felipe; Mannarino, Veronica de Gusmão; Longo, Carlos Roberto Juliano; Silveira, Elizabeth; Murashima, Mary Kimiko; Capello, Cláudia; Rego, Marta Lima, Getulio Vargas Foundation – FGV Online, **"The use of Business Games as final subject and theme for student monographs in FGV Online courses"**

- Thomaz, Sueli Barbosa, UNIRIO/CEDERJ, **"The Re-Signification of the Work of the Public Education Network Teachers: The Special Case of the Cederj Partnership in Distance Education"**
- Tonelli, Alessandra; Laurindo, Rosemeri, Universidade Regional de Blumenau – FURB, **"The Learning Process in Blended Learning Courses"**
- Vasconcellos, Liliana, Foundation Institute for Administration – FIA, Leme Fleury, Maria Tereza; Casado, Tânia, School of Economics, Management, and Accounting / University of São Paulo, **"The Influence of Student's Learning Style in Developing Competencies through Online Education"**
- Versuti, Andrea C., UNICAMP and UNICOC; **"A Proposal for the Development of Printed Material for a Distance Pedagogy Course"**
- Vida Noronha, Robinson; Torres Fernandes, Clovis, Instituto Tecnológico da Aeronáutica, **"Execution Obstacles of a Structural Communication Exercise"**
- Vilas Boas, Ana Alice, The Federal Rural University of Rio de Janeiro, **"The Federal Rural University of Rio de Janeiro"**
- Villardi, Raquel; Gomes de Oliveira, Eloiza da Silva; M. M. Sá, Marcia Souto; Cardoso de L. Rêgo, Marta; Santos, Lázaro; Nunes, Raquel S., Universidade do Estado do Rio de Janeiro, **"The Importance of Interaction in Collaborative Learning: Development of Tutors for an e-Pedagogy"**
- Wagner, Paulo Rech; Tavares Franciosi, Beatriz Regina; Lopes Leite, Leticia, PUCRS, **"Technology Acquisition in the Faculty Skill Development Course in Distance Education of PUCRS Virtual"**
- Walker, Robert K., Ágere Cooperação em Advocacy and Universidade Católica de Brasília, Eghrari, Iradj R., Ágere Cooperação em Advocacy, Marques, Luis Gastón L., Faros Tecnologia Aplicada à Educação, **"Distance Learning In-service and Pre-service Courses as an Instrument for Strengthening Citizenship Rights"**
- Zanette, Elisa Netto; Ribeiro dos Santos, Cleusa; Giacomazzo Nicoleit, Graziela Fátima; Fiuza, Patricia Jantsch, Universidade do Extremo Sul Catarinense, **"The Challenges and Possibilities of implanting Distance Education in Higher Education: the experiences of a multidisciplinary team"**

Canada

-Lentell, Helen, Commonwealth of Learning, **"Reflections on the meaning of quality in open and distance learning"**

- McGreal, Rory; Tin, Tony; Cheung, Billy, Athabasca University, **"Digital media at Athabasca University – Canada's Open University – Going Mobile"**
- Villa, Genny; Kerr, Barbara, Concordia University, **"Cultural issues and considerations for online instructional design and learning"**

Chile

- Ramirez, Camilo Pena, Universidad Tecnica Federico Santa Maria, Sede Vina del Mar; **"Business Plan for a Distance Learning Campus of a Prestigious, Traditional and Accredited University in the Chilean Education System Working in a Highly Competitive Scenario"**

China

- Dingquan, Ji; Nong, Qin, Shaanxi Radio and Television University, **"Modern Open and Distance Education: The Eden of the Lifelong and Workplace Learning in Remote Regions in West China"**
- Zhang, Zhigang, National Education Examinations Authority, **"Reorganization of Social Higher Education Resource: System Innovation by Self-Taught Learning Education Examinations"**

Colombia

- Vásquez, Ruth Molina; Briceño Castañeda, Sergio Ramiro, Universidad Distrital Francisco José de Caldas, **"Virtual Learning Network: A Continuing Professional Development Strategy for Teachers"**

Cuba

- **"The work that is done in Cuba to increase the quality in the use of Technology for Information and Communication"**

Denmark

- Andersen, V., Risoe National Laboratory, **"Distant Education of Medical Doctors for Dealing with On-Site Emergency Situations"**

Germany

- Hees, Frank; Backhaus, Wolfgang; Sattari, Sanaz; Henning, Klaus, RWTH Aachen University, **"A web-based knowledge map for higher education"**

India

- Kulkarni, Yogesh, Vigyan Ashram (Indian Institute Of Education), Gaikwad, Madhav, K.T.H.M. College, Nashik, **"ICT based learning strategies for Educating nomads"**
- Kumar, Sunaina, Indira Gandhi National Open University, **"E-books – Need, enrichment, ability Sub-title: How e-books can facilitate the variously abled distance learner"**

Indonesia

- Suparman, Atwi, Universitas Terbuka, Indonesia, Indonesia Open University, **"Enhancing Learning Support System through the Use of Information and Communication Technology: a Case at Universitas Terbuka"**

Iran

- Monajemi, Ebrahim, Payam Noor University, **"What kind of technology is the most useful in improving the quality of teaching and learning in developing countries?"**
- Zahra, Ostadzadeh, Ministry of Science, Research & Technology, **"Education and Social Development. With Focus on the Human Development and Science & Technology Situation in Iran"**

Italy

- Ghioni, Fabio, Telecom Italia Group, **"The Future of Distance, Flexible and ICT-based Education: Cyber Games"**

Macedonia

- Gopal, Parthiban, Universiti Sains Malaysia, **"E-Supervision: A Boost for Post Graduate Studies at Universiti Sains Malaysia?"**

- Murugaiah, Puvaneswary; Zakaria, Norraihan, School of Distance Education, Universiti Sains Malaysia, **"Video Conferencing at Universiti Sains Malaysia: An Effective Teaching-Learning Tool . . . Or Is It?"**
- Trajkovik T., Vladimir, Davcev P., Danco, Faculty of Electrical Engineering, **"Mobile Learning in Engineering Education"**

Malaysia

- Zakaria, Norraihan; Murugaiah, Puvaneswary, School of Distance Education, Universiti Sains Malaysia, **"Navigating Through Distance Education: A Malaysian Experience"**

Mexico

- Valenzuela, Jaime R., Tecnologico de Monterrey – Virtual University, **"Quality Standards in Distance Education Course Design: Lessons Learned from the Work of a Task Force from the Tecnologico de Monterrey's Virtual University"**

Nepal

- Sharan Sah, Prem, Pokhara University, **"Creative Wings in Distance Education Technologies"**

New Zealand

- Rajasingham, Lalita, School of Information Management Victoria University of Wellington, **"Re-Focusing Universities and Improving the Quality of Higher Education for the Knowledge Society"**

Nigeria

- Omofaye, Joel Oladipo, Federal University of Technology, **"Challenges Facing ICT Infrastructure and Successful Online Education in Africa"**

South Africa

- Duvenhage, CJ; de Beer, KJ; Baird, NH, Central University of Technology, **"Quality Standards related to Universities of Technology's Distance Education"**

- Louw, HA; Prinsloo, P, Unisa, **"Higher Education in the Service of Humanity: Reflections on Engagement toward Development"**

Sweden

- Hansson, Henrik, Stockholm University, **"The digital learning landscape: Traps, tricks and survival tactics"**

Switzerland

- Andrade Marson, Guilherme, National Center of Competence in Research in Molecular Oncology – Swiss Institute for Experimental Cancer Research; Debard, Nathalie, EuroVacc Foundation; Kraehenbuhl, Jean-Pierre, EuroVacc Foundation; Py, Pascal, EuroVacc Foundation; Cornneille, Yan, EuroVacc Foundation; Richard, Laurent, EuroVacc Foundation; Meystre, Alain, EuroVacc Foundation; **"Fostering E-Learning in Medical Education: the EuroVacc Team Experience"**

UK

- Conole, Gráinne, The Open University, Carusi, Annamaria, Oxford University, de Laat, Maarten, Exeter University, Darby, Jonathan, Southampton University, **"What can we learn from the demise of the UK e-University?"**
- Inamorato dos Santos, Andreia, The Open University-UK – Institute of Educational Technology, **"Pedagogical Principles in Course Design and the Learner Experience: A 'Discourse Models' Perspective"**
- Knight, Peter, The Institute of Educational Technology, The Open University, UK, **"Quality, enhancement and on-line distance education courses and programmes"**
- Malalasekera, A., Loughborough University, **"Use of Information Technology to Convert a Full Residential Part Time Masters Programme into a Partial Distance Learning Programme"**
- Needham, Gill MSc Econ, The Open University, **"Towards independent lifelong learning and active citizenship: getting Information Literacy into the curriculum"**
- Okada, Alexandra; Buckingham Shum, Simon, Open University – Knowledge Media Institute, **"Knowledge Mapping with Compendium in Academic Research and Online Education"**
- Sclater, Niall, The Open University, **"Putting the Open University on the Internet"**

USA

– Aldridge, Susan C.; Parker, Mark L., University of Maryland University College, **"Evaluating quality in fully online U.S. university courses: a comparison of University of Maryland University College and Troy University"**

– Bunch, Meredith; Shaffer, Ruth E.; Buckley, Lauri A.; Gladfelter, Jamie; Uskova, Maria, Midstate College, **"eLearning Assessment: A Study to Determine the Value of eLearning Best Practices for Quality Student Outcomes"**

– Clemo, Lorrie, Wolford, Karen, State University of New York College at Oswego, **"Can Specialized Learning Communities Increase Civic Life? Possible Applications for Distance Learning"**

– De Feis, George L., Monroe College, Iona College, Pace University, Juele, Lilia R., Community College of Philadelphia, **"Learning Outcomes Based on Constructivist Designs Applied to Online (Distance) Learning (With a Case Study on the Course 'Management Science')"**

– El-Mansour, Bassou, Indiana State University, **"Distance Education and Preparing HRD Professionals: A Case Study of a United States-Based HRD Program"**

– Edgerton, Thomas; Gonzalez, Rosendo, SkillEdge, LLC, **"Extreme Application Development, Learning Models, and Risk Management"**

– Garcia, Fernando Leon, City University, USA, Rebro, Jan, City University (Slovakia), **"International Partnerships for Capacity Building"**

– Gayol, Yolanda, Fielding Graduate University & NASA/GFSC, Boubsil, Ouanessa, University of Maryland University College, **"Evaluating Performance, Usability, Accessibility and Inclusion of Multimedia Educational Products Developed at the National Aeronautics and Space Administration"**

– Khan, Rana, University of Maryland University College, **"Best Practices for Successful Online Delivery of a Science-Based Program"**

– Kinuthia, Wanjira, Georgia State University, **"Cultural Diversity: An Examination e-Learning in the Face of a Flattening Globe"**

– Kolstad, Max C., State of Arkansas Department of Information Systems, Guimarães, Paulo Ovídio I., University of Brasilia, **"Arkansas Statewide Interactive Video Service: Education as an Anchor Tenant"**

– Ntloedibe-Kuswani, G. S, Syracuse University, Tau, O. S., University of Botswana, **"Promoting Quality in Distance, Flexible and ICT-base Education"**

– Porto, Stella C.S.; Frank, Michael S., University of Maryland University College, **"Ensuring Technological Quality in Online Programs at University of Maryland University College"**

- Stanchev, Peter L., Kettering University; **"Converting a Regular Learning Course into Distance Course"**

Venezuela

- Rada Cadenas, Dora M., Universidad Pedagógica Experimental Libertador-Instituto de Mejoramiento Profesional Del Magisterio, **"Participation of Teachers in the Virtual Forum: Pedagogical Use of the Technological Resources"**

Abstracts available for ICDE Members Only:

Africa

- Adekanmbi, Gbolagade, PhD, Centre for Continuing Education, University of Botswana; **"Promoting Quality in Distance Education Programmes in Africa"**

Argentina

- Espíndola, Martha, Universidad de la Cuenca del Plata; **"Educational Materials Under the Magnifying Glass: A Comparative Study of Text – Based and Virtual Distance Education"**
- Fainholc, Beatriz, Dr., Universidad Nacional de La Plata – Fundación CEDIPROE; **"Collaboration Towards Creating Capacities through ICT Distance Education Programs: A Search for Epistemological Coherence between their Design and its Practice"**

Australia

- Boitshwarelo, Bopelo, Deakin University; **"The Draft Botswana ICT Policy and its Implications for Quality Distance Education Delivery"**

Austria

- Benimeli Bofarull, Enrique, Salzburg University of Applied Sciences; Muendler, Anke, Salzburg University of Applied Sciences; Haber, Peter, Salzburg University of Applied Sciences; **"Transnational Online Project Management Curriculum Model for Engineering Students"**

Brazil

- Almeida Amorim, Joni de, Universidade Estadual de Campinas (UNICAMP – FEEC); Moura Silva, Eliane, Universidade Estadual de Campinas (UNICAMP – IFCH); Kosicki Bellotti, Karina, Universidade Estadual de Campinas (UNICAMP – IFCH); **"Citizenship, Culture and Basic Digital Literacy: Lifelong and Workplace Learning in Brazilian Schools"**
- Andrade, Sônia Regina, Universidade Regional de Blumenau; Ramos, Daniela Karine, Universidade Regional de Blumenau; Bizzotto, Carlos E. N., Universidade Regional de Blumenau; **"When the Teachers Turn Pupils in the Distance: the Formation of Teachers for the Education Modality in the Distance"**
- Aquino de Araújo Mendonça, Gilda, Centro Federal de Educação Tecnológica de Goiás; Furtado de Mendonça, Alzino, Centro Federal de Educação Tecnológica de Goiás; **"The Influence of Multilateral Organizations in the Elaboration of Distance Education Public Policies in Brazil"**
- Araujo, Marcia S., Fundação Universidade Federal do Rio Grande – Colégio Técnico Industrial Prof.;" **Projects of Learning as a Strategy for Environmental Education in High School Philosophy Classes"**
- Baginski, Batista Santos Roberto, Centro Universitário da FEI; Bernal Barbeta, Vagner, Centro Universitário da FEI; **"Distance Education and the Cognitive Reorganization of Students Who Failed in a Course"**
- Barbeta, Vagner B., Centro Universitário da FEI; Santos, Roberto B. B., Centro Universitário da FEI; **"The Role of Distance Education in Promoting the Quality of On-Campus Courses"**
- Barros Fernandes de Oliveira, Rocilda de, ITEO – Instituto Teológico João Paulo II; **"How to Survive as a Teacher in the University"**
- Batista de Lima, Tereza Cristina, Universidade Federal do Ceará – UFC; Firmo de Souza Ferraz, Serafim, Universidade Federal do Ceará – UFC – FEAAC; **"Supervising Junior Researchers in Virtual Environments Based on the Perspective of Collaborative Learning"**
- Bechara, Fabiana, Praxis Soluções Educacionais; Priscilla Ferreira, Ana, Praxis Soluções Educacionais; Miranda, Elisa, Praxis Soluções Educacionais; Araujo Calçada, Marcia, Praxis Soluções Educacionais; Almeida, Maria Angélica, Praxis Soluções Educacionais; **"The Pedagogic and Technologic Meeting: A Challenge for Corporative Education, a Reason for Distance Education Tutoring"**
- Bulla, Gabriela, UFRGS; Santos, Letícia G., UFRGS; Yan, Qiaorong, UFRGS; Polonia, Eunice, UFRGS; **"The Collaborative Construction of an Online**

Newspaper by Portuguese as a Second Language Learners Using ICT: Being Just Modern or Effective?"

- Cacique, Aldemir, RM Sistemas S.A. – Belo Horizonte, MG; **"Structuring Content Generation for Distance Education in Corporate Environments"**
- Campos da Rocha Ferreira, Aline, QuickMind Knowledge Management; Mahaut Rodrigues, Aline, QuickMind Knowledge Management; Barros de Souza Mendes, Clara, QuickMind Knowledge Management; Miguel, Luciana, QuickMind Knowledge Management; Dallari, Marcia, QuickMind Knowledge Management; **"The Usage of Supportive Tools to Enhance E-Learning Courses"**
- Campos Olivier, Barbara, QuickMind Knowledge Management; Ramos Barbosa, Claudia Cristina, QuickMind Knowledge Management; Araújo Lessa Paiva, Danielle de, QuickMind Knowledge Management; Nogueira Martins, Flavia, QuickMind Knowledge Management; **"Simulation: Innovative Practices Proposal for Corporate Training Programs"**
- Cavalcanti, Carolina M. C., Universidade de Santo Amaro; Inocencio, Doralice, Universidade Presbiteriana Mackenzie; **"Professor's Training in Distance Education as a Necessary Mechanism to the Construction of New Paradigms"**
- Duarte Segenreich, Stella Cecilia, Universidade Católica de Petrópolis; Apparecida Campos Mamede-Neves, Maria, Pontifícia Universidade Católica do Rio de Janeiro; **"Lifelong and Workplace Learning for Elementary Education Teachers Using E-Learning: an Experience of Double Digital Inclusion"**
- Escovedo, Tatiana, Catholic University of Rio de Janeiro (PUCRio); Ancelmo Saramago, Filipe, Catholic University of Rio de Janeiro (PUCRio); Fuks, Hugo, Catholic University of Rio de Janeiro (PUCRio); Pereira de Lucena, Carlos Jose, Catholic University of Rio de Janeiro (PUCRio); **"Applying the WebBased Instruction in Musical Education"**
- Fernandez, Consuelo Teresa, Serviço Nacional DL Aprendizagem Industrial-Senai/SP; **"The Rebellion Against E-Learning Templates, or the Importance of Being Creative in E-Learning Systems"**
- Ferraz Rodriguez, Maria Isabel, DATAPREV; Oto de Souza Lieberenz, Ricardo, DATAPREV; Bastos de Castro, José Luis, DATAPREV; **"Design for the Real World to Provide Accessibility and Welcome Insightful Learners to Virtual Collaboration and Distance Education"**
- Ferreira Amaral, Sergio, Faculdade de Educação-UNICAMP; Colombo, Marcelo, Lantec/Faculdade de Educação/UNICAMP; Souza, Karla Isabel, Lantec/Faculdade de Educação/UNICAMP; **"Use of Interactivity in Digital TV Applied in Education"**

- Ferrer Maia, Ivan, Departamento de Multimeios, Mídia e Comunicação, Instituto de Artes – Unicamp; Oliveira Rangel, Flaminio de, Departamento de Multimeios, Mídia e Comunicação, Instituto de Artes – Unicamp; Armando Valente, José, Departamento de Multimeios, Mídia e Comunicação, Instituto de Artes – Unicamp; **"Me, you, him . . . us? Cooperative Relationships in Distance Education Environments"**
- Ferreira Franco, Jorge, Universidade de São Paulo; Deus Lopes, Roseli de, Universidade de São Paulo; Ferreira Franco, Nilton, Universidade Presbiteriana Mackenzie; Rodrigues da Cruz, Sandra Regina, PMSP; **"Enhancing Learning, Research and Content Production Skills through Information Visualization Systems and Web Based Technology Synergy"**
- Fichmann, Silvia, Escola do Futuro – Universidade de São Paulo; **"Strategies for Inservice Teacher Training Using Online Collaborative Learning: A Case Study"**
- Fraga, Cecília, QuickMind Knowledge Management; Dias, Alessandra, QuickMind Knowledge Management; Gomes, Beatriz, QuickMind Knowledge Management; Portilho, Danielle, QuickMind Knowledge Management; **"Problems and New Perspectives of Basic Content for the Development of Online Material"**
- Furtado de Mendonça, Alzino, Centro Federal de Educação Tecnológica de Goiás; Aquino de Araújo Mendonça, Gilda, Centro Federal de Educação Tecnológica de Goiás; **"The Role of the State in the Formulation of Public Policies About Distance Education"**
- Gama, Carmem L. G., MSc, Federal University of Paraná; Scheer, Sergio, PhD, Federal University of Paraná; **"A Systematic Approach for the Development and Use of Numerical Methods Learning Objects"**
- Garrido, Susane, UNISINOS; Schlemmer, Eliane, UNISINOS; **"Reflections About Project for On Line Education"**
- Gonçalves Martins, Janae, Dra, Universidade do Vale do Itajaí – UNIVALI; Silva Miranda, Andréa da, M.Eng., Instituto Virtual de Estudos Avançados – VIAS; Rodriguez, Alejandro Martins, Dr., Instituto Virtual de Estudos Avançados – VIAS; Bosco da Mota Alves, João, Dr., Universidade Federal de Santa Catarina – UFSC; Beber, Bernadétte, M.Eng., Universidade do Vale do Itajaí – U N I V A L I ; Scudelari de Macedo, Claudia Mara, M.Eng., Pontifícia Universidade Católica de Curitiba – Paraná; **"Interlinking of the Concepts of Accessibility and Usability in the Conceptualization of ICT's"**
- Grassi, Daiane, SENAC/EAD/RS; Camargo, Luiza Ester, SENAC/EAD/RS; Dal Santo, Ricardo Melo, SENAC/EAD/RS; Macedo, Alexandra L., SENAC/EAD/RS; Majdenbaum, Rivka, SENAC/EAD/RS; Santa Maria, Gládis

Aparecida, SENAC/EAD/RS; Silva, Odilia da S., SENAC/EAD/RS; **"Optimal Distance Education: Faculty Development Based on SENAC/RS/EAD Institution Qualities"**

- Jönck Pedroso, Gelta Madalena, Universidade da Região de Joinville – UNIVILLE; **"Model of Distance Learning Programs Implementation in Comunitarian Universities Based on Critical Factors of Success"**
- Leite, Lígia Silva, Nova Southeastern University, Universidade Católica de Petrópolis; **"Getting to Know the Virtual Doctoral Student: Theoretical-Practical Perspective"**
- Lucena, Alex, EduWeb; **"Rio de Janeiro's Police Utilizes E-Learning as a "Weapon"**
- Liberato, Almir, Dr., Amazon Federal University; Barreiros, Nilson, Dr., Amazon Federal University; Colares, Jackson, Master, Amazon Federal University; Oliveira Soares, H., Graduated, City Department of Education; **"Knowledge Production by Post-graduate Students in an Educational Technology Course Accredited by the Federal University of Amazonas"**
- Lino Tarcia, Rita Maria, Centro Universitário Salesiano de São Paulo; Barbosa, Anderson Luiz, Centro Universitário Salesiano de São Paulo; **"The Process of Taking Pedagogical Decision in the Different Phases of the Distance Education: from Production to Implementation"**
- Lupion Torres, Patrícia, PhD in Production Engineering-PUC-PR; Ferreira Ramos, Andréia, Coursing Masters in Education-PUC-PR; Tavares Franciosi, Beatriz Regina, PhD in Computer Science-PUC-RS; **"A Study On Pedagogical Aspects of the Learning Objects"**
- Mallmann, Elena Maria, Universidade Federal de Santa Catarina; Roncarelli, Doris, Universidade Federal de Santa Catarina; Nunes, Ingrid Kleist Clark, Universidade Federal de Santa Catarina; Catapan, Araci Hack, Universidade Federal de Santa Catarina; **"Pedagogical Mediation and Virtual Environments of Teaching-Learning"**
- Martins Pompeu, Randal, Ms.C, Universidade de Fortaleza (UNIFOR) Mestrado em Informática Aplicada (MIA); Bezerra da Silva Filho, Jose, Dr., Universidade de Fortaleza (UNIFOR) Mestrado em Informática Aplicada (MIA); **"EAD Through the Internet at the University of Fortaleza"**
- Matta, Alfredo, Fundação Visconde de Cairu-FVC & Universidade do Estado da Bahia – UNEB; Paiva, João, Universidade do Porto (Portugal); Mondlane, Alberto, Academia de Ciências Policiais – ACIPOL (Mozambique); **"Basis for the Construction of an International Community of Learning in the Portuguese Language"**

– Mazur, Alcione, Serviço Nacional de Aprendizagem Industrial-SENAI-PR; Simões, Marlete C., Serviço Nacional de Aprendizagem Industrial-SENAI-PR; Schnefert, Denise, Serviço Nacional de Aprendizagem Industrial-SENAI-PR; Bentes, Roberto de F., Serviço Nacional de Aprendizagem Industrial-SENAI-PR; **"Preparing Teachers for the Integration of Disabled People: an Experience of Distance Education at SENAI-PR"**

– Miskulin, Rosana G. S., IGCE/Unesp/Rio Claro; Rocha C. Silva, Mariana da, FE/Unicamp/Apoio Fapesp; Rosa, Maurício, IGCE/ Unesp/Rio Claro; **"Communities of Practice Supported by Virtual Communities and its Contributions for the Re-significance of the Teachers' Pedagogical Practice"**

– Notargiacomo Mustaro, Pollyana, Universidade Presbiteriana Mackenzie; **"An Interdisciplinary Approach to the Development of Learning Networks in a Virtual Environment"**

– Oliveira Pan, Maria Claudia de, Consórcio CEDERJ/UERJ; **"In the Meshes of the Net: Reading the Hypertext"**

– Oliveira Rangel, Flaminio de, Departamento de Multimeios, Mídia e Comunicação, Instituto de Artes – Unicamp; Ferrer Maiam, Ivan, Departamento de Multimeios, Mídia e Comunicação, Instituto de Artes – Unicamp; Valente, José Armando, Departamento de Multimeios, Mídia e Comunicação, Instituto de Artes – Unicamp; **"Autonomy in Distance Education Environments"**

– Papi, Cathia, Laboratoire Interuniversitaire des Sciences de l'Education et de la Communication (LISEC); **"How Social Affective Background Influences Open and Distance Learning?"**

– Pimenta, Sophia Roslindo, FGV; Bonadia, Sandro E. F., FGV; Pizzi, Fernanda Fortuna, FGV; Capello, Cláudia, FGV; Carvalho, Felipe, FGV; Freitas, João Carlos, FGV; Rego, Marta Cardos, FGV; **"E-Learning Contribution to Social Inclusion: A Case Study Concerning Accessibility"**

– Pimentel, Mariano, Catholic University of Rio de Janeiro (PUCRio); Escovedo, Tatiana, Catholic University of Rio de Janeiro (PUCRio); Fuks, Hugo, Catholic University of Rio de Janeiro (PUCRio); Pereira de Lucena, Carlos Jose, Catholic University of Rio de Janeiro (PUCRio); **"Investigating the Assessment of Learners' Participation in Asynchronous Conference of an Online Course"**

– Pires, Marco Tulio B, MD, PhD, Professor Adjunto, Faculdade de Medicina da UFMG, Diretor Médico da Bibliomed; Cohen, M. MD, MBA, Assessoria de Saúde da CCSIVAM; **"An Electronic Medical Library in the Amazon: The Bibliomed – SIVAM Experience"**

- Rabetti Giannella, Taís, Núcleo de Tecnologia Educacional para a Saúde (NUTES/ UFRJ); Farias Culmant Ramos, Vinicius, Núcleo de Tecnologia Educacional para a Saúde (NUTES/UFRJ); Struchiner, Miriam, Núcleo de Tecnologia Educacional para a Saúde (NUTES/UFRJ); **"Research and Development of "Constructore", a Web Course Authoring Tool: Analysis of Educational Materials Developed by Science and Health Graduate Students"**

- Ramos, Daniela Karine, Universidade Regional de Blumenau; Bizzotto, Carlos E. N., Universidade Regional de Blumenau; Andrade, Sônia Regina, Universidade Regional de Blumenau; **"Webconference: the Interaction as Pedagogical Strategy in the Distance Education"**

- Rezende, Paulo Sergio, SENAC/SP; **"Contextualizing a Scenario: New Technologies and a Portuguese Course for Refugees in Brazil"**

- Rodrigues Gonçalves, Maria Ilse, Faculdade Senac Minas Gerais; **"The Collaborative Construction of Knowledge and Its Difficulties in the Discussion Forums Involving Online Learning"**

- Rondelli, Elizabeth, Universidade Federal do Rio de Janeiro; Rohden, Fabíola, Universidade do Estado do Rio de Janeiro; Vaz Cavalcanti, Karla, Letteris Digital Consultoria; Coutinho, Laura, Didak Consultoria; **"Gender and Diversity at School – the Process of Production, Execution and Evaluation of a Nationwide Online Course"**

- Santos Nonato, Emanuel do Rosário, Universidade do Estado da Bahia; Rodrigues Matta, Alfredo Eurico, Universidade do Estado da Bahia; **"An Approach to the Development of "Hyperreaders""**

- Silva Vellasquez, Fabrícia da, Universidade do Estado do Rio de Janeiro – UERJ; Santos Abreu, Diana dos, Universidade do Estado do Rio de Janeiro – UERJ; Villardi, Raquel, Universidade do Estado do Rio de Janeiro – UERJ; Cardoso Lima da Costa Rego, Marta, Universidade do Estado do Rio de Janeiro – UERJ; Santos Barbosa, Suelen dos, Universidade do Estado do Rio de Janeiro – UERJ; Leite Lucas de Azevedo, Viviane, Universidade do Estado do Rio de Janeiro – UERJ; Fernandes de Souza, Valéria, Universidade do Estado do Rio de Janeiro – UERJ; **"Learning By Distance Education On The Net: A Positive Perspective Of The Technology's Use"**

- Smith Pilla, Bianca, Universidade Federal do Rio Grande do Sul; Keiko Nakayama, Marina, Universidade Federal do Rio Grande do Sul; Binotto, Erlaine, Universidade do Planalto Catarinense – UNIPLAC; **"Characterizing E-Learning Practices in Companies: an Exploratory Research in Brazil"**

- Szpigel, Sérgio, Universidade Presbiteriana Mackenzie; **"Using a Social Constructivist Virtual Learning Environment to Improve Student Understanding in Quantum Physics"**

- Tavares Franciosi, Beatriz Regina, Pontifícia Universidade Católica do Rio Grande do Sul; Kohls dos Santos, Pricila, Pontifícia Universidade Católica do Rio Grande do Sul; Ferreira Ramos, Andréia, Pontifícia Universidade Católica do Paraná; **"E-Learning Skill Development Course: A Refreshing Look Into E-Learning"**
- Todescat, Marilda, Dr, Universidade Federal de Santa Catarina; Santos, Neri dos, Dr. Ing., Universidade Federal de Santa Catarina; Spanhol, Fernando, MSc, Universidade Federal de Santa Catarina; **"Long Distance University in Santa Catarina – A Hypertext Model"**
- Tricai Cavalini, Luciana, Epidemiology and Biostatistics Department, Community Health Institute – Fluminense Federal University; Kawa, Helia, Epidemiology and Biostatistics Department, Community Health Institute – Fluminense Federal University; Laubisch Muller, Adrian Maciel, Computer Sciences Institute – Fluminense Federal University; Oliveira Fernandes Valente, Karen, Computer Sciences Institute – Fluminense Federal University; Loures Quirino da Silva, Leonardo, Computer Sciences Institute – Fluminense Federal University; Mansur Motta, Thaís, Medicine College – Fluminense Federal University; **"E-Learning in Epidemiology: A Pilot Project"**
- Valda Sales, Mary, Universidade do Estado da Bahia; do Rosário Santos Nonato, Emanuel, Universidade do Estado da Bahia; **"Lifelong Qualification of English-as-a-Second-Language Teachers of the Public Schools of Bahia: an E-Learning Experience"**
- Vieira Monteiro, Alexandra Maria, MD, PhD, Medical School, State University of Rio de Janeiro; João Junior, Mario, MSc., Medical School, State University of Rio de Janeiro; Curi Gismondi, Ronaldo, MsC., PhD., Medical School, State University of Rio de Janeiro; Sarmet dos Santos, Alair Augusto, MD, PhD, Medical School, Fluminense Federal University; Cavalcanti Albuquerque, Silvio, Pernambuco's Materno-Infantil Institute; Sakuno, Telma, MD., Medical School, Federal University of Santa Catarina; Nobre, Luis Felipe, MD., PhD., Medical School, Federal University of Santa Catarina; Filgueiras, Tereza, MD., Medical School, Federal University of Minas Gerais; **"Prospective Evaluation of a Teleducation Program Using Videoconferencing to Enhance Radiology Resident Education. A Medical School of State of Rio de Janeiro University, Brazil, Teleteaching Initiative"**
- Waisman, Thais, Waisman Tech; Oliveira, Julio Augusto de, Genius Instituto de Tecnologia; **"T-Learning (Distance learning Through TV) in the Amazon State: the Interactive TV Distance Learning Opportunity for Isolated Areas"**

Canada

- Ally, Mohamed, Ph.D., Assoc. Prof., Athabasca University; Schafer, Steve, Director Library Services, Athabasca University; Tin, Tony, Electronic Resources Librarian, Athabasca University; Hutchinson, Maureen, Acting Manager, Learning Services and Course Production Coordinator Centre for Innovative Management, Athabasca University; **"Mobile Library (M-Library): Delivering Distance Education Materials on Mobile Technology"**
- Baker, John, Desire2Learn, **"Overview and Demonstration of Brand New Teaching and Learning Tools"**

Cape Verde

- Sousa, Sónia; Lamas, David, Universidade Jean Piaget de Cabo Verde; Hudson, Brian, Sheffield Hallam University, United Kingdom; **"A Study on the Importance of Fostering Trust in a Distance Learning Community"**

China

- Fanghong, Li, Central Agricultural Broadcast and Television School (CABTS); Yichun, Zeng, Central Agricultural Broadcast and Television School (CABTS); **"China Rural Distance Education and Construction of the New Countryside"**
- Liang, Qiuxia, National Education Examinations Authority; **"A Brief Introduction to the Assessment System of China's Self-taught Higher Education Examinations"**
- Luyi Sun, **"Evaluation: A Principal Method to Promote Quality of Distance Education"**
- Yingxin, Chang, Central Agricultural Broadcast and Television School (CABTS); Fanghong, Li, Central Agricultural Broadcast and Television School (CABTS); **"Teaching and Learning Support Service to Rural Distance Education in China"**
- Zhang, Zhenhong, Knowledge Science and Engineering Institute, Beijing Normal University; **"An Effective Way of Emotional Support and Raising Motivation in Distance Education: Periodical Questionnaires and Annotated Announcement"**

Costa Rica

- Corrales, Maricruz, PhD., Universidad Estatal a Distancia (UNED); **"Online Learning Strategies to Students: a Grounded Theory Study in Hispanic Universities With Developed Virtual Campus"**

Germany

- Cycon, H.L.; Schmidt, T.C.; Regensburg, H.; Palkow, M.; Wählisch, M., FHTW-Berlin, **"New Scenarios for Distributed Video Based Distant Learning"**

Estonia

- Kusmin, Marge, Tallinn University; **"Thematic Networks in Estonian e-University"**

Finland

- Liukkunen, Kari, University of Oulu; Pohjonen, Juha, Open University, University of Oulu; **"Tools for ICT Strategy Processes in Teaching: The Finnish Universities National Strategy Service and Web Tool"**

India

- Kanakasabha, Ramana, Assoc. Prof. of Telugu, Dept. of Telugu Studies, Faculty of Arts, Dr. B.R. Ambedkar Open University; **"Quality Assurance in Human Resource Development in Distance Education : a Case Study of Dr. B.R. Ambedkar Open University"**
- Ramachandraiah, Magham, Dr., Ph.D., Prof. of Botany, Dr. B.R. Ambedkar Open University; **"India's Distance Education System – Does It Contribute to Country's National Development?"**
- Rao, B. Sunder, Prof., Additional Director, GRADE, Dr. B.R. Ambedkar Open University; Meduri, Emmanuel D.K., Consultant, GRADE, Dr. B.R. Ambedkar Open University; **"Technology Driven Distance Higher Education in India: A Case study of Dr. B. R. Ambedkar Open University (BRAOU)"**

Indonesia

- Pannen, Paulina, SEAMEO SEAMOLEC; Mustafa, DINA, SEAMEO SEAMOLEC; **"E-Pedagogy: Design Consideration for ICT-based Open and Distance Learning"**
- Pannen, Paulina, SEAMEO SEAMOLEC; **"Widening Access to Higher Education: Open and Distance Learning in Higher Education Setting in Indonesia"**

Iran

- Hosseini, Mirza Hassan, PayameNoor University; **"Education and Human Resource Development via Distance Education in Iran"**

Japan

- Ozkul, Ali E., Ph.D., Anadolu University, Turkey; Aoki, Kumiko, Ph.D., National Institute of Multimedia Education, Japan; **"E-Learning in Japan: Steam Locomotive on Shinkansen"**
- Yoshida, Masami, Professor of Chiba University, Faculty of Education, Japan, Advisor of Thailand Cyber University Project, Commission on Higher Education, Ministry of Education, Thailand; Tiranasar, Ampai, Lecturer of Chulalongkorn University, Faculty of Education, Thailand; Sombuntham, Supannee, Director of Thailand Cyber University Project, Commission on Higher Education, Ministry of Education, Thailand; Theeraroungchaisri, Anuchai, Deputy Director of Thailand Cyber University Project, Commission on Higher Education, Ministry of Education, Thailand; **"Applied Study of LMS to Develop a Transactional International Course"**

Korea

- Han, Tae-In, KGIP (Korea and Germany Industry Park); **"A Study on Process Based Quality Assurance Framework for E-Learning"**
- Kang, Kyong-son, Korea National Open University; **"How to Overcome Social Barriers for an Up-credited Open University?"**
- Kim, Yong, Korea Education Research Information Service; Kwak, Duk-Hoon, Korea National Open University; Lee, Seung-Jin, Korea Education Research Information Service; Jung, Sung-Moo, Korea Education Research Information

Service; Hwang, Dae-Joon, Korea Education Research Information Service; **"National Master Plan for E-Learning Quality Assurance in Korea"**
- Kwak, Duk Hoon, Korea National Open University; Shon, Jin Gon, Korea National Open University; **"Evaluation of Face-to-face Schooling System for Higher Quality of Education in Korea National Open University"**
- You, Hyo-soon, Korea National Open University; **"Effectiveness of Blended Tutoring System in a Mega Distance University: a Case of Korea National Open University"**
- Youn, Young-Ja, Ph. D., Korea National Open University; **"The Current Situation And Future Prospect of the E-Learning Collaboration Activities of Korea National Open University"**

Malaysia

- Noor, Nor Azian Mohd., Asst. Prof. Dr., Institute of Education, International Islamic University; Agboola, Abdulhameed Kayode, Ph.D, Institute of Education, International Islamic University Malaysia; **"Effective Integration of E-Learning Tools Among Lecturers in a Tertiary Institution: A Perceptual Survey"**

Morocco

- El Kamoun, Najib, STIC Laboratory, Chouaib Doukkali University, Faculty of Sciences; Bousmah, Mohammed, STIC Laboratory, Chouaib Doukkali University, Faculty of Sciences; Berraissoul, Abdelghafour, STIC Laboratory, Chouaib Doukkali University, Faculty of Sciences; **"Online Environment for the Project-Based Learning Session"**

New Zealand

- Karamat, Parwaiz, The Open Polytechnic of New Zealand; Michalski, Konrad, Athabasca University, Canada; **"Adoption and Implementation of Internet Technology to Education"**
- Smart, Susan E., The Open Polytechnic of New Zealand; **"An Investigation into Delivery of On-line Courses within an Early Childhood Teacher Education Distance Programme in New Zealand"**
- Tiffin, John, Victoria University of Wellington, **"Globalisation, Localisation and the Quality of Education. Keynote Presentation ICDE Rio de Janeiro 2006"**

Norway

- Beck, Eevi E., Education Research Institute, University of Oslo; Hatlevik, Ove E., Education Research Institute, University of Oslo; Stokke, Mona H., Educational Technology Group, USIT, University of Oslo; **"Experience-Based Faculty Development Seminars"**
- Halvorsen, Kjell A., Norwegian University of Science and Technology; **"A Holistic Approach to the Development of ICT Literacy"**

Portugal

- Carvalho, Ana Amélia A., University of Minho; **"Learning Objects Structured According to Cognitive Flexibility Theory"**

Puerto Rico

- Melendez, Juan, University of Puerto Rico, Rio Piedras Campus; Castro, Anadel, University of Puerto Rico, Medical Sciences Campus; Sánchez, José, University of Puerto Rico, Rio Piedras Campus; Vantaggiato, Antonio, University of the Sacred Heart; Betancourt, Carmen, Bayamon Central University; **"Examining Distance Education as an Innovation (a Study in Progress)"**
- Vantaggiato, Antonio, Universidad del Sagrado Corazón; **"Web-based Education: Towards a Manifesto"**

Romania

- Niculescu, Rodica Mariana, University Transilvania of Brasov Romania; Usaci, Doina, University Transilvania of Brasov Romania; **"A New Methodological Approach to Assessing Students' Competences in Direct Education and Distance Learning a Comparative Study Focused on the Quality Dimension of Assessment"**

Singapore

- Aggarwal, Neelam, Ph.D., SIM University; **"Creating Quality Courses: Challenges, Context and Commitment"**

Spain

- Barbera, Elena, Open University of Catalonia; **"Netfolio: a Tool for Mutual Assessment at the University"**

Sweden

- Åström, Eva, Swedish National Agency for Higher Education; Johansson, Magnus, Swedish National Agency for Higher Education; Andersen, Michael, Danish Evaluation Institute; Hansen, Tommy, Danish Evaluation Institute; **"National Evaluations of Quality in Flexible Education – the Cases of Sweden and Denmark"**
- Sigrén, Peter, PhD Candidate, Centre for Learning and Teaching, University College of Borås; **"Artifacts of Technology in Multimedia Produced Distance Courses"**

UK

- Banks, Frank R J, The Open University; **"Research and Development of a Costing Toolkit for Distance, Flexible and ICT-based Education for Teacher Development in Africa"**
- Doody, James, University of Durham; O' Reilly, Derek, University of Durham; Cardiff, John, ITT Dublin, Ireland; Magee, Patricia, ITT Dublin, Ireland; **"Reflections on Teaching and Learning in a Virtual Learning Environment Using Learning Objects in Face-to-face and Distance Learning Programmes"**
- Gaskell, Anne, The Open University; Kelly, Patrick, The Open University; **"Learner Support and Quality Enhancement at The Open University UK"**
- O' Reilly, Derek, School of Education, Durham University; Doody, James, Institute of Technology Tallaght, Ireland; **"Do Students Benefit from Having Their Lecture Notes on the www?"**
- Murphy, Linda, The Open University, UK; Shelley, Monica, The Open University, White, Cynthia, Massey University, New Zealand; Baumann, Uwe, The Open University; **"Developing effective language tutors: are generic competencies enough?"**

USA

- Boubsil, Ouanessa, University of Maryland University College; Goff, Don, University of Maryland University College; **"A Distributed Model for Recruiting, Training and Retaining Faculty: The Postdoctoral Fellowship in Information Assurance Online"**
- Feldman, Andrew, American Public University and University of Maryland University College; **"Technology, the Senses, Social Context, and Socrates' Legacy for Professors of the Information Super-Highway"**

- Juele, Lilia, R., Community College of Philadelphia, **"Designing Constructivist-Driven Learning Environments for Online Teaching and Learning"**
- Larson, Linda, Dr., McNeese State University; Lewis, Barbara, Dr., McNeese State University; VanMetre, Sharon, Dr., McNeese State University; Pearce, Gayle, Mrs., McNeese State University; **"What Is a Quality On-Line Posting? A Study of Inter-Reliability of an Online Discussion Grading Rubric"**
- Masalela, Regina K., Northern Illinois University; **"Contextual Motivational and Deterrent Factors of Faculty Participation in Online Learning at the University of Botswana (UB)"**
- Nelson, Patricia A., The University of Akron, College of Education; Pennisi, Eileen J., The University of Akron, College of Education; **Training Programs for Teachers: The Chilean Experience"**
- Serdyukov, Peter I., National University; Hill, Robyn A., National University; Weegar, Mary Ann, National University; **"Integrating Real-life Experiences in E-Learning"**
- Serdyukova, Nataliya, National University; Serdyukov, Peter, National University; **"Time Efficiency of Online Adult Learning"**
- Stone, Theodore E., Ph.D., University of Maryland University College; **"Equipping the Online Faculty Member's Toolbox: Engendering High Tech/High Touch in the Online Learning Environment"**
- Uskov, Vladimir, Dr., Bradley University (Peoria, IL, U.S.A.); Uskov, Alexander, Bradley University (Peoria, IL, U.S.A.); **"Innovative Streaming Technology and Courseware to Promote Quality in ICT-Based Education"**
- Uskov, Vladimir, Dr., Bradley University (Peoria, IL, U.S.A.); Uskov, Alexander, Bradley University (Peoria, IL, U.S.A.); **"Promoting Quality in ICT-Based Education: Perspectives for 2006-2010"**

Zambia

- Kruger, C. G., North West University South Africa; Spamer, E.J., Prof., North West University South Africa; **"Teacher Upgrading Through Distance Education in a South African Context"**
- Merwe, Annie van der, University of Pretoria; Gouws, Susan, University of South Africa; **"Preparation for Examination and Renewal of Knowledge: Resolving the Refailing Issue Through Re-education"**